Tales of the Old
HORSEMEN

"MANDE'S GRY."

JOHN PALEY

TALES OF THE OLD
HORSEMEN

Jennifer Davies

David and Charles

ACKNOWLEDGEMENTS

I thank all who have contributed their reminiscences to this book. Without you there would be no book.

I owe thanks too, to the following individuals and organisations for their kindness and help: His Grace the Duke of Beaufort; Big Pit Museum, Blaenafon; Birmingham Canal Navigation Society; Black Country Museum; Brooke Hospital for Animals in Cairo; numerous ex-cavalry regiments; Circus Friends Association; Forestry Commission; British Horse Loggers' Association and Hereford College of Agriculture; Imperial War Museum; Charles Martell (grandson of Sir Dymoke White); National Waterways Museum; Welsh Industrial & Maritime Museum; and last but not least, the Welsh Pony & Cob Society.

I am also grateful to all those people who have loaned books and photographs from their own collections, and to the staff of Ledbury Library for their kindness in obtaining reference material.

I am pleased that John Paley agreed to illustrate this book and thank him for his superb drawings. For her invaluable help I thank my editor Sue Hall who initiated the Tales of…series.

Designers literally make books and I am grateful to Sue Cleave for making this one. Indeed, I am indebted to all who have supported this venture and hope that they will feel it has been worthwhile.

The author and publishers would like to thank the following individuals and organisations for supplying photographs.

Page 1("Mande's Gry"=my horse) Frank Cuttriss/courtesy of Len Smith; pp10, 13, 14 & 15 Arthur Showell; p19 Charles Martell; p20 Arthur Showell; p23 Mike Roberts; pp30 & 32 Les Elliott; p36 Frank Cuttriss/courtesy of Len Smith; p37 J.Golden Short/courtesy of the Ninth Century Trust, Lyndhurst; p42, 43, 44 & 47 Jim Cradock; p58–9 Stanley Bywater; p67 'Caggy' Stevens; pp68, 69 & 72–3 The Bob May Canal Collection; p76 & 77 'Caggy' Stevens; p80 Hereford and Worcester County Libraries; pp83, 84, 85, 86, 88, 89, 91 & 92 Emmie Yelding; pp94, 95, 96 & 102 Edward Martin; pp109, 110 & 111 National Coal Board; p114 Welsh Industrial & Maritime Museum; pp120, 121 & 123 Jack Croasdale; pp125, 126 & 127 Alaister McLean; pp 130 & 131 (top) Mr & Mrs George Read; p136 Brooke Hospital for Animals in Cairo; pp137 & 140 Western Morning News; pp143, 144, 145 & 146 Portsmouth Evening News; pp147, 148 & 149 Jack Dowdeswell; p150(btm) Jack Knight; p151 Jack Dowdeswell; pp154 & 156 Hector Skyrme; p157 from Saddle Room Sayings by William Fawcett (pub Constable & Co, 1931)/photo Graphic Photo Union; pp161, 162 & 163 Mr & Mrs Jack Williams; pp173 & 174 Wynne Davies; pp182 & 183 Jim Seymour; p184 Arthur Showell; p188(top) William Brooks. All other photographs by the author.

The extracts and illustation from the Badminton archives on pp50, 52, 54–5 and 56 appear by courtesy of His Grace the Duke of Beaufort. The blacksmith's account on p106 is reproduced by permission of Hereford and Worcester County Record Office. The painting of Jack Dowdeswell on p150 is by Michael Weir.

The extract from John Masefield's King Cole which appears on page 8 is reproduced by kind permission of Bill Masefield and The Society of Authors.

A DAVID & CHARLES BOOK
David & Charles is a subsidiary of F+W (UK) Ltd.,
an F+W Publications Inc. company

First published in the UK in 1997
Reprinted 2005
First paperback edition 2006

A catalogue record for this book is available from the British Library.

ISBN 0 7153 0469 0 hardback
ISBN 0 7153 2419 5 paperback

Typeset by ABM Typographics Ltd, Hull
Printed in United Kingdom by Butler & Tanner Ltd
for David & Charles
Brunel House   Newton Abbot   Devon

Visit our website at www.davidandcharles.co.uk

David & Charles books are available from all good bookshops; alternatively you can contact our Orderline on 0870 9908222 or write to us at FREEPOST EX2 110, D&C Direct, Newton Abbot, TQ12 4ZZ (no stamp required UK mainland); US customers call 800-289-0963 and Canadian customers call 800-840-5220.

Contents

INTRODUCTION

One fine day in the late 1930s a circus stopped to set up and perform in a small West Midlands town. That morning a local boy called Bill Masefield watched the circus people putting up their tents with his father. An elderly man was bent double, hammering in a tent peg.

Bill's father asked him, 'Who was that chap I used to see when I was a boy? He did an act in which he strapped baskets onto his feet, and then jumped onto a galloping horse.' The man straightened up and replied, 'Me, Sir, your humble servant.' The boy suddenly realised they were talking to 'Sir' Robert Fossett, the great Victorian circus owner and horseman. It was a meeting Bill has never forgotten, and he told me about it almost sixty years later.

Indeed, 'Sir' Robert crops up again in the stories told by his grand-daughter Emmie Yelding in this book. However, there are many men and women who are *not* famous but who, during their lives with horses, have acquired such a depth of skill and knowledge they deserve to be remembered; and even more so when you realise that some of their professions, such as those involved in working with horses in coal mines, or riding them into battle, or using them for commercial haulage on canals, are no more.

Conversely, whilst horse handlers of the old school take a step back into retirement, the horse is becoming ever more prominent in our lives. They have been reintroduced to forestry work, and have become increasingly important in the leisure and tourism industry. Their popularity is such that whereas forty years ago the Shire horse, for example, was almost an endangered species, it is now bred to such an extent that supply is exceeding demand, albeit demand is high. Indeed, Shire horse centres have opened all over the country. They demonstrate the work horses used to carry out in agriculture and industry. Some centres also breed, break and train

horses to harness, and keep other breeds of horses as an added attraction for tourists.

A riding school on the Isle of Wight carried out a survey recently and discovered that within a square mile of its premises there were three hundred horses! Every year sees numerous new events, including festivals, parades and ploughing matches, which have proliferated to complement long-established horse shows.

Yes, horses are numerous and loved; but the memories that people hold of them from their old working days are more fragile. Here I return to the boy Bill, who half a century or more ago met Sir Robert Fossett. He had an uncle who was as famous as Fossett, but in a different sphere: John Masefield, who was appointed Poet Laureate in 1930. He also loved the circus, incidentally, as anyone who reads his poem *King Cole* will find. However, he is best known for his poetry, and one of his works refers poignantly to the brevity of our lives. However, it finishes thus:

> *'But gathering, as we stray, a sense*
> *Of life so lovely and intense*
> *It lingers when we wander hence,*
>
> *That those who follow feel behind*
> *Their backs, when all before is blind*
> *Our joy, a rampart to the mind'.*

And that, in a way, is what this book attempts to record; the trials, and often the joys, of the old horsemen and women, which are here passed on to the many horse-lovers of today.

JENNIFER DAVIES
Ledbury, 1997

A ROYAL COACHMAN

Arthur Showell, Hampton Court Mews, Surrey

A cobbled forecourt and rainwater pipes embossed with the date 1570 confirm the venerability of the place in which Arthur and Yvonne Showell live. The complex once formed the stables and coachhouses of one of the royal palaces; it still is, in fact, part of that palace, but nowadays the coachhouses are garages and the stables and grooms' quarters are comfortable flats.

Yvonne is a kind, hospitable person. She is quietly proud of Arthur's achievements in life and keeps a book of newspaper cuttings which mark occasions in his career. Arthur's life with horses deserves recording. It culminated in his becoming HM the Queen's head coachman at Buckingham Palace Mews. He held this post for twenty-three years before he and Yvonne retired to their flat by the Thames.

Arthur is compact in build. When he talks, his rounded features are bright with enthusiasm and he laughs cheerfully. However, it is obvious that he can stand his ground when he feels it is needed.

For ease of telling, it is simplest to break Arthur's story into three parts.

GROWING UP IN JERSEY

Both Arthur and Yvonne are Jersey born and bred, and they still visit and love the island. Jersey acknowledges Arthur too, for not so long ago when their Philatelic Bureau published a stamp to honour a royal occasion, they used a photograph of Arthur on its presentation pack: it shows him in full livery driving the Queen in the Ivory Phaeton to the Trooping the Colour. Arthur describes his early history thus:

'I was born in 1926. My parents never had any money and there was no such thing as the

Arthur as a young boy in St Helier

Pony Club, so because I loved horses, I used to go round all the local stables in St Helier just to get as much as I could of what in those days they called cartage. They'd let you drive the horses and I used to learn a lot from watching them. For example, the way they loaded their vehicles. They'd put two tons of coal or sand or gravel from the sea on a two-wheeled vehicle. It had to be balanced correctly so there wasn't too much weight on the horse's back. As the loaded cart approached a hill the carter would usually stand on the shafts; that stopped the shafts going up in the air when the horse climbed the hill and also kept the weight on its back. Some people would say, "Look at that lazy so-and-so making the horse pull him up the hill". They didn't realise that he'd walked a couple of miles, just to make sure that there wasn't too much weight on the horse's back during the journey.

'I'd help take the horses down to the beach on a Sunday morning, too. If the tide was right, the carters would get me to jump on their horses' backs and take them into the sea and swim them. The carters would each bring an old dandy brush with them and when their horse came out, brush all the feather on its legs and give each one a good clean up because they used to think that salt water was a good remedy. Nowadays people turn hosepipes on their horses' legs for tendons and suchlike, but in those days we took them into the sea.

'I spent a lot of time with a firm called Pitchers. They used to have horses what we called vanners which were a cross between a riding horse and a draught horse and which could be put into a four-wheeled van for haulage. They also had a livery yard with about twenty horses of all kinds, and they owned a bus company which did island trips. One of their vehicles was a sixteen-seater horse-drawn car called a "Tantivy".'

Arthur was thirteen when the war broke out. He describes the effect on Jersey when the Germans first moved in to occupy it: 'The island was in full swing with plenty of food in the shops, and when the German troops arrived and saw so much stuff they bought it all up quickly and sent it back to Germany. Well, it wasn't long before the shops were empty. Pitchers had a shop down in the Parade and they were sensible because before it was too late, they shut shop and took everything home. Put it under the floorboards.'

Pitchers and other horse haulage firms actually benefited from the German occupation, because with petrol being short, horse-drawn vehicles were in demand. As Arthur recalls:

'Everybody started looking for landaus or any kind of horse-drawn carriage that was laid up in the manors around the island; there was quite a lot of carriages to be got hold of. Old Boss Pitcher was a bit shrewd and got himself a variety of vehicles like landaus, barouches, wagonettes, funeral carriages, horse hearses, more coaches and vans and a useful vehicle called a brougham, and went into the cabbing business. People could ring up for a carriage and pair or a single horse to go somewhere. Riding for pleasure completely stopped. The only time you got a ride in those days was when you jumped up and rode bareback to the blacksmith's shop.

'One of the bad things was that there wasn't much food for the horses. You couldn't get a lot of oats, and although it was grown locally, hay went up to £40 a ton. That doesn't sound much today, but in those days wages were 30s [£1.50p] and £2, so there's the difference. Horses were in such poor condition their collars had to be small so that they fitted around their shoulders. You had to force these collars over the horse's head – in fact you tried to open them up by putting them on your knee and pulling at them, and some people would put them on the floor and push down from the pointed end. It was always a struggle to get the collar on, but I thought that was natural, I just thought, well, the horse has got a big head and that's it. It was only after the war that I learnt different – in fact, when I went to work in Hampshire for Sir Dymoke White. His horses were in such good condition and their necks so big but the collars went easily over the heads and correctly fitted the shoulders. It was quite an eye-opener to me.

'We used to mix molasses with the horses' food, a sweet substance like black treacle, and were often so hungry we'd eat a bit ourselves! Mangolds was another horse food – a root similar to a swede – and the prickly shrub with a yellow bloom called gorse. We called that furze or fuzz. We'd bundle it up and put some risers on the van to cope with the high load. We put it through the chaff cutter, but because of the spikes on it we used to wear a pair of thick gloves and use a stick or something to get it through. Some of the heavy horses had a moustache on the upper lip and people used to say: "He's a good fuzz eater", because the moustache would protect him!' Arthur chuckles at this memory. Still considering gorse, he adds: 'Horses sometimes suffer from lampas, a swelling of the gums in the upper jaw. But it was said that horses fed on gorse never had it – and gorse was a good treatment for it, too. I also found out in later years that if you had a horse with severe colic and were lucky enough to have it recover, it would of course still be out of sorts and would take a long time to get eating again. However, if you got a nice bundle of gorse and strung it up in the corner of the stable, then a horse would somehow get some comfort from it and start picking away at it.'

Going back to their wartime days in Jersey, Yvonne describes the household food they had: 'We were existing on swedes, a few potatoes, but mainly swedes. My grandmother could get Jersey milk, so she used to bring it to the boil and then skim off the cream and make butter; so she always had plenty of butter, but no bread so we fried the swede. We had boiled or fried swede for breakfast, and would then go out into the garden and be sick all the way.' Arthur takes up the tale: 'There was a curfew on the island. I think six o'clock in the morning you were allowed outside your house, and you had to be in at ten o'clock each night or nine o'clock in the coastal area. It was a good job there *was* a curfew, otherwise horses would have been worked day *and* night!

'There were no lame horses on Jersey, they just all knew one another and were nodding, saying "Morning!" to each other as they went by. They really worked, those horses, I'll tell you that right now, even if they were bloody lame they still went. Actually the funny thing about a lame horse is, you can walk him along and all of a sudden he'll start bucking and kicking and when you move him on he'll still muck about. We had one horse that was definitely lame but it worked for several years like that. You see there was nothing to move anything and they needed transport. I mean, people were lame too, they were hungry and weak but everything had to be kept going.

'As I say, Pitchers really came into their own. They supplied the undertakers with the hearse and the funeral coaches, and they also did weddings, private cab work and supplied horses for the farms for doing a bit of ploughing.

'Although these horses were not in the best of condition by any means, they were *fit* and quite hardy, that is, they could trot for quite long periods and would very rarely sweat. But when you had a chance to stop and you threw a rug over their backs, we always used to have a knee rug for the cabbing work, that was their signal that they were going to get a rest and they'd stand really quiet.

'But occasionally a horse *did* take charge and gave you a bit of a frightening experience. I can remember a chap called Jack Coutanche and myself when we were both about sixteen or seventeen and we were both on a brougham with no passengers, returning to the stables. The horse was a rather well bred cob of about 15.2hh. Anyway, we hit this patch of cobbles, six to eight feet square, and as the wheels went over it vrrrhhmmm, suddenly this cob took off. I can remember the brougham started swaying from left to right and this horse was *really* galloping, you know his hind legs were touching the vehicle, with us both hanging on with a hand round the brougham lamps. I think we finished up with a rein each, pulling at it, but went another four or five hundred yards coming up to a rather nasty cross-roads until we managed to stop him – although he was on the pavement. I think I took the reins and Jack led us back home. We were both utterly exhausted – you'd be surprised how exhausted you are when you're frightened for your life!'

He did other jobs for Pitchers besides cabbing: 'You could be up at the gas works with a heavy horse carting coal. You'd load it with a sort of slack which was a dusty type of coal, then cart that and tip it around the purifyer. If you were on your own you would shovel and cart 12 tons, that's eight loads a day. I think I was about sixteen in those days. I used to come back of a night and put the horse in the stables with the other carters; and when I got home there wasn't always a lot to eat, and I'd be just about bushed so I used to have a wash and go to bed. Then my mates used to come round to meet me to go out, but I would be too tired to go – and I put up with all this just for the pleasure of actually working with horses, you know.'

There were also stints of coal hauling in the docks. It was dangerous work, as Arthur explains:

'You backed the horse and cart into the quay, and the only thing to prevent you going over into the boat below was six to eight inches of woodwork which went round the pier head. Today it would frighten me to bloody death! And the noise was terrible, engines going and

A Jersey farmer leads his horse onto the weighbridge

shovels. You'd stand in your cart and could just see the ears of the horse. For safety you put the reins through a piece of string which was attached to the high part of the riser, so if the horse made a dive forward you could make a grab for the reins. Men in the boat loaded the coal into baskets, and operators using a steam-driven winch and derricks would swing the basket at you, and you'd catch it and tip it in your cart; then you'd drop the basket down and it would go back to a chap to fill it again. A full basket weighed 3cwt. The great art of loading was to make a wall at the back of the cart: you'd put the lumps of coal there, or if you were loading slack, you would stamp on it to compact it there.

'It was a bit precarious when you got on to the top of the load and were getting the last two or three baskets. But if you had a good chap on the derrick, he could nearly hold the weight of the basket whilst you tipped it. Then the great thing was to try and prevent any of the coal rolling off onto the horse's back and frightening it.

'As soon as you were loaded you'd jump down and prepare to move off. You always started the horse off by going to his head. You never see people doing it now, but you held his head and felt his mouth so you'd got hold of him, then you put your right hand on the shaft and asked him to move by putting a fair bit of pressure on his mouth. If he decided to come towards you quickly with the weight, or stumbled and went down on his knees, you'd push yourself off him with your right hand – otherwise he'd fall on you, particularly as the cobbles were really slippery and also there was a crane track to get over. If you had an obliging horse it would just *lay* on the collar – but a smart one who was sharp at getting away would make a plunge, and they'd all got to do it for the first time!

'You'd go onto a weighbridge, then on towards a store. Sometimes in summer it would be bright sun, but in the store there'd be no lights at all, just a few candles twinkling in the dust. The store was long and narrow, with often barely enough room to turn the horse

Arthur and his mates enjoying a pint after joining up

round, and here there would be chaps called trimmers. They wore chokers, and they would throw the coal up high because the higher it went, the more they got in.

'You'd turn the horse and back the load up, and they used to hold their shovel on the near side of a sort of horseshoe hollow they'd dug out and say "On the shovel, son"! And you had to get your wheel in line with this chap's shovel as you backed it in. Then they would knock out the tailboard of the cart and the coal would come out – but you didn't want too much to come at once, and that's why the wall you'd made was useful, because that kept the cart reasonably balanced. If the load shot out you had all the weight of the fore cart on the horse's back which would make it difficult to tip the cart. You also had to make sure that your horse stood still, because you didn't want it to pull forward and drag the coal out into the open area. If it did, the trimmer would probably have put his shovel on your head as *he'd* have the work of throwing it all back!

'Once the cart was tipped, you just moved the horse forward pace by pace very slowly until it was clear. When it was, a good thing to do was to put a lump of coal under one of the wheels and tell the horse to pull forward; as it went up and over the coal the jerk it made used to pull the cart back upright. If your face fitted and you did it right, possibly the trimmers would give you a hand to put the heavy tailboard back on. Then you'd come away, and then go back and do the same all over again.

'Another job which I did was shop deliveries. There was a chap on the island called Bert Mills, a bit of a flash character with a grey horse who used to do a shop round for a big multi-store called De Gruchy; they sold things like furniture and china, anything to do with the home. But after a period of time during the occupation the Germans decided to deport English-born people and Bert Mills was sent abroad; Pitchers took over the horse, and so then I drove it on the shop round.

'The horse was called Rosa; she was an exceptionally fast-walking animal, and this was good, because you didn't want a lot of trotting when horses weren't getting enough food. But I think she had kidney trouble, because about once a month or more she'd collapse, go straight down as you were walking along. I found the knack of unhooking her without undoing too many straps. I used to undo the back strap so it would free the breeching and free the hames from the hame strap under the collar, although the traces were still attached. Then I'd loosen the belly band if I could. I'd get two or three people to help me get on the wheel of the van and on the shafts and roll it back, and it used to just slide away. Rosa would lay quiet; and if, after looking her over, I couldn't see any injuries, I'd give her a shout and she'd get up, we'd put the bits and pieces on her and carry on as usual. In wartime people didn't waste their money on vets.'

On one occasion in 1942 Arthur, Bert and Rosa were involved in an accident with a lorry on a blind corner; Rosa ended up with her two forefeet through the lorry cab window and herself on top of the bonnet. The accident was reported in the local paper and recently was re-reported in their '50 years ago' column. Family members on Jersey sent Arthur and Yvonne this latest paragraph and Yvonne has added it to her cuttings collection.

In quieter mode Arthur, Bert and Rosa used to deliver to a lady out on a farm. 'She'd give us a glass of milk and two little cakes each,' Arthur recalled. 'I can remember devouring my two cakes, but Bert used to always leave one of his for "manners". One day I didn't do the round with Bert because I got upgraded, and Jack Coutanche went in my place. I said to Jack "Did you have your cake?" He said "Old Bert said he'd better leave one for manners, but I told him 'Manners don't bloody need it, but I do', and I picked it up and ate it.'" Arthur splutters with laughter at this memory and adds, 'I'd been dying to do that for years.'

In addition to working for Pitchers, Arthur spent some time with another Jersey horse firm called Martlands, which worked solely with heavy horses. However, it is Pitchers he remembers best, particularly the harness room and tack cleaning by a coke brazier. He also recalls how their horses were kept: 'Nowadays you don't see people grooming like we used to. Grooming was a ritual, and it was pleasant to

Arthur in his army days: every inch the dashing soldier

watch a chap who could groom, you know, seeing him moving in a rhythm, and he'd "get a sweat on", as we say. The old grooms used to blow a bit, you know what I mean? Sort of "pwssh" when they were grooming, and every time they touched the horse with the brush they went "prrrhh, prrrh"[Arthur vibrates his lips to make the noise], so the horse half expected a hand on him, especially if they were doing the ticklish area around the stifle. I mean, those old grooms used to blow even when they carried a bucket. Sounds daft, but they did.'

In 1946, aged twenty, Arthur joined the army for a dare and came to England. He eventually ended up in a Royal Artillery Riding Troop at St John's Wood in London and in the King's Troop. In February 1952 he was selected to be sergeant in charge of the gun team which accompanied King George VI's coffin from King's Cross station to Westminster Abbey where it was to lie in state. He received the Royal Victoria Medal for performing this task.

After seven years in the army he left and did a couple of jobs involving horses. Then Yvonne's uncle died in Jersey and Arthur and Yvonne returned to the island. Their stay wasn't too happy, however; work was difficult, and eventually Arthur ended up working in the docks. But he still took the magazine *Horse and Hound*, and one day saw an advertisement which was to open a new chapter in his life.

FOUR IN HAND WITH SIR DYMOKE WHITE

The advertisement was for someone to look after hunters on the Norfolk estate of Sir Dymoke White. Arthur answered the advert. A letter came back asking if he knew anything about driving horses, to which he replied that he did. Sir Dymoke then wrote to say he thought him too experienced for the Norfolk job, but to come for an interview to fill the post of head man at his Hampshire estate.

Arthur recalls: 'I was working on a potato or tomato boat in the docks and that boat was going back to Southampton and I managed to book myself onto it.'

At the interview they spoke about driving horses, and Arthur told Sir Dymoke how to use couplings, the buckle on the top of the driving reins. He explained: 'If you get a horse that works harder than the other, you can pull him back two holes on his coupling to hold him back or you let the other one out to let him work more, or if they're going along a bit one-sided, you can play with your coupling.'

This information was new to Sir Dymoke. Arthur then met Billy Belbin who had been stud groom on the estate for forty years and he showed Arthur the horses and carriages. Sir Dymoke was President of the Coaching Club.

Sir Dymoke's final comment was: 'You're a little chap you know, and these are big horses.' Arthur replied: 'Ah well, if you've any doubts best that we leave it.' Sir Dymoke didn't, and Arthur was engaged.

Looking back, Arthur says: 'I had nine and a half years there, and they were the happiest in my life.' Billy Belbin taught him to drive a four-in-hand and when another groom left, a friend of Arthur's from Jersey called George Abbot came and joined them.

Arthur remembers some of Sir Dymoke's vehicles:

'He had a yellow and black coach, and a black Lawton coach which was the best one, the one used for showing; the yellow and black one went to Ascot or anything like that. Ascot week is in June, but on the Saturday prior to that there was Richmond Horse Show, and on the Thursday, the Coaching Club dinner at Hurlingham. We used to go up on the Thursday, the

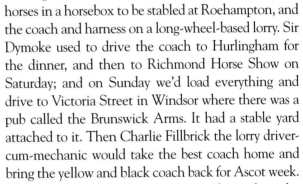

horses in a horsebox to be stabled at Roehampton, and the coach and harness on a long-wheel-based lorry. Sir Dymoke used to drive the coach to Hurlingham for the dinner, and then to Richmond Horse Show on Saturday; and on Sunday we'd load everything and drive to Victoria Street in Windsor where there was a pub called the Brunswick Arms. It had a stable yard attached to it. Then Charlie Fillbrick the lorry driver-cum-mechanic would take the best coach home and bring the yellow and black coach back for Ascot week.

'At ten o'clock in the morning we'd start from the Brunswick Arms on our way to Ascot. The Queen used to give us permission to go down the Long Walk. Some days we'd pick up the Queen's chaplain; in his garden he'd have a little table laid out with glasses of sherry, and we'd stop on the verge and the chaplain's wife would hand these round.

'The minute we stopped I'd jump down, because that's something that you *do* in private service. As the coachman, I'd hold the offside wheeler (one of the horses nearest the coach) so if Sir Dymoke who was sat up on the coach wanted anything, I could talk to him. George would go and hold the two leaders. There was always somebody to hold the horses, and that's why we went nine and a half years with Sir Dymoke without any accident. If we came to any potential difficulty at all, at a cross-roads, for instance, one of us would get down and run ahead. Sir Dymoke was an old character and you got what you worked for, but he *appreciated* what you did, and that was the quality I liked in him.

'Occasionally whilst we were at the chaplain's, the Queen would arrive with a riding party. In those days it was quite a considerable party, the Duke of Beaufort and probably twelve or fourteen others. That's where I was first introduced to the Queen by Sir Dymoke; it would have been 1961, something like that.

'On Ascot race days we'd get to Ascot at twelve o'clock. Sir Dymoke loved going up the High Street with all the traffic and hustle and bustle, and he'd have George blowing the horn all the way! At the racecourse we didn't drive up the main drag, as the Queen does; we would take the horses and coach into the car park, and then had special permission to put the coach into the paddock. This is adjacent to the race course, so you could sit on the coach and watch the horses gallop by.'

Arthur carried on to explain that after he and George had put the coach in place and made sure that it looked tidy, they would take the horses to a barn in Ascot. It was Crown property, and was also where the Royal Mews horses were temporarily kept for the occasion.

After they had watered, fed and groomed their own horses, and rubbed up the harness, Arthur used to wander up and look at the royal ones. Colonel Miller (later Sir John Miller) was the Crown Equerry in charge of the Royal Mews, and he'd say to Arthur 'Come and have a look' and Arthur would ask him all sorts of questions about the horses in his care.

Sir Dymoke, Arthur and George went to many shows – the Royal Show at Aldershot, Romsey, the White City – and won many prizes. They usually took part in the coaching marathon, which was judged on presentation. Marks were given for the condition and matching of the horses, the cleanliness of the harness, and the correct fitting of various appointments on the coach; for example, the whippletrees (or swingletrees), the pivoted crossbars to which the traces are fastened, had to be attached so that the screws faced the outside, and the umbrella basket had to be on the nearside of the coach.

The horses pulling an exercise brake was also a familiar sight on the roads around Sir Dymoke's Hampshire estate. In Arthur's words:

'Stansted Hill was a lovely drag of about a mile. You could get horses pulling into their collars, the four of them, but they would be light in your hands, you didn't have to hold them back; we used to put about a half a ton of sand in bags in the brake, the equivalent weight of a full complement of passengers.

'The hardest thing when you're training horses is to get all their heads straight, and not "bossing" – that is, going to the left and to the right – and never mind how you play with the couplings, alter curb chains and lower or raise the bit, you can still have problems. A horse might be experiencing pain in the mouth, but it can't *tell* you what's wrong; this depends on your horsemanship, and learning how to cope with it.

'Some horses prefer one side rather than the other. If you've got a horse to go well on the left side, *leave* him, don't change him over. All horses to my mind like to go on the right-hand side, left is for traffic-shy ones.

'It's the two wheelers, the two at the back which do the pulling. They reckon that the one in the gutter moves you off, but how many times do you stop in the gutter?

'Another thing, if you had a big horse, say, half-an-inch taller than the other horse, you put him in the gutter so that the two looked matched to anybody walking round them. It was also the practice to have, say, 16.2hh wheelers and 16hh leaders, so that the leaders looked that little bit smaller and more cocky, you know.'

At this point I ask Arthur about the care of the coach.

Driving in the Itchen Valley in 1958

'The Head Coachman looked after it, because you've got to wash it after every time it's been out – that night, if you can, even if it's only to wash the mud off the wheels. There's nothing worse than cow dung for sticking onto it! You must be careful cleaning that you don't bring the paint off. There's also little flints in the grass which chip away at the paint on the felloes – that's the woodwork which goes round the wheels – but there's not a lot you can do about that.

'We had a carriage jack, they're made of wood, for raising the wheels to clean them. We used a scrubbing brush on the ironwork. The iron on the outside of the old coach wheels is proud to the wheel, projecting about an $\frac{1}{8}$in to a $\frac{1}{4}$in so that if you came up against a curb the tyre would rub but the woodwork wouldn't. If people put iron on wheels today they have it flush, but it shouldn't be.

'Front wheels are always worst to clean; they're smaller than the back and they never have the brake block on them to help get rid of mud.'

I ask Arthur if he used detergent:

'You're not supposed to, they say plenty of cold water for varnish, but Charlie Fillbrick found me something called DEB. It used to really freshen the coaches each time, so I always used it – but Sir Dymoke never knew we used it, he'd have gone bloody barmy!

'What about looking after the interior – did you have to keep it aired?'

'Yes, coaches are few and far between, and there's not many that are really kept nice inside. You see, once you take away the inside they are not original any more, so you try to keep 'em to what they were, keep them hand-brushed and chuck in a dozen mothballs during the winter.

Arthur on duty at a show with Sir Dymoke White and his sister Miss Pauline

'On top of a coach the upholstered seats have straps to keep them in place. Sir Dymoke was very keen that the straps were always buckled *behind* and not in front, because of the buckles tearing trousers or a lady's skirt. When I used to do a bit of judging, that was one point I used to go for.'

Arthur generally went with Sir Dymoke to Aldershot Horse Show; they usually showed the coach and horses there. It was normal practice that, prior to the show, the coach owners and their guests lunched in the officers' mess of the local barracks. Arthur describes the scene:

'At a given time, people like myself would get coach and horses together, drive it up outside the barracks and then the owners would come out, each to his own coach. Old Sir Dymoke would look along and say: "Arthur, you make me feel a proud man today." Things like that were marvellous, you know; and you hadn't even started, hadn't had a prize.'

On show day in 1968 Arthur was on the back of the coach as usual, with Sir Dymoke driving and his sister Pauline beside him. They approached the show ground and their progress was monitored, because a part of the judging was to appraise a coach's arrival to see if the horses were fit. Arthur relates what happened next:

'We were trotting, and I was sitting at the back, and the next thing I heard was Miss Pauline calling "Arthur, Arthur!" – and Sir Dymoke had fallen backwards; and do you know, those horses stopped quick as anything, although we'd been trotting.'

A doctor was called and Sir Dymoke taken to hospital, where he died. Arthur finishes this sad incident:

'A chap came up and says to me "If I was you, the best thing to do is to load up and go home" – and that remark really brought me up short because *nobody* had told me what to do for nine and a half years. Sir Dymoke never told me what to do, he knew he never had to, we just talked roughly about what was going to happen. He used to say, perhaps to Miss Pauline: "I haven't seen Arthur for ten days but I bet when we get there he'll have it all put together."

ROYAL COACHMAN

Sir Dymoke White's collection of vehicles was dispersed to museums and Arthur was approached by several people offering him an appointment. Amongst them was Colonel John Miller of the Royal Mews in Buckingham Palace Road; he offered Arthur an assistant stud groom post, looking after polo ponies at Windsor. Arthur was taken on as royal staff, but for a while he had to stay on Sir Dymoke's estate; in the meantime he was sent various young horses to train.

Arthur's first meeting with the Queen was singularly lacking in pomp and circumstance. 'It was coming towards Ascot week, and it was decided that the horses should go up to Windsor so that the Queen could see them. I remember the Queen coming in when I was first there, and I was waiting for someone to introduce me and no one said anything. Then she came again, and still no one said anything. Anyway, the next time I just said to her "Good morning, Your Majesty"; and she replied "Oh, good morning, the horses are looking well". And we had a chat, and she asked me about different things, and that broke the ice. Princess Anne started coming down too, and she was quite friendly to talk to, so that helped as well.'

A little later Arthur was invited to come to London and take up the post as the Head Coachman. Arthur was delighted: 'I quite fancied myself driving the Queen up the Mall and carrying out all those sorts of duties as the Head Coachman. To be honest I had criticised them in the past – I think all was not as efficient as it could be – so I said to myself, well go on up there, put it right, have a crack at it.' And so he did.

'For twenty-three years,' Yvonne explained. She had made some delicious sandwiches to sustain Arthur and myself through his reminiscences, and having cleared away the plates and taken them to the kitchen, had come back to join us.

I ask Arthur how he had settled into the new job:

'It was a case of going there and trying to weigh it all up. Horses are horses and harness is harness, although state harness has got ornamental pieces on it – ornate brass, and rosettes on special occasions – and of course the Mews were open to the public; this meant that I would have to allocate from my workforce men to stand around on duty. Part of the daily regime was that a messenger brougham used to go out. It was drawn by a single horse and picked up the Queen's Messenger at the Court post office and took him around to various banks and offices. Usually it was a plain brougham, and the driver wore black livery in the summer and in the winter a drab coat. But on a member of the royal family's birthday, the messenger went out in a brougham painted in the royal colours, and the driver wore scarlet and had gold lace on his top hat.

'There was a lot to think about because there was the actual exercise of the horses each day, and vehicles for visiting dignitaries. For example, when an ambassador came to present credentials to Her Majesty, I'd arrange for a state landau pulled by two horses to take the ambassador to the Palace and return to his embassy. A High Commissioner had a semi-state landau, drawn by four horses. It was postillioned, that is, the horses were ridden. I'd also have to allocate horses for the daily jobs done by the brougham. Obviously the longer you were there, the easier it became to get into routine, but sometimes it was a job to remember that perhaps there was a covered brake wanted for the following day – that's a pair of horses – or horses required for an investiture. You really had to read your diary.

'For staff, I had three coachmen under me. A coachman is in charge of a stable with, say, eight horses and four men, that is a senior liveried servant and three men with him. New recruits were called junior liveried helpers. The next step up was to be a senior liveried helper, which was the equivalent to the rank of coachman. There was also a day man: his duty was to turn out the messenger brougham, then spend the day picking up droppings and keeping everything as tidy as possible. Talking of duties, after I'd been there a while I trusted certain men to do manes and tails, and they did it well. In fact a lady wrote to ask me where I'd got the stocking netting which went over the horses' tails – but there wasn't any, it was the way they'd been pulled! We pulled the tails hard over the dock and kept them bandaged. On special occasions the manes were plaited and rosettes of ribbons were attached; usually these were crimson, but on the Queen's Silver Wedding we had silver rosettes.'

I ask Arthur how he coped with organising and preparing the horses for major ceremonial occasions.

'Well, there was a chap called Alfie Oates and he'd been there many years. I made him a coachman because he was quite knowledgeable about it all and helpful, and *he* showed me one thing and another. Also, I think when I went in there first you know, I earned the respect of the men. I could ride and drive horses as good as anybody, if not better, and I knew how to feed and clip. So they used to tip me off and say "Don't forget this or that tomorrow!"

'I did make some changes to bring things up to the standard that I liked and knew. Exercise on the road and in Hyde Park had been at half-past six in the morning but I found that, understandably, with such an early start, the men were keen to get back for their breakfast, and the exercise time for the horses wasn't as long as it should have been. So I made it a half-past eight start, after men and horses had been fed and watered, and then they stayed out until at least ten o'clock. There was a bit of opposition to this at first because the later they went out, the more traffic would be about; but when I was in the King's Troop we used to go out in the traffic, so I thought, we'll see.

'I made structural changes, too! For example, in each corner of the riding school there was a big lump of iron sticking out – I think lamps had hung on them years ago. I had these cut out because they were in line with the horses' heads. I gave some of the men riding lessons in their own time, and found that most were keen to learn.

'All the Mews bridles were blinkered – this was usual in a driving bridle, to keep the horse looking forward and not shying at things going on around it – and in the riding school where it was the practice for a man to ride one horse and lead another, if you gave a bit of instruction, say "Turn left", the horses couldn't see each other and they would bang their heads together, which obviously they didn't like a bit; so I adapted the bridles to be open ones.

'I was also keen to use looseboxes as much as possible. Most of the horses lived tied up in narrow stalls, and big horses – and we had some which were 17 to 18hh – haven't got room to lie down in a stall. And just imagine it, if you were one of these horses, if you were lucky you had two hours' exercise a day and on Saturday just one hour, and if you were in a stall you spent *all* the other hours tied up looking at the wall! No, you'd be better off moving about, particularly if you were a bit arthritic, or perhaps you want to lay down and stretch out. So without breaking up the sets of eight horses too much, I tried to put all I could into looseboxes. The sets of eight were two teams of four which were kept together as much as possible because they generally worked together and would do so better if they knew each other really well.'

I ask Arthur if it was difficult to buy coach horses.

'Yes, very difficult. At first Sir John Miller bought the horses, but latterly I did and it was a

One of Arthur's proudest moments, driving the Queen at the Trooping of the Colour in 1987

case of travelling all over England, Holland and Germany to find them. It's nice if you can buy 'em all broken to harness but there's very few you get like that.

'When the Fédération d'Equestre Internationale started, Prince Philip was the President and he asked Sir John if he would take part in FEI competitions: he said he would, and I started training the horses. It was a different thing altogether to the coaching I'd done with Sir Dymoke. For example, a lot more discipline was required in the horses. In a three-day driving event there would be dressage one day, cross-country the next and cone driving on the final day. For the dressage phase you used the best carriage and had nicely turned out livery; the test involved making circles and turns to the left and right. Day two was a marathon, a test of cross-country driving and you didn't turn out as smartly for this. It was usually over a distance of twenty-four kilometres, or fifteen miles, and was split into timed sections: one was straightforward driving, another at walk, a third at a fast trot. Cone driving on the final day was best "bib and tucker" again in the ring, and it involved manoeuvring the horses and carriage round cones topped with tennis balls; if you dislodged a ball you were penalised. There was a time limit.

'We started out with Sir John doing the driving, and we did reasonably well, competing in Switzerland and Germany and winning gold medals. They have a presentation class at each show and we always had the best turn-out of anybody in Europe, and in the world, you know!'

Arthur talks generally about horse-drawn vehicles today: 'Driving is really making a comeback. At Windsor Show there could be eighty turn-outs, and all beautifully presented and turned out. And it takes some doing to win in the private driving turnout because people who have just the one outfit really take a pride in it, and get the harness on the kitchen table and clean it all to the last buckle; and those who can afford staff have a groom to do that sort of thing. Yes, it's all coming back, which is rather nice.'

Here, Arthur describes his much tried and tested training methods.

'You must get the right horse first; one that's five or six years old is best, a horse that's big enough to look well in a carriage, with bone and substance, the nicer looking the better. Also a good head and a nice bold eye, a good front and shoulders, and well shaped feet. Good round quarters not wasting away, a straight mover, and if possible, a horse with some presence which carries itself well. Most important of all – a horse with the right temperament.

'Training time varies; it might be six months for a good horse, some take a year, some two years – some are never any good.

'It is best to try them out at the sellers' premises or have them on approval.

'If a horse had been ridden and well handled you can start further up the ladder when breaking him. Introduce the harness piece by piece and lunge him with the harness on. Introduce two lunge reins, and walk behind him and drive him about so he responds to your voice and to a gentle touch of the whip. What you're trying to find out is how good his temperament is – is it going to kick or get stroppy?

'Put on an open bridle [without blinkers] to start with so he can see you and gains confidence in you. Then you introduce a closed bridle [with blinkers] though be cautious with the horse then because he can't see you until you are in front of him. Finally you put on a whole set of harness.

'It's better if you can have someone to help you at this stage. Put the traces onto a collar and hames and extend them so the straps from the traces go at least four feet behind the horse. As you're driving behind, say to the other chap "Just lay on the traces so he feels pressure on his shoulders" – just some weight, because it's surprising how just a little weight worries a horse at first.

'After you've done that a few times, the man holding the traces should lower his hands and let the traces touch the horse around the hocks and fetlock joints to see if he'll kick and to get him used to the feel of the traces when turning left and right. Then without the assistant pulling on the traces, take up two lightweight but substantial poles ten to twelve feet long and put them through the tugs of the harness on either side of the horse. The assistant holds these at the back of the horse taking their weight, and gently squeezes the poles against his sides, preparing him for the shafts he'll feel when he is put into the breaking cart.

'I usually have a plastic container, say a half gallon orange juice container, filled with nuts and sugar, and all the time I'm playing with the horse on the long rein I rattle the carton so he looks at me whilst I'm stood in front of him, cocks his ears and I'll feed him from it. Eventually I tap the container over his back, his neck, his quarters and he knows he's got nothing to fear from the tapping, he *likes* it. This also prepares him for the rattle of iron-tyred vehicles.

'When you're happy about all that, put long traces on, that is, extended pieces on the traces. The idea of having long traces is so that if the horse jibs, that is, gets worried and steps back and gets his leg over a trace, there's enough play on the trace to avoid it coming up and touching his stifle, because that'll make him kick.

'Next, hook onto the whippletree either the branch of a tree or a rubber tyre; get your assistant to put string around it. Then drive the horse forwards – to start with your assistant should pull the tyre or branch until the horse has got going, then he lets the rope out gently so the horse picks up the weight until he's pulling the object himself.

'If the horse is going well and you feel that he's stopping and standing at your command nicely the next stage is to put him into the breaking cart, a two-wheeled vehicle; this stage should be carried out in a manège, or enclosed space. Before you do so, however, you should go over for a short period what he's learnt before. Then have the breaking cart brought over. You will need two men, one on either side of it, and also a third man (generally myself) facing the horse, and with a hand placed one on each side of his mouth; bring him round gently to look at the breaking cart, then line him up four feet or so in front of it.

'With the two chaps helping, pick up the shafts and lay them high in the air over the horse's back; then pull the cart quietly towards the horse. Pat him on his quarters to let him know something is going to happen.

'The two shafts must go down together, so the two helpers have got to work as one. Put in the tugs. As soon as the near side (left) shaft is in place, do up the belly band so the shaft doesn't tip into the air; each helper takes a trace and hooks the horse up with the traces so it's connected up on both sides, but they must do this together.

'Do the breeching up loosely. I always have a kicking strap, because it prevents the horse bucking in the carriage. I also always use a bearing rein when putting the cart to the horse, though a loose-fitting one; this is because when a horse kicks he puts his head down, so the bearing rein stops him putting his head down. At this point you're still in the riding school. As soon as you think you've got the horse right, have a man on the left side, a man in front (usually myself) and a man on the right.

'I take the reins and get up into the breaking cart; it's open at the back so you can get in and out without climbing over the horse's backside. It has long shafts, and a rein rail of 2ft 6in to 3ft in height; this takes the weight of the reins from the mouth to your hand and also helps to prevent the horse getting his tail over the reins.

'Two men then go to the horse's head; normally you'd have a lead rein, so as not to interfere with the rein I have – it would go to a stable headcollar, a nylon collar under the bridle, so if the bridle broke there'd be something to hold on to. The other man is on the near side rein which is attached to the bit. You want as good a man on the ground as the one driving the vehicle!

'I then ask the horse to move forwards by using the words "Come along", "Walk", "March", and I used to tell my helpers that all I wanted to do was walk the horse forwards three paces only.

'When you stop the horse the two men have to have equal feeling on the reins as well as I have. The reason is that if the one on the left pulls hard the horse's quarters go to the right and touch the shafts which could start him panicking and kicking.

'I shout "Whoah" for stop. I do this two or three times, gradually increasing the steps.

'When the horse is taking two or three paces forwards, the man on the right-hand side would walk backwards with the rein in his hand so the horse could look at him all the time. That man would slip back to the horse, and the other man walk forward three paces and so on. When I felt that the horse was doing it OK I'd say "Let him walk on…".

'A horse doesn't know how to turn in shafts – it's not a normal thing for him. If you pull on the left rein his head goes to the left but his quarters go to the right, and then his shoulder is against the shaft on one side on the left and his quarters on the right-hand side – so he can't turn. The man on the left should pull on the shaft, and the man on the right, taking care not to jam his fingers, pushes the horse gently. If there's a problem, go back again, one step at a time, and just rock the horse so it puts one leg over the other. When you've done that, start walking forwards again. It takes some time for a single driving horse to learn that he must use the weight against the left shaft to push himself round.

'The next stage is to bring the horse and cart out of the riding school, and at the Royal Mews I drove it round the yard so it could see motor cars and hear traffic sounds.

'The above is training for a *single* horse. When you're training it for a pair, you put that single horse through all its training before putting it as a pair in a carriage with an old experienced horse. Some people might think this is too cautious a move, but I did this for my living, and if there was a mishap it was no good me having to say to the owner "I've just smashed up your carriage!". So that's the way I did it.

'I always bandaged up the tail of the old experienced horse like you do a polo pony. That stopped it flicking its tail onto the young horse which might have thought it was a whip, or that the old horse was going to kick, because when the young one was out in the fields he'd discovered that horses always flicked their tails before kicking him.

'Another way of forestalling trouble and getting a horse used to the other flicking it was at the long-rein stage, to get a fly whisk – that's like a hunting crop handle with some horse hair on the end of it – and flicking it around his back so he's used to the feel of another horse's tail. The better you can prepare him, the better the job in the end.

'I always put the old experienced horse on the off side to start with, not the gutter side, and the new horse on the near side, because horses are used to being handled from the left rather than the right. Also he's not near the traffic and you are not in the path of traffic if you've got to get off and handle him.

'I would have two good chaps to help do up the pole straps loosely – that is, in the first hole – so if the old horse fidgeted and walked forward the carriage wouldn't hit the new one up the backside. The nearside trace always went on first – once a pole strap is on and an outside on, the horse is locked in. If you put the inside on first, he can swing his arse towards you. Then you do the inside one and tighten the pole strap as necessary. Couple the reins up across to their heads.

'Then take the reins and climb up onto the box, with the same procedure as for the single horse, that is, a man in front of the head of the new horse, and a man with the old one. You make them go three paces first, then six, then go around the yard.

'When you are pleased with the new horse working on the left-hand side, change and put him on the off side, following the same procedure all over again. With a four-in-hand you do that to all the four horses, that is the two in the front (the leaders) and the two in the rear (the wheelers).'

THE ROMANY HORSE DEALERS

Les and Edna Elliott, East Midlands

According to recent statistics there are around 100,000 gypsies in the UK and about half of these are nomadic. However, many of their traditional stopping places have been lost to development, and their freedom to linger anywhere has been legally curtailed as the Criminal Justice Act of 1994 gives the police and landowners the authority to move nomads on. It also relieves councils of the responsibility to provide sites for vans. Gypsies cannot even live in caravans on land they have bought for themselves.

Gypsy crafts have also suffered over the years. In winter people buy fresh flowers air-freighted in from abroad, not wooden ones hand-made by gypsies. Tumble driers and plastic pegs have spelt the demise of gypsy willow-made pegs, and few people today have their knives and scissors sharpened by gypsy knife-grinders. Collecting and selling scrap metal, trading motors and buying and picking fruit are more likely to be today's gypsy occupations.

However, amongst all these changes one traditional gypsy trade endures: horse dealing. Gypsies and horses are inseparable – in fact the gypsy language of Romani gave us the word 'jockey', a derivation of 'chookni' meaning a whip. Each year gypsies flock to horse fairs around the country. There's one at Appleby in Cumbria, and another in Barnet, North London; Abergavenny horse sales cater for Welsh custom, and Gloucestershire has Stow-on-the-Wold horse fair each May and October.

Stow received royal permission in the early twelfth century to hold a weekly market in the town, and in 1476 Edward IV granted a charter for two fairs to be held there, one in May and one in October. At first these fairs were mainly for sheep, as Stow was a prosperous woollen town, but over the years they became the usual rural servant hiring fairs which included the

Les at Stow Fair,
a place to catch up with old friends

selling of produce and animals. The horse-selling side received a boost when local auctioneers concentrated on this aspect, and Stow's fame as a horse fair grew from there. The auctioneers have now moved their horse sales out of the town, but the gypsies still continue to bring their horses to Stow each spring and autumn. They purchased a field in which to park and conduct their business, but at the time of writing this, they are forbidden by law to use the field and so the selling and buying takes place in the lower part of the town.

Many gypsies arrive a week in advance of sale day and park on the verges and lay-bys in readiness. Some local residents believe they are harmless and consider they add colour to the town's yearly calendar; to others, however, they are clearly a nuisance. On the day of the sale one or two shops display singularly few goods and prop up the following terse message in the window: 'Closed because of the Horse Sales'. Also a few of the town's smart hotels have a bouncer on the door; they let in well heeled foreign tourists, but anyone considered less desirable would think twice about crossing the threshold. When I turned up in my quest for a gypsy horse dealer, the only place which seemed to be enjoying the custom brought by the sale was a fish-and-chip shop: situated near the hub of the sales, the queue and bustle around it never diminished all day long.

Beyond the shop the clatter of hooves on tarmac frequently sent people scattering. The cause would be either a seller hurtling along in a horse-drawn buggy (with the object of showing off his horse's paces) or a young gypsy buck for the same reason running down the road and leading a smartly trotting pony.

Even in the throng of so many horse copers I found it difficult to pin down a gypsy prepared to talk about horse dealing. A few referred me to a family of brothers, but when I found the eldest, he assured me he only dealt in scrap. Ten minutes later I saw him slapping his hand down on a deal and passing a bundle of notes to a young man who had five donkeys tethered to the car park railings. Eventually someone suggested that I make my way down the road, for somewhere at the bottom, parked in an old-fashioned gypsy caravan was Les Elliott, a renowned and thankfully, communicative horse dealer.

The journey down hill wasn't simple, because of the hundreds of people thronging the trade stalls which stood on either side of the road. And threading my way through the crowd it was easy to see what attracted them: there were stalls of every different sort and kind – set with the prettiest Wedgewood and Doulton china, and glistening with cut glass; stalls with piles of frilled linen and pillow cases; stalls selling leather belts, bags and clothes, each piece brightened by brass stars and buckles; stalls of buckets, bowls and bins all decorated with flowers (and a snip for £20 a set of three); stalls hung with pictures of horse-drawn caravans and mugs decorated with horse's heads; useful stalls selling iron kettles and the wherewithall for cooking out of doors, plus the odd bundle of leather ferret collars; and any number of shoe stalls.

Beyond, the crowd thinned, and here I found Les Elliott and his wife Edna. But it was impossible to talk to them. Edna, with the traditional scarf covering her head, was cooking sausages over an open fire on the grass verge, every now and then turning to fetch a bread roll or an extra cup from their old-fashioned flat-bedded dray parked close by. Les stood by the fire. He had dark wavy hair and a moustache, and wore a red spotted handkerchief round his neck, a red check shirt and was surrounded by people. It was this multitude that Edna was catering for.

Later, I learned that like most Romanies, Les and Edna have a great many relatives, and that the only times they really all meet up nowadays are at fairs, weddings and funerals. And there were friends too, some already installed by the fire, others passing by and stopping to chat en route.

I made my way to Les and asked if we could talk about horse dealing. We spoke briefly, and I photographed him by the shafts of a neighbour's caravan and also Edna, sat against their own dray which they towed behind their big wagon. However, it was obviously going to be better if I could see them on another day which wouldn't be quite so hectic. Les agreed and said that he and Edna had just acquired a house for over-wintering in. His health and the fact that they weren't as young as they had been had prompted this move, although Les really preferred travelling winter and summer. They would be there until March, then away again.

A few weeks later I arrived at their house. Edna gave me coffee and sandwiches on beautiful china. The house, warm and spotless, was alive with canary song: there were at least a dozen of the birds, some pale lemon yellow, others with flushes of orange to their feathers, each in an individual wooden cage in an annexe by the sitting-room. Apparently they had even more upstairs.

This is Les's story in his own words:

'The Elliotts go back a long way. Someone looked it up once, and it's on record that in 1746 a Mrs Elliott with three children was stopping in Coate's lane on the borders of Nottinghamshire. She was in a rod tent – benders as they call 'em today – and had three boys. It's also on record that in 1796 an Elliott family was camping four miles further up the road. I say "Elliott", though in fact the family name used to be "Elit"; over the years it's got modern with people writing it and adding an "o" and an extra "l" and "t". I don't know whether I am an Elit or an Elliott because I haven't got a birth certificate.

'Both me grandfathers used to buy horses out of the coal pits. They'd clean them up, and feed 'em and brush 'em down, and soon they could see the ones which was going to survive. They'd say well, that one's all right, but the other two've got to be put down – some would be too old to eat, others'd be too lame, you see. They just fed 'em up and looked after 'em and brushed 'em and watched them over a week or fortnight, and if they could see they was going to alter they knew they'd got one that was going to survive. Then they'd go perhaps into a pub and say "Oh, I've got three hosses – I'll swop you for that one"; and so they'd swop 'em, and they'd keep on like that and the next man 'ud have 'em.

'Hosses was cheap and everything was horsepower, there were no motors. You could go up a lane and lay in the middle of the road and you'd perhaps see one car a week.

'My father's name was Everett Elliott, and he was a horse dealer too. I was the youngest of thirteen, and we lived in what they called a "Palace on Wheels" – well, we didn't all live in it

Les' grandmother, Kazia Booth

because some of my older brothers and sisters had moved out. The caravan's proper name was a "Reading", and it had straight sides, two great big windows and a big mollycroft roof [a small roof on top of the main one; it has windows in it which help to give light and ventilation to the van]. The wood on the van was carved.

'The caravan I've got today is different. It's a Ledge, Bill Wright, and is named after the man that made them. It hasn't got straight sides, it's got ledges, and it's all mahogany wood inside, and inside the cupboard there's sunflowers carved in the wood. I think mine's the only one of its type that's still travelling today, anyway that I know of; it's about 120 years old, and used to belong to my cousin's great-grandfather. Two horses pull it, and one horse pulls our flat-bed-ded dray.

'The first time I ever seen a horse was when I was two. We were stopping at Derby on a piece of ground that used to be called Brexall Ground; there was everybody on it, people out of towns what hadn't got no houses. It was like a shanty town, and there were a lot of gypsies on there; in them days there were no money to be had, so they had to do as best they could. I remember me Dad fetching up a hoss. I was stood at his side and he give me this halter to hold, and when I looked up all I could see was this big head looking down at me; and me Dad said "Oh, it's a horse, it won't hurt you" – and ever since I've had hosses.

'One day when I was about six or seven my Dad said to me "I want you to take the horse up to the blacksmith and have it shod." I used to stutter when I was a little boy, and I was leading the horse to the blacksmith trying to get the words out, and the blacksmith said to me, I were crying, he said, "What h'ever you crying for?" I said, "Me Dad said to take the hoss up to the blacksmith and have it shot."

'Any road, he shoed it – and I've still got a mark in me leg today where a piece of iron flew off the anvil and went into me leg. The blacksmith was making the shoes, cutting and bang-ing, and he did tell me to go back from the forge – but I was so inquisitive I didn't take notice and all of a sudden I felt it like a red-hot bullet, straight into me leg here; I still got the mark. The blacksmith just chucked some water on it and said "That'll learn you"; and it did!

'Then me Dad come and he said "You're a long time shoeing this horse." "Yes," he said, "I've had to make the shoes special for this one – and you're lad's been crying half the day, thought you said have the hoss *shot* instead of *shod*". "Oh, did he," he said, and hit me up the ear-hole.

'Men were all hard in those days; there was no "I'll buy you this", or "I'll buy you that". Everybody was hard, it was survival, remember.

'When my Dad was horse dealing he used to dress up with leggings and a suit, and a cap or bowler hat and smock, and say he was a horse dealer. In them days people wouldn't buy off a gypsy, they used to think we was doing nowt but stealing; that's why we never used to buy coloured horses only blacks and browns, because people wouldn't buy them off him because they'd think he was a gypsy and he'd stolen them. Now it's gone the other way and gypsies favour coloured horses. When he went dealing my Dad would leave the waggon and travel in a horse and trap.

'People got to know his name, and would ask him to get them, say, a quiet horse for driving; and he'd ask about until he found one. Then he'd deliver it clean, brushed and respectable, with its mane hogged, teeth cleaned and harness polished, like you'd expect a new car to arrive today.

'If someone was selling, on the other hand, he'd give them a hard luck story, saying, "Well, the horse trade's not very good ma'am" (if it was a lady) and he used to say to me "There's nothing better than to be clean, and polite to people, civility gets you through the world" – and he was right.'

At this point Edna came in from the kitchen with a tray, and held it out to show three fruit cakes. They were not the conventional shape, but flat, traditional gypsy cakes, and they looked and smelt wonderful.

'Come out all right, ain't they, hey? Done on the top, they ain't so good as them done on a fire outside, but they turned out all right.'

Although Edna likes her electric cooker she maintains that an open fire cooks food better. She can cook roasts, stews, soups, pies and puddings on the grid over her camp fire, in fact she thinks that there isn't a dish she can't cook on it. She returned to other delicious smells in the kitchen. Les continued his reminiscences:

'The first day I went out with a horse and cart I think I was eight. My Dad give me the reins to drive the hoss and the hoss took off, run away with us. Me Dad jumped off to grab its 'ead, and it was too fast. I never forget it. Dad roly-poly'd in the road, and a policeman come past on a bike and he kept pedalling and trying to grab the back of the dray, but he couldn't make it and we went over a railway bridge. Eventually I pulled the rein on me right-hand side, and hoss and cart went into a fence, and the hoss started kicking and got out of the harness.

'In fact the hoss eventually came to a bad end: it put its head through the fence on the railway siding – in them days it were like iron bars – to get grass, and summat must have frightened it because it tried to jerk its head back through and broke its neck. The knacker man had to come and shoot it in the field. Did you know that the bullet goes straight through an 'oss? They shoot it straight in the centre of the head, but you can't stand behind it because the bullet goes straight through, down its back and out the other end. It's dead as soon as you hear the gun go "click".'

Les breaks off here, and going into the annexe gives each canary some fresh lettuce. He returns and we resume:

'We used to travel all over. When the war was on we was round Derby and Nottingham, but when the war finished we went all over.

'Any horses that we bought at fairs were bought, as they still are today, by the raising and dropping of the buyer's hand on the seller's each time a price is mentioned. You went up in price until a purchase price was agreed – and a man's word was his bond, it was a gentleman's agreement.

'Purchased horses were tied behind the back of the waggon. There was also a pony and cart on the back, for the wives, the women, to drive out in for their business to go selling. They wus as clever as the men at dealing, and would buy any cheap horses. I mean, horses them days weren't a lot of money; you could buy one for 15s, 75 pence nowadays – although even 15s would have taken a long time to earn.

'My wife Edna didn't buy horses, but she did sell a couple of mine. She'd say "Oh, my husband's got one for sale"; and she'd sell a waggon too if she had a customer. She sold two of mine.

'When I was a lad you weren't allowed to tether horses on the main road, so we travelled on the back lanes which were quiet. I didn't get any schooling because we used to pull the waggon in the end of a lane and they'd say to me "Right, go to the top of the lane and sit there until we send for you and send someone else up." Then they'd loose the horses off the back of the waggon, and they would graze between the waggon and me sat up the end. There was no tethers for them. When they got too far I'd have to send them back.

'I spent hours and hours, all day, like that, and if it rained it was just too bad. I'd make a fire under the hedge. If there was two of you, one would try and catch a rabbit and we'd roast it.

'When the horses had eaten that part of the lane off, they'd put the waggon hoss in and bring it to where we had our fire and then we'd walk down the road another half a mile and that's how they used to do it.

'Sometimes they'd forget to send for you, because there was no set time. Then when they remembered they'd give a certain whistle, and like a sheepdog, you'd be listening for that whistle and come back; or perhaps they'd send someone up with a pot of tea and some bread and cheese or bread and lard, you got whatever you got. But whatever it was, you were grateful.

'At night-time we used to put the horses in a farmer's field. We used to watch him put his lights out and then we'd put them in the field, and we used to fetch 'em out before he got up, and would go round the field and pick all the droppings up so he never knew. Some of the farmers used to know we'd done it and they used to fetch a policeman and all sorts. We used to have to move, then, when they fetched a policeman.

'There were no friendly farmers in them days, in fact no friendly nobody. People were suspicious of us as soon as we pulled in, and if you had two nights in a place you were fortunate. You see, years ago everyone had horses and living vans and so many used to congregate in one

A much-treasured photo of Les' mother and father

spot – and when one van moved off, another would draw in; and people in the neighbour-hood would get fed up seeing 'em, and they'd think it was still the same lot parked. But the bitterness against us is dying with the old people. The young generation now if they see me with my horses and my traditional gypsy waggon, they say "Isn't that beautiful!" [Les pauses and says with a grin:] It's a pleasure for me to be a gypsy now. Years ago you used to be terri-fied. Although even today I still can't stop somewhere for a week without getting nervous! Yes, we were always on the move, but in a way we liked it. Riding the horses behind the wag-gon, mares and foals coming on, dogs running at the side, the waggons going on. Nomadic people just going where we wanted.

'Looking back, life wasn't too bad in the summer, but in the winter I'd go to bed when it were dark and get up when it were dark – I used to think I'd never been to bed. And then as I growed up, somebody else would take on the job of minding the horses when they grazed. There'd be two or three families of us together, you see. And they'd say: "Right, you goo today and fetch some peg sticks." And I used to get the peg knife and go and fetch a load of peg sticks, cutting them out of the hedge from willa trees. Then the men and the young gals would help to make the pegs.

'I'll show you some; I still make 'em you see. Then we used to make wooden flowers out of elder, they used to look like big white chrysanths.'

To show me what he meant, Les held one hand as if it grasped a knife and the other as if he held a piece of elderwood, and then proceeded to use the "knife" to peel down the strips of wood. He explained that it was like a petal on top of a petal – it all had to be done quickly until it formed a round ball which curled underneath and looked just like a *real* chrysanthemum.

'We used to make and sell no end of these. See, in them days there were no silk flowers like there are today, no flowers what you could buy out of season, although you can buy flowers all the year round now. We used to make 'em, dye them different colours with clothes dye, say red and yeller, and people used to buy 'em to put in their winders. The women used to go out with them, and I used to go out with them.

'When you got old enough, to go out to fend for yourself, that's it, you had to do it, and you didn't get no help from nobody. But it wasn't all work. We used to sit round the fire and talk, and make a conversation up. There were no wirelesses, see, and we weren't allowed to go to dances – and we didn't have the money to get nowhere. I mean, our clothes were all old, somebody else's leave-offs. And we always used to have one of these on [indicates his red neckerchief].

Les unties and reties the neckerchief in the ordinary way, saying at the same time that this wasn't the way his mother used. Untying it again, he showed me *her* method which involved first, putting it round the front of his throat like a vicar's collar, bringing the two ends from behind his neck and tying them in front.

'This way kept me neck warm, and also hid the dirt on the collar of me shirt because there was no time to wash, and anyway, sometimes the clothes we got wasn't fit to wash, there was nowt left to wash.

'I used to wear a man's coat and roll the sleeves up, men's trousers and roll the bottoms up – and to this very day you'll see some gypsy men walk about with their trousers turned up because they're too long. I mean anybody's cast-off clothing was very helpful to us, you know.

'The blankets we had were those old grey and blue army itchy blankets, and they used to make me mad! No soft, warm pillers and soft warm beds, I tell you it was very hard. I mean, every morning you got up you'd got to have a fire outside, you'd got to wash outside, winter and summer.

'I once remember me and me cousin laid under one of these waggons; we used to put a sheet round the wheels, and two bales of straw under it and a couple of pillers, if we'd got 'em. We'd lay under there and then in the morning me Dad'd say, "Hey up, boy!" – and if you didn't hear him, that was just too bad for you because he wouldn't shout twice, only the once. One morning I couldn't open me eyes because the sun was shining in them. I woke me cousin up, and we sat up and looked at each other like two mongooses. I said "There's summat missing – where's waggin?" We found out it was about seven o'clock, and my Dad had put the hoss in and pulled the waggon over us, took the sheet down. But the next morning when he shouted, then we said, "Yeah, all right!"

'It was his way of training you. You couldn't afford to lay in bed all day, who's going to feed yer? Oh, they was hard times – and the gals wus brought up just as hard as the boys, they didn't have a soft, easy life. When they got married they had a child in the sling, a basket on their arm, and perhaps another child dragging behind them.

'I tell you, we used to sell and buy anything, horses, chickens, anything you could make money out of – and that was the way our people was brought up. But I do remember me Dad turning down some money once. When the war was on, two lads from the army came to him and asked if he had a horse and cart they could hire. He said we had, and I fetched up the horse and we put the harness on and put it in the cart for 'em; but then they said "Which way do you pull to turn left and right?", and me Dad asked if they'd ever driven a horse before. When they replied that they hadn't he said "You're not driving this one, then" – and wouldn't let them have it.

'As it turned out, somebody else come that day and my Dad sold it for £9, the horse, harness and the cart, and that was a lot of money in them days. As it happened I got a good hiding on that occasion, because when gypsy menfolk were dealing you wasn't allowed to speak, you just stood there and looked and listened; but I was going to tell this man that there was a brake on the dray, thinking this would help me Dad in selling it. Oh, he gave me such a fourpenny 'un, and told me "When you're a man, then you can butt in; until then, shut up!"

'I wasn't allowed out with him when he went horse dealing. In fact mostly I went out with me Mam, because the men wouldn't have you with them; in them days children couldn't go in pubs, and a lot of business was done in pubs. When I did go out to buy horses, although I wasn't very old, about thirteen, I went on my own.

'I might find a horse, but not have enough money for it, so I used to go back to me Dad and say "There's a pony down in the village I can buy," and I used to add a little bit

'Off to the 'oppin.'

on it for myself, I'd perhaps put 3s or 4s on the purchase price, which was a lot of money in them days. It warn't the truth. Then I'd bring the horse back and he'd say "Oh, that was all right then." Then he'd say, "How much have I got to give for it?" So you'd add a little bit more on top of what you'd already paid, and by the time you'd finished you had a good bit of profit out of it.'

'But some of the old men, they'd say "Oh, I've got a man as 'ud buy that pony off you, but he can't come and get it, so I'll take it up this afternoon." And they'd put the halter on it, and that would be the end for you. And it were no good saying "Where's me money?" Because they'd just say "Money, money! You don't get fed for nowt, you know!" No, they didn't feed you, you fed yourself.

'The horses' food we used to buy off the local farmers. You'd have say, perhaps, six pennyworth of corn and six pennyworth of hay, and in them days you could buy enough to keep two horses for perhaps a shilling. A truss of hay was as much as a man could pick up. Nearly as big as that sofa [indicating a medium-sized sofa in the sitting room]. Then they'd have a few oats, and you'd feed them like that.

'The winters in them days was a lot harder than they are today. In 1947 Edna was in a caravan on top of that hill, out there in the distance. She, her Dad and Mam and three brothers were snowed up there for six weeks. They dug themselves out eventually. My family was snowed in at Melton Mowbray.

'By that time I'd left home. I couldn't get on with my Dad. He'd keep saying to me "It's time you brought some money in, about time you done this . . ." you know. I left when I were fourteen, just walked off. I went to me aunts and uncles who were travelling like us, though I used to see me Mam regular. I got me own horse.

'When I married Edna we had a pony, a trap and a tent, and were very fortunate to have these. She come with what she had on her back, her parents were poor as well, and she was the oldest out o' nine of 'em so they didn't have nothing to offer. We got married in a registry office, though some people in those days jumped the broom.

'We used to travel through Derbyshire and Nottinghamshire and up to the North. If we

Gipsy camp

could get a living, and there was plenty of grass for our hosses and somewhere to stop, we'd stop. Just shift round local lanes in the area. If it was hard we'd move on.

'Remember our wireless thing we had, Edna?'

Edna comes in from the kitchen. 'It was a good wireless,' she replies. 'Black polished wood. And we had a trugunda (gramophone) with a brass horn . . . Used to be able to get two records for a penny when I was a kid. They were second-hand, ha'penny a piece . . . George Formby, Slim Whitman, everybody.' Les and Edna swop record reminiscences. Then we get back to horses because I ask Les if gypsies have a special way with them.

'We're more horse people than a lot. I mean we can tell whether they're going to make good 'uns or bad 'uns. That black and white one on there' (he points to a photograph on the wall which shows his waggon and horses) 'He's only a yearling on there, but now he's three years old. I broke him in meself and he pulls that waggon, and he's really a good horse, it's very rare I have to use a whip.'

'And,' I ask, 'any secret gypsy remedies if a horse falls ill?' Les thinks, then replies:

Well, you'd boil up the mallow plant in a bucket and then strain the water off. It looked a dirty green, and you used to bathe a horse's leg in it if it had a sprain. The liquid was good for human sprains, too. The remedy for colic or a broken leg was a bullet.

'Sometimes a horse would throw a spavin, though I haven't seen one for years. They were usually caused by hard work and the horse would generally go lame on one or both hind legs. In the old days if it was lame on one they used to do summat to the other leg because how could you go lame on two feet?

'Then there's sweet itch, which isn't a pain but rather an irritation. Have you ever had an allergy which makes you scratch your whole body? Well, its similar to that, only it's continuous day and night. It starts in the spring, and lasts from the first of the leaf until the end of the leaf. The horse would rub against anything, a door, a fence, rub and rub until it bled, and you had to be careful where you tethered it. The irritation would start in the top of the tail where the hair is broke and after rubbing it would spread, but only where the harness fits, that is in the mane, on the shoulders, on the back and on the tail. There are powders and treatments

37

today to treat sweet itch, but the only thing we could use to ease it – didn't cure it, but eased it – was waste oil put on with a rag.

'Also sometimes you'd get a horse with a splint and it would go lame. If it had two splints it warn't too bad, it just used to be a bit "pudgy" [pottery] in front. Some horses had a parrot mouth, you know the jaws wouldn't meet properly and it was difficult for them to eat. We believed a lot of that was caused by people putting halters on them and leaving the halter on and their heads grow'd but the 'alters didn't, though I'm told this is not so.'

'Do gypsies use Romani commands to their horses?' I ask.

'No, English,' Les replies. 'Because if you're selling horses to English people you kakka rokker (don't speak) Romani, you've got to say "Whoah, stop". But,' he adds, 'we talk Romani between ourselves. For instance a horse is a "grasni", and a farmer's field is a "puff". In fact it's very rare we talk English, only when out getting us a living, buying and selling.'

Edna is busy preparing food for some afternoon guests. I beg a few more minutes, and ask Les if it isn't a pleasure to have the comforts of a house during the winter (it's their second winter under a tiled roof).

He replies: 'Sometimes, you're right.'

I enquire when they'll be off on their travels again.

'Tomorrer, if *she* would.'

'But you'd lose your TV and comfortable bed and central heating.' To which Les replied:

'Edna likes the house, it's not so hard for her as on the road – there she has to get a living. Also in the house it's all there for her, light at a switch, and water. But I'm losing me freedom (then quietly so that Edna doesn't hear), and that's more important than all this lot put together.'

He looks through the window. 'We'll go off in the early spring. At present my horses are a distance away, but I've always had 'em where I can see 'em because they know my footsteps, if it's dark at night, they'll whinny, they know it's me. They'll come over and they won't leave me, none of 'em will.'

O, I am not of gentle clan,
I'm sprung from Gypsy tree
And I will be no gentleman,
But an Egyptian free.

GEORGE BORROW

A STALLION WALKER

Jim Cradock, Willingham-by-Stow, Lincolnshire

In a tiny village near Gainsborough in Leicestershire, 84-year-old Jim Cradock is the proud possessor of a very particular sort of stick. In spite of its age – it is over a century old – its polish and fine workmanship are pristine. This may be because Jim's father never allowed any of his three boys to touch it – and they were tempted to because with a few deft movements of the hand, a tall honey-coloured ruler would emerge from one end of it, and at the top of this a brass bar inset with an elfin-size spirit level could be flipped up until it lay at right-angles to the ruler.

Jim's father used the stick to measure the height of a horse, and that brass cross-bar placed across its withers helped him to settle many a dispute as to just how many hands high an animal was.

Originally Jim's father had been a farmer at Brompton near Northallerton in Yorkshire. He had kept a herd of dairy cattle and some pigs, although horses were always his special love. I met Jim with his wife Minnie in their bungalow. We sat in the sitting-room where there was a dresser of beautiful old china, which Minnie had used in the days when they had a big farm-house kitchen. She admitted that they found the confines of the bungalow strange at first, but at least it was snug. Jim settled in his chair and began by telling me of his father's involvement with horses:

'He had Clydesdales and Shires which he would break in when they were two-year olds, and then sell as work horses to the local towns. They went to pull everything. Also the army used to hire hunters from him, and other horses for officers' parades. He made enough money in the summer that way to hunt his own mare, Rachel, in the winter.

'When I was thirteen I left school and began to help on the farm. But then in 1927 we got foot-and-mouth disease, and that meant the end of the cows and the pigs – even the dogs and cats had to be killed because by law, all four-legged animals on an infected farm had to be destroyed.'

Minnie interjects: 'Jim's mother went out and milked all the cows before they were slaughtered to relieve the discomfort they would feel as a result of having a very full udder. But of course, all the milk had to be poured down the drain.'

Jim continues: 'A big trench was dug in one of the fields, and after they'd been slaughtered, all the animals were put in this pit and burnt.

'Losing the herd we lost our milk round – and we'd been the first TT [tuberculin tested: tested free from the tuberculosis bacillus] milk in Yorkshire, too. There was an epidemic of foot-and-mouth at the time. A huge number of cattle were coming in from Ireland: the Irish would send their store bullocks over to this country to be fattened ready for slaughter, and one theory is that these brought the virus with them. That's how our cows might have got it.

'It was over a year before we could buy more cattle. And then, just as the farm was picking up nicely again, the herd contracted yet another viral disease, known as contagious abortion – that is, cows aborting their calves. That was terrible, because of course you have to put them in calf so they produce milk. We didn't know what caused it but the vets' bills started to pile up and some of the cows had to go to the knacker's yard; and finally we had to give up because there was just no money left.

'My father got a farm manager's job at Hadleigh in Essex, but I decided to go and work for an uncle. He paid me 4s a week, and apart from the family I was the only workman. However, after a year I decided to join my father.

'In 1933 my father moved to become the manager of some farms at Worlaby, near Brigg in Lincolnshire, and I and my two brothers went with him. It was at Worlaby that I had my first experience of stallion walking, when we bought, on behalf of the estate owners, a two-year-old Clydesdale stallion. He was a lovely dark-brown horse called "Worlaby Fashion".'

Jim goes over to a drawer in their sideboard, and pulls out a photograph. It shows a smartly dressed young man standing in front of a stallion, hand raised so the rein is held beneath the horse's chin so that it stands still for the camera. There's no doubt that the beautifully turned out animal is the star of the picture: Worlaby Fashion, and of course the young man is Jim. He explained how he worked with the stallion:

'Tenant farmers would ring up or talk to you at market, saying they had a mare they wanted to put in foal and asking you to take Worlaby Fashion to the mare. The stud fee was £2, but if the mare didn't get in foal they had a free service the following year.

'I never had a proper route with him. If it was somewhere a long way off, well, we had a lorry on the farm and popped him in it and away; but a lot of the time I walked him around. It was always local, I didn't have to stay away overnight. The season for serving mares was from April to July, and I then broke him to work on the farm. He'd work as hard as any of the other horses.

'There was a wonderful stockman called George Wilson at Worlaby, and he used to be a stallion walker. I remember him one morning going down on his bike to a Thoroughbred stallion which was so vicious no one could travel it. But George was quite fearless, and went into the horse's box and before it finished tossing its head, he had hit it with an ash stick between the ears. He tamed it and travelled it, then.

Jim with Worlaby Fashion

'My father died in 1936, but we stayed on, my elder brother Chris by this time being foreman. Soon after I was invited to go to Forshaws, a firm which kept a large number of stallions; in the season they sent these stallions out, each with a walker, all over the country. They were a family business based at Carlton-on-Trent, near Newark in Nottinghamshire. The men on their farm used to be up at 5.30 each morning training horses, and they only had stallions.

Billie Taylor, an old-fashioned Shire man, must have put a word in for me to the firm, because one Sunday when I came back from chapel Richard Forshaw was sat in his car waiting for me. This was probably a good start because the Forshaws were big churchmen. Tom Forshaw, Richard's uncle and the main man in the firm, was sixty years in the church choir. He was also practically teetotal. He'd have a glass of sherry but would fill it half with water. They used to say if you went to Forshaws and said "I'm a teetotaller" they'd take you on.

'Anyway, Richard said to me: "I wonder if you can do us a favour. The man who was going to take 'The Dean' to Wem has chucked it in, I don't know why. Can you get to our place for Tuesday morning?"

'So I went to their premises, and they asked how I wanted my wages. "Oh," I said, "I'll just have a bit and then square up at the end." Then they gave me a little card to carry – they gave one to all their men, and although I can't remember the exact wording on it, it was something like:

Keep away from Public Houses,
Look after your horse first,
Get him settled first,
Get to bed early.

' "The Dean" was one of their champions, and he was a grand old lad, not in the least temperamental – because stallions can be a handful, you know. Forshaws had one which, for some reason, became very upset when it was travelling and pulled violently against the man who was travelling it, and he ended up losing his arm altogether!

'On my first day I walked The Dean from the farm down a short cinder track to a railway siding; there were several boxes at the siding, and the place used to be busy with mares coming in during the season. In those days there were railway waggons which could take up to three horses. We took a train to Wem: the Wem and District Agricultural Association had arranged The Dean's visit to the area with Forshaws, and initially we stopped at the Talbot Hotel, The Dean in a box in their stable yard.

'The following day was market day in Wem, so I rose early and groomed The Dean, and took him to stand in the market so that farmers could come and look at him.

'A card had been printed with The Dean's particulars, also such commendations as "He has proved himself a sure foal-getter and a sire of many prize-winners", and there was a list of all his own prizes. He'd won the 16.3hh class – the "Little Horse Class" it was called – for four consecutive years at the London Show. On the back of the card was the route I was going to walk him – that is, leave Wem on a Monday, and where I'd be travelling that day, ending up for the night at Hodnet. There were details for my travels each day of the week, and that I'd arrive back at Wem the following Saturday. Sunday was to be a rest day, and on the Monday I'd go off following the same route I'd taken the week before. That was to be my schedule for the "season", April until June.

'I had a pocketful of these cards to give out, and the association had also put my route in the local farming paper. It was information farmers wanted to know, because not many kept a stallion. Most farm horses were mares, and it was an opportunity for owners to mate them with a good quality stallion and breed a foal which they could sell, or keep on to work for themselves.

'When I set off on my travels I didn't know where I was going as I'd never been in the parish before, and I had to ask directions; but I soon got to know the route, and discovered I had some wonderful places to visit. We used to walk about ten to fifteen miles a day. Occasionally I'd stop and have a word with a roadman, and The Dean would graze for a while on the verge – or men working horses in the fields would come up and have a natter with me.

'We had a list of places to visit, but this was added to as we went along. For instance when I was stopping the night somewhere, very often somebody would ring up and ask to speak to "the groom". They'd say, "I've a mare and I'm sure she's in season and you'll be coming past my gate, could you drop in?" Or perhaps a farmer would send someone to meet me as I was walking along the road and ask me to go to a mare at a farm down a lane. They'd almost always assure me that it wasn't a very long lane – but sometimes it was over a mile, and then I had to come back again, so that was another mile!

The Dean

'The Dean would serve eight to ten mares a day, but it was really very difficult to get him interested if the mare was suckling a foal. As a stallion man you had a certain procedure to follow: first, to serve a mare you needed a good fence, or preferably a gate. You took your horse one side, and someone would bring the mare to the other side, but with her head first and not the other way, because until she had been given the chance to meet the stallion she might start to kick or smash the barrier down. They'd put their heads together and smell each other, and you'd let 'em nibble one another. If the mare was in season she'd whinny and pass water and suchlike. Then you'd take the tackle – that is, the rug

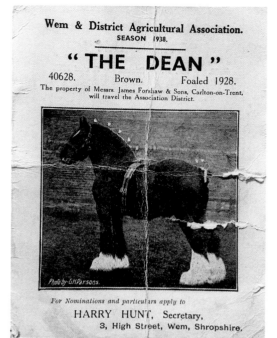

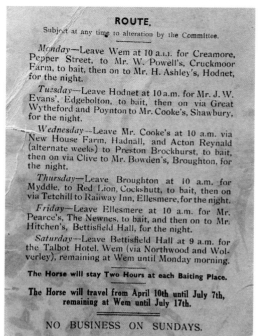

The Dean's stallion card

and whatever else he was carrying – off the stallion and the gate would be opened.

'You'd push the mare's tail aside, and tie it back with small pieces of string. The stallion would then mount her, and you'd guide his penis into her. When he was finished you had a bucket of water and you always washed his penis straightaway. The mare then went away and you hoped that was the end of it. But because you travelled the route regularly, if after three weeks the farmer thought she'd come into season again, you'd go back. And if she wasn't interested in the stallion, then she'd probably taken.

'It was important that mares were clean, otherwise the stallion might contract an infection; sometimes I'd have to refuse to let him serve a mare if it had a discharge. Perhaps they'd brought her along too soon after she'd had a foal. It had to be ten days or over after foaling; you're not supposed to serve them for three weeks, but you can serve them at ten days after they've foaled as long as they're clean.

'It's interesting, if there were any women around, they'd be the first to come and watch proceedings– but girls didn;t like to go out with stallion walkers; I knew a chap whose girlfriend found out where he worked, and she pushed off straightaway!

'Some of the earlier stallion men used to drink quite heavily, and they did give the occupation a bad name. I must have followed on the heels of one like this, because at one place they swept me out of the yard with no dinner – and once at Hodnet when I hadn't fixed up any lodgings, the publican refused to accommodate either me or the horse because he'd had some rough stallion men in the past. On that occasion I went down to the village: it was a cold night, and I was lucky to be offered a box for the horse on a farm on the outskirts, and a room for myself over a butcher's shop. This was with a Mrs Dodds, and I went there for three seasons.

'My wage was £2 a week, and my lodgings had to come out of that. I usually paid 2/6d for bed and breakfast so this didn't leave much over, but if I was going to a farm they always gave me lunch, and if I went into a pub they served a ploughman's lunch. A pint was 6d.'

On the day of my visit Jim was looking immaculate in polished brown brogue shoes, checked sports jacket, light-coloured flannels, a maroon sweater and maroon-patterned tie. This prompted me to observe that stallion walkers had the reputation for always being very smart.

Jim nodded: 'Yes, that was part of the job – you had to look smart.' And Minnie added: 'Jim always liked good breeches – there's nothing worse than badly cut breeches.'

Jim nodded again in agreement, and said, 'I always bought my own clothes. There was a good breeches maker in Wem, and I also bought my leather leggings there, which I've kept, by the way.' He slips out of the room and returns with the leggings. They fasten with buckles, and are still soft and polished.

'I bought these for 10s and this brush to clean them for 6d. I remember Mr Hunt the secretary saying to me when we finished the first season, "You're the best groom we've had, you always have a collar and tie on!" ' Jim then continues his recollections of travelling The Dean:

'I carried my clean loose collars, a bar of soap, a towel, a pair of socks and my shoe polish and brush in a pack on The Dean's back. He also carried a dandy brush and comb, and ribbons and raffia for himself. The ribbons, known as *caddis*, were blue and white, the Forshaw colours. My morning routine was first to give him a good brush, then to plait his tail, which had been docked, with raffia; the plait was looped up "Toby jug" style. Then I tied ribbons to the underside of his tail. I also plaited his mane, and every so often put in a wire and a ribbon.

'At night I never washed him with a bucket of water, no matter how hot the day had been, because I was afraid he'd get pneumonia. Usually when walking he'd wear a light rug called a quarter sheet, because a stallion should never be allowed to get wet on the loins for fear he caught a chill. On particularly hot days I would put sawdust on him straightaway in the evening, to stop his coat drying matted with sweat; I would then brush the sawdust out. On other occasions I've used chippings, anything like that.

'He would wear his shoes out quite quickly, and as Forshaws were very strict on this I used to check them frequently. If he needed shoeing I got it done at Ellesmere on a Friday night, at the forge of two brothers who were blacksmiths there.

'The Dean came to recognise Wem, and he'd whinny when we came into the main street every Saturday. He loved his big box at the Talbot Hotel and as soon as he arrived he would roll in it.

'I'd get my hair cut, and do my laundry at weekends. On Saturday nights I always made a bran mash for The Dean and put two teaspoonfuls of special powder into it, the recipe for which came from the old Worlaby stallion man, George Wilson. I've lost the piece of paper now, but I used to take it to the chemist and he'd make up the mixture. I think it was a combination of minerals and salt, and it did seem to keep him looking really fit.

'At the end of the season, if men took their horses home in good order, Forshaws gave them an extra £3. The bosses also told us always to keep an eye open for good colt foals, and fillies which would make decent broodmares – and if we told them where one was, they'd go and buy it. The deal used to be sealed with a smack in the hand. Forshaws had a wonderful name for reliability: if you made a bargain with them there was no need to write it down.

'At the start of the second season when I arrived at Wem station I felt quite emotional

because I knew people would be looking out for me; and at the end of one season I was given £4 which the farmers had clubbed together to give me as a sort of thank-you present. I did three seasons at Wem with "The Dean", and then the war came. At the beginning of the war you weren't allowed to buy food for horses, and all the Forshaw stallions went to the knacker man. We plaited their manes and tails up before we sent them, and it was really one of the most distressing things I had to do – we were all so upset. The horses made £3 apiece at the knackers. Six months later the ruling had changed, to the effect that horseflesh was eligible for human consumption to help eke out meat rationing, and this meant that Forshaws could have made £120 a horse.

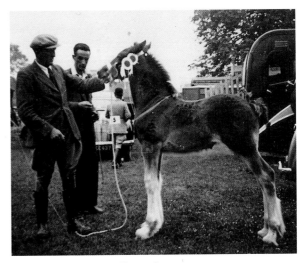

Both well turned out!
Jim and an entrant at a local horse show

'I went back to the big estate in Lincoln to do a bit of shepherding, and became head man of all stock. I had a horse to ride, and also used to break in horses for work. There were frequent farm sales, and a lot of horses at these, and the local auctioneer usually wanted someone to plait up their tails to make them look smart; so on Saturdays I would do this as well as my ordinary work.

'I took Minnie to visit Wem after we were married, and we went to see the butcher's wife, Mrs Dodds. Her daughter, who'd been only a little girl when I lodged there, remembered me: when she opened the door she called, "Mum, here's Mr Dean!" '

Jim still walks: having worked out of doors all his life he likes to get out of the house. Every day, if he's able, he takes one of his collection of sticks – although not his father's precious measuring one – and sets off on a mile and a half tour of the village. He stops to talk to people on his way, and he has certain places that he always visits: a bit like old times, really.

---

*A*t the farm of Dick Jones, a farmer now local to Wem, there is still a loosebox called 'the stallion's box' because the travelling stallion was always lodged there. He also tells the following story:

'My family came to the farm in 1936. Its previous owners had been a family named Anwyll, and the Anwylls had sixteen Shire stallions which they would hire out for stud to different areas through the Shire Horse Society; they would go all over the country. Also, there is a field on this farm which the older locals advise me never to put sheep in, maintaining that if I do they'll always go lame because it's the field the sixteen stallions were put out into when the "season" was over. The Anwylls used to let the field's thorn hedges grow to ten or twelve feet across so that the horses had plenty of shelter, and the grass was left to grow as long as hay so that in July and August there would be plenty of grazing.

'In the early 1930s the Anwylls bought a grey foal from up the Severn Valley. It was called Ervell Lady Grey, and they sold it to Chivers Farm, Histon, for the then colossal sum of 750 guineas.'

William Pugh, retired farmworker from near Bridgnorth, Shropshire; observes: 'I always remember the stallion walkers as being little men – unless they looked so because the stallions were so big; little with bandy legs, but smart in breeches and polished leggings.'

THE STUD GROOM

Brian Higham, Badminton, Avon

The last time they met, Brian Higham recalls that HM the Queen told him: 'Every time I see you Brian, you personify Badminton.'

And he does, because in his capacity of stud groom Brian rules over the 11th Duke of Beaufort's stable yard. His charges include thirty horses looked after by eight girl grooms, and every day Brian himself will be seen somewhere on Badminton estate exercising the Duke's horses or in the stable yard overseeing their welfare. Hunting evenings in particular involve checking over each animal thoroughly for cuts and bruises sustained whilst out with the famous 'Blue and Buffs', the alternative name for the Beaufort Hunt and taken from the colours of the hunt livery.

Brian's weathered face is serious, and he betrays a feeling of nostalgia as he looks around the stable yard: 'I often think this is probably the last place where things are run on traditional lines. In the past all big houses had stable yards like this, but over the years the cost of keeping them running has proved too much. I'm glad this place is being written about, because it can't go on for ever.'

A native of Snainton in the Vale of Pickering in Yorkshire, Brian came to Badminton in 1959. He is from a long line of men whose professions have lain with country estates. One of his ancestors was a gamekeeper, Matthew Pateman, who worked at Ebberston Hall for Squire George Osbaldeston, a gentleman famous for being the 'hunting squire of England'. A century later, and Matthew's kin, Bert Pateman, was carrying on the tradition of working for a hunting man, but further south: Bert was employed by the 10th Duke of Beaufort on the beautiful Badminton estate a few miles from Tetbury in Gloucestershire. In his thirty years of service to the Duke he worked as whipper-in; then kennel huntsman and finally huntsman. And when, during that time, an extra hand was needed in the stable yard at Badminton, Bert spoke up for his sister's boy, Brian Higham.

Brian was living in Yorkshire at the time, and recalls being interviewed for the job by the Duke himself when he was judging at the Great Yorkshire Show. And thus it was that he came to Badminton as second horseman and second man. Uncle Bert is now dead and Brian is in his thirty-eighth season. 'A season starts from the first of May,' he explains, adding 'I've been stud groom since 1966. This means I am in charge of the stables and the grooms, and that it is my responsibility to produce fit horses for the Masters and Hunt staff and guests for the whole season.'

Brian is married, and he met his pretty American wife, Sherry, when she had sought his advice whilst on a horse-buying trip from the States; they live in a spacious cottage a stone's throw from the stable yard. Its entrance bedecked by flower baskets, the cottage is entirely in keeping with the picture-postcard beauty of Badminton village. The single village street is flanked by houses built of mellow Bath stone, their woodwork painted yellow-buff, the estate colour. The street's timeless appearance is a fitting introduction to the old-fashioned stable yard beyond. Even so, Brian hasn't forgotten his Yorkshire humour: 'Musn't forget my cap, there's woodpeckers about,' he is wont to say, setting that accessory firmly on his head en route from cottage to stable-yard door.

The handle set into the yard's huge door is fashioned in the shape of a stirrup, and like the rest of the estate woodwork, the door itself is painted buff to match the buff of the Duke's hunt livery. It opens onto a vast square yard with buildings on all four sides. There

Badminton village with the Estate Office in the background

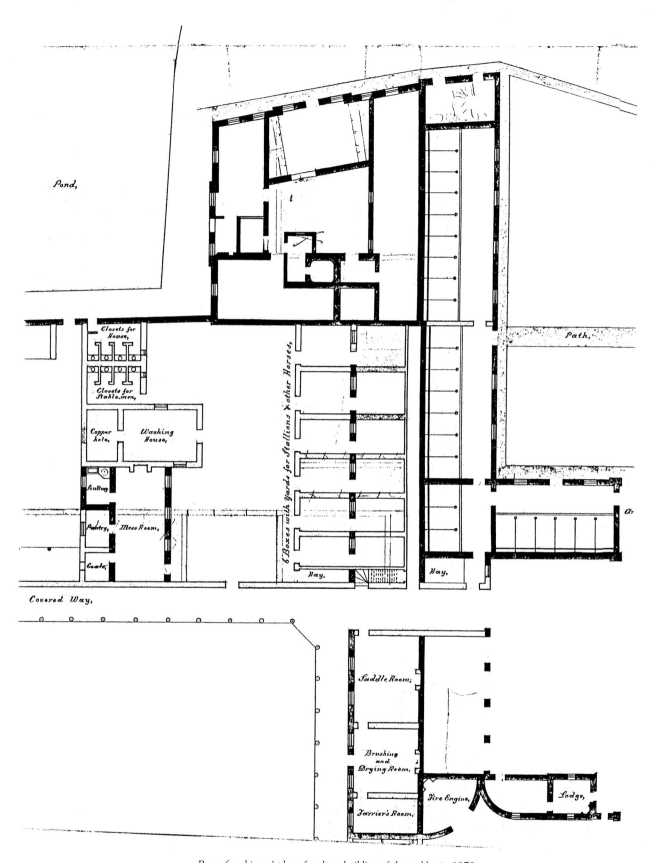

Part of architects' plans for the rebuilding of the stables in 1878

is a wooden tower on the north side, on its roof a weather vane in the shape of a fox stretching its iron forepaws perpetually in the direction of the wind. The yard was built in 1887 and the weather vane also dates from that time: thus a glance at this very same vane would have shown a Victorian stud groom the way the wind was blowing, and helped him to work out how to keep an even pressure of air within the stables. He did this by opening and closing the windows according to the horses' comings and goings – because heaven forbid that his equine charges be subjected to draughts! Brian no longer practises such niceties, but is full of admiration for the way the stables are built:

The weather vane with a hunting theme

'Years ago they knew all about animals requiring good ventilation. The stables here are very warm and airy in the winter, and cool and airy in the summer. They're high, 14ft to the eves, and this gives plenty of room so that the dust can get above the horses. A lot of stables today have low ceilings, and horses will develop respiratory problems from that sort of housing because the dust from the hay and straw, and probably the sprays and fertilisers used on them, can't get out.'

Each doorway from the yard leads into a line of looseboxes. Outside each box is a polished brass hook for hanging a headcollar, and the latch on each door is also brass; and every Sunday all the brass throughout the stables is cleaned. Brian admits with pride that there is not a stable in the country still run on such traditional lines. An iron saddle horse is fitted to each loosebox post; when not in use these fold away so there is no risk of the horses knocking against them.

Halfway up the stable wall nearest the yard, iron racks hold brushes and forks: stored safely in this way, they pose no risk of injury should a horse get out in the night. With equal care for safety, the water taps in this same wall are set in ornate Victorian iron alcoves. Brian also points out the doorways, which are all built wide so that horses don't knock their hip bones as they are led in and out.

As well as the stables, the yard is extremely well appointed as regards rooms where all the different tasks concomitant with running a high class yard can be accomplished. Thus the tack man works in a 'cleaning room' complete with a copper and a sink. There is a glass case lined with baize which holds clean spurs and bits, and polished oak stands where saddles can be racked up to air. When the tack is clean it is stored in the 'best tack room'. The one at Badminton is panelled in wood to the full height of its 20ft [6m] high walls, with saddle trees, complete with saddles, set one above the other from head height to ceiling; the higher ones are reached by a long wooden ladder. Other saddles are stored over old wooden 'Toblerone'-shaped rests, polished bright by use. The room is heated by rows of ninteenth-century, 4in iron hot-water pipes.

Within the rich gloom Brian says 'The "best tack room" can be the holiest, even now, and in times past no one would have been allowed in here except the tack man. He would always have been immensely proud of his work, and would have kept everything in immaculate order. Pride was an essential ingredient in every sort of job then – and there was nothing wrong with being proud, that's where it's a changing world today.'

He picks up some of the tack: 'Leather today is tanned differently to how it was years ago; it's not as good, and it doesn't last as long. And you never saw numnahs, the saddle-shaped piece of sheepskin or fabric that people put beneath their saddle nowadays. That's because in the old days a saddle was made to fit the horse for which it was intended, and it had a linen lining with a bit at the back blancoed white. Today the linings are leather. At one time when this place was in full swing there was a saddler's shop at Badminton – of course in those days there was also the carriage harness to see to, and all that worn by the farm horses.'

On the north side of the yard is the feed store. A bit like the quality leather, there have been changes in this department too. Brian explains: 'In the last thirty-five to forty years feed merchants' policy has been increasingly to compound feedstuffs into nut or cube form. Before that feed was mainly provided as chaff and oats, or chaff, beans, oats and different types of clover. They used to pour molasses over the feed, too, whereas now molasses comes in the compounds. However, I would say that in general, horses look better today than they did years ago.

DESIGN FOR STABLES FOR 48 HORSES   PLATE 1

VIEW OF THE PRINCIPAL FAÇADE

'As regards feeding, a big yard would have a yard man, and some still do. He'd make the mash with a hand-turned chaff cutter, in the days before there was an electric machine to do it. We have an old mash house here, with metal coppers which would be warmed by lighting fires underneath them.'

Brian's office is at the far end of the east side of the yard. One of the doorways from it is in direct line with a doorway leading to a row of looseboxes running down the south side, and with both doors open there is a clear view down the whole row. Brian says that you do have to walk along the boxes to check them properly, but there is no doubt that both now, as in years gone by, from this doorway vantage point a stud groom can keep a fairly close eye on stable lads and lasses!

The office has a black chest-high Victorian desk, and rows of old books. These include diaries from the mid-nineteenth century which record carriage runs between Bath and Bristol, and also various wage-books. Brian opens one dated 1908: 'There were forty men here then, so there'd 've been over a hundred horses. The stud groom received 27s and there was even a woman paid to do the mess-room!'

Various old veterinary aids hang on the office wall and Brian lifts a few down. 'This is a drenching horn – years ago one reason for drenching was to alleviate colic. You'd put the prongs of a pitchfork through the horse's headcollar and, standing on a bin, use the horn to pour a mixture down his throat. Another old remedy was nutmeg and horsehair to get rid of parasitical worms; horses can't be sick like humans, so the idea was to purge them. Those who knew how would make up balls of medicine, and a skilled man could put a ball down with his hand or use one of these balling guns – this bar goes on the back of the tongue and is then pressed down.' Brian then proceeds to describe the yard and the running of it, both as it used to be, and as it is now:

Brian with a 'baller'; one of the old tools kept at Badminton. It was used to open a horse's mouth so a draught or pill could be inserted

'There's a wash-box in the yard. Not that we always wash horses, but we might want to wash one that's injured. There is also a room known as the "pharmacy". It's never been in use in my time, but it still contains old blue poison bottles and apothecary scales, and there used to be a handwritten book of horse cures in it, many of which we still use. For example in a wet season a constant problem is mud fever, basically an inflammation of the skin because of mud getting into the pores; a horse's legs may swell, and bad cases can't hunt. To treat it we mix up copper sulphate, meths, vinegar and water and apply it for three or four days, and this works better than a lot of the modern treatments. And an old way of drying the mud and wet quickly from a horse's heels is to apply sawdust or bran – bran is thought to be best because there's a soothing quality in flour.

'I still boil up the herb comfrey and bandage it around swollen knees. In fact you can use any sort of brassica for this, because they all have great drawing qualities.

'There's an old saying, "If a horse has got a headache, check his feet", and it's remarkable how true this is. If a horse is "footy" I may use cow dung to ease the pain – and pig dung is useful too, but for another reason: if a horse is biting his rug, smear some on the spot, and he'll soon stop!

'As regards the general care and management of horses, there used to be men in these sorts of yards with job titles you never hear today. For example a "nagsman" was someone who would "make" the young horses – he would "nag" 'em about, ride 'em hunting and make them at home before they went hunting properly with their owners or their guests.

'Then there were "strappers"; today we call this sort of person a 'groom' though part of the strapper's job was to "wisp" or "strap" a horse, and this is rarely done nowadays. He would make a "wisp" out of hay or straw, depending on the quality of the forage, by twisting it round until it was quite substantial, and then he would slap or "bang" the horse with it over its neck, quarters and loins. It didn't hurt the horse but it was said to help build up his muscles. Old-fashioned people still do it, but it's all about time and labour, and today a girl groom probably looks after four horses so she hasn't got time to do it.

House

1901				£ s d		£ s d

Stables continued — Brought Forward £ ... 2313 | 5 | 7 ... 3147 | 17 | 6

Date	Name	Description	Sub-amount	£	s	d
12 Jany	Geo. Williams & Son V.S.	examining horse at Tattersals		1	1	-
12 Jany 11-6-9 11 July 12-4-6	A. Turpin	Chemist		23	11	3
21 Jany	J. & G. Lock	Livery hats & hunting caps for second horsemen		19	13	-
4 July 36-13-6 19 Dec 32-11-6	W. E. Cross	Livery for coach establishment £69 - 5 - 0				
4 July 13-2-0 19 Dec 153-1-6	— do —	— do. hunting -do- 166 - 3 - 6		235	8	6
21 Jany	Bartley & Sons	top boots for coachmen and second horsemen		33	13	9
21 Jany	Thos. Callow & Son	horse thongs, crops &c		19	6	6
22 "	The reps of the late E. H. Baker	saddlery ½ year to Christmas 1900 255-5-6				
16 April 55-5-2 5 July 17-6-8 29 " -19-0 8 Oct 137-17-0	Shattock Hunter & Co	saddlery 211-7-10		466	13	4
9 Feby	G. Dallimore	Shoeing horses at Semington		2	10	-
9 May 32-13-6 12 July 12-18-0 27 Aug 6-9-6 3 Sep 6-14-10	Peat Moss Litter Co	Moss litter		58	15	10
16 May 2-2-0 12 Dec 2-8-0	Excec. of late E. Sharp	standing and feed for hound van horses 4-10-0				
16 May 1-16-0 30 Nov -18-0 12 Dec 1-16-0	R. Careless	-do- 4-10-0				
16 May -12-0 12 Dec 1-4-0	T. Blackman	-do- 1-16-0		10	16	-
31 Oct	Hood & Moore	forage for London carriage horses		47	15	6
3 July	A. Thompson	vetches 4-14-0				
" "	H. Butler	-do- 23-4-0		27	18	-
12 "	Musgrave & Co Ld	mangers		6	18	6
12 Sep	Gillett & Johnston	a new turret clock 105-0-0				
12 Oct	T. Long	winding up -do- one year to 29 Sep 1-6-0		106	6	-
13 Sept	J. Slade	carriage of goods		-	7	-
31 Oct	Cotterell Bros.	wall paper		-	3	10
26 "	W. E. Spencer	hunter		63	-	-
				3437	5	7

License Duties

19 Jany	Collector of Inland Revenue	for 45 male servants 33-15-0				
		Carried Forward £ 33-15-0		3437	5	7 ... 3147 17 6

Account

		Brought Forward £	33	15	–	3437	5	7	3147	17	6

Stables contd
Licenses

17 Jany	Collector of Inland Revenue	9 – 4 wheel 2 horse carriages	18	18	–						
"		1 – 4 wheel 1 horse do.	1	1	–						
"		3 – 2 wheel 1 horse do.	2	5	–						
"		Armorial bearings	2	2	–	58	1	–			

Repairs

fortnightly from 19 Jany	C. E. Lewis	tradesmens work and for shoeing, one year to the 28th Decr 1901	177	8	1						
	A. Perks	whitewashing	2	16	7						
6 Sep	Jno Turnor	painter	30	–	–						
9 Nov	J. Clark & Sons	cow hair	6	2	6						
14 Dec	E. Russell	smith	–	17	9						
16 "	May & Hassell	timber	15	15	–						
18 "	Thos Reynolds &	Ironmongery	15	1	–						
21 "	W. D. Patterson	do.	8	10	6						
	S. & J. Cole	Carpenters	12	16	–	269	7	5	3764	14	–

6912 11 6
3147 17 6
3764 14 –

Kennels

	W. Dale Huntsman	one year's salary to Christmas 1901	200	–	–						
	do.	Miscellaneous Xpenses	76	11	8						
30 July	do.	Xpenses to Peterboro' Show	13	12	2	90	3	10			
	J. Maloney 1st whip	one year's wages to Xmas 1901	80	0	0						
5 Oct	do.	expenses	1	6	5	81	6	5			
	T. Newman 2nd whip	one year's wages to Xmas 1901	60	0	0						
5 Oct	do.	expenses	–	7	0	60	7	–			
	W. Chiles Kennelman	one year's wages to Xmas 1901	52	0	0						
	do.	273 hides at 1/.	13	13	0	65	13	–			
	W. Dale	underkennelmens wages one year to 28 December 1901	101	7	–						
		Carried Forward £				598	17	3	6912	11	6

An extract from the House, Park and Farm accounts, Badminton archives

A healthfull drink for a horse.

Boyl half a dozen cloves of Garlick for some time
in 3 pints of Ale, being straind, add half an ounce
of Elicampane, y[e] like quantity of Bay-berries, w[th]
Diapente, & Turmorick, w[ch] wth an ounce of Venice
Treacle, & 2 spoonfulls of honey make into a drink

Probatum est.

For y[e] Scratches.

Cut away y[e] hair, rub off y[e] scabs, & wash y[e] horses legs w[th]
old urine, Alome, & salt, mixt together, & heated, as hot as
y[e] horse can endure it, y[n] take y[e] tops & buds of Elder, & y[e] green
berries of bryers, boyld in a pottle of Stonewort, to w[ch] add
a good quantity of Alome, & wth this, wash y[e] part griev'd
twice or thrice y[e] day. Probatum.

Or.

Let y[e] horse blood in y[e] Fetlock vein, suffring him to blee
pretty freely; y[e] next day wash & clean y[e] part wth warm
water then cliping away y[e] hair anoint it wth this oyntm[nt].
Take Verdigrease, & green Copperas of each 2 Ounces, & 4 of
Honey well pounded & mixt together.

Some wonderful remedies for horses from the Badminton archives

'Strappers also used to have certain ways of doing things: for instance it was tradition to put an odd number of plaits on a lady's horse; and the length of a hunter's tail was also important – the correct length was one inch above the chestnuts when the horse was stood square. Now you see all lengths, and nobody would care if it was touching the ground or not; but years ago grooms were immensely proud of the horses from their yard, and they'd be watching others very carefully, too.

'There was also much more emphasis on "spit and polish" and finishing touches. Strappers would take the trouble to weave straw round a pitch-fork handle and lay it across the doorway so that the stall looked tidy. Another trick was to outline the estate crest in sawdust at the box entrance. Actually I've never seen that done, but I've heard old chaps talk of it.

' "Jockey" Matthews, who's sadly passed on, could remember all the old ways – he was a proper little strapper fellow. He used to ride second horse to the 10th Duke; before that, 'Jockey' used to take the 9th Duke out in a donkey cart when the Duke couldn't ride because he had gout and weighed twenty stone.

'There's a blacksmith's shop in this yard, and I've heard it said that there was once a tailor's premises, probably in the estate yard – there was so much livery in those days. The second horsemen used to wear green coats: before horseboxes it was their job to hack the horses to a meet, and also to take fresh – or "second" – horses to a pre-arranged spot part-way through the day, for the Duke and each of his party.

'Big yards like this would also have one man solely responsible for clipping and trimming, probably someone very experienced who didn't ride any more. He would do this in a clipping box, and would be hugely proud of his skill. Nowadays, well, you could go to a meet today and think some of the horses had been clipped with a knife and fork – but nobody takes any notice because so many people just don't know the difference.'

Brian chuckles. Needless to say, Badminton horses keep up the traditionally high standard in their clipped appearance. The final touch for a really smart job is to singe off the longer "cats-hairs", particularly in the spring, and sure enough, there is an old brass singeing-lamp amongst Brian's tools. He explains how the handle of the lamp is filled with meths, and how, lit by a match, a wick within the lamp feeds a flame. The flame then fans out in the shape of the bristle end of a paintbrush. Deftly and quickly Brian demonstrates, running the flame over one of the horse's coats, burning off any stray long hairs.

'There won't be many people singe today, I would imagine,' he observes. 'But it's very practical in the spring when you stop clipping, because as the horses' summer coats come through they also grow these cat's-hairs down the back of the legs and under the jaw in particular, but all over the coat, too. Singeing these off makes them look much neater, and they love having it done because it's warm. I've never had a horse you couldn't do, once it realises the lamp's not actually going to burn it.'

Brian also prefers the traditional methods for breaking in young horses, and at certain times of the year he can be seen in the lanes around Badminton walking behind a young horse which he is controlling with long reins. 'You have to handle them well from birth, and again, it's all about time – some people are inclined to try and break a horse too quickly, and this doesn't always work. Of course, you can always try the old horseman's remedy to make a horse obey you: that is to get a foal's "false tongue", a piece which is present in the afterbirth, once a foal's been born. Some old chaps used to dry this out and carry it in

their pocket, and this was supposed to make any horse respect the man carrying it!'

Brian considers the question of what makes a good hunter:

'Everybody has his or her own ideas. I like the Irish Draught/Thoroughbred cross, which has a bit of limb and a good temperament. And for people that can ride them, Thoroughbreds – they wear well because often they've got enough bone, and plenty of spirit – an ounce of blood is worth an inch of bone, as the saying goes! I was fortunate enough to be given the 10th Duke's horse, Jupiter; and the one I have now, a grey called Lord, was given to me by the 11th, the present Duke. In fact it's not part of my job to go hunting, and if I do go out it's a perk.

'Our routine is to bring in a few horses from grass in June, early July, ready for autumn hunting, and these are in use by the end of August. They need seven to eight weeks to get reasonably fit. Nowadays these could be any horses, though years ago you probably kept a few horses that weren't sound enough to go the whole season and used them just to September or October. All the horses are up before the end of July. Hunting proper starts in November, but most of the horses won't be really fit until mid-December.

'Years ago they didn't turn the horses out in the summer at all; they had enough labour to keep them ticking over in the stable. They used to bring them vetches and grasses from the fields, and kept them on very light work, so they were never allowed to go right down, to become really unfit. Of course, in those days the season was longer – they used to catch a May fox here, the season finished at the end of that month, and autumn hunting started at the end of August; so it didn't pay to put the horses out fit and well, and then they would be really gross and soft by the time they were brought back in.

'I am no chauvinist when it comes to looking to the future: a stud groom was always a very respected position, still is. Most big hunts have probably got a *man* stud groom still, but they are becoming fewer because hunts have cut down the number of horses – it's all down to

The 10th Duke of Beaufort

59

The first vet's inspection takes place in front of the house at Badminton, before the trials start

costs, again. I think eventually a good lady could do the same job, and often does in some cases. In fact, I think in general girls do a very good job and work equally as many hours today as men did in stables years ago.'

When he's not to be found in the stable yard Brian is generally away judging horses at shows in different parts of the country. Or he could be buying horses in Ireland, and meeting his old friend Mick O'Connor there. Mick is a breeder and dealer of some repute, whose customers include the British army: 'Sefton', whom the nation grew to love in the early 1980s following his injuries from an IRA nail bomb at a London barracks, was originally one of Mick's horses.

Brian's own judgement when it comes to choosing a horse for purchase is highly respected, so much so that he was entrusted with negotiating the purchase of a pony for Princess Beatrice, a gift from her grandmother, the Queen.

When the occasion demands it, Brian is a smartly dressed man. For a day at Cheltenham races he wears a bowler hat, and considers it sensible, secure headwear in windy spring weather. He also wears his bowler when he mingles amongst the crowds keeping an eye on things during the four days of the famous Badminton Horse Trials.

The horse trials take place at the beginning of May and are, of course, a major event in his calendar. During the weeks leading up to them, he arranges for all the stables to be thoroughly washed out, disinfected and put ready for the international influx of competitors' horses which will inhabit them. Even an individual horse's preference for straw, paper or shavings as bedding is taken into account!

Riders appreciate this care, and also Brian's presence. Karen Dixon says: 'Brian Higham is one in a lifetime. To the riders that have the pleasure of returning to Badminton later in the year after the horse trials, to train as part of the British team, he is an intricate part of the place. Not only his knowledge of horses, his local knowledge is enormous too – as is his character and his heart! And he is always one for a new joke, particularly if it's rude; he never fails to make you laugh!'

She adds: 'Over the last fifteen years he has been of enormous support to me, and become a good friend. Long may he remain fit, healthy, and one of the cornerstones of Badminton.'

Mary King (née Thomson) has been competing at Badminton Horse Trials since 1985. She, too, admits that arrival time at the stable yard is laced with joke-swapping: 'Brian generally has a new crop to tell!'

Like Karen, she also meets Brian when she is part of the British team training at Badminton. Mary remembers that on the last such occasion, which was prior to the Olympics, Brian and Sherry, in a typically kind gesture, invited all the girl grooms round to their house. Indeed, during Trials week itself, the Higham household is swelled by visiting Masters, farriers, friends from Ireland and any number of people connected with horses. Such happy, chaotic interludes are part of life at Badminton.

To make a horse follow his master, and to find him out and challenge him amongst ever so many people.

Take a pound of oatmeal, to which put a quarter of a pound of honey, and half a pound of liquorice, make a little cake thereof, and put it into your bosom next to your naked skin, and then run and labour yourself till you sweat, and so rub all your sweat upon your cake; then keep the horse fasting a day and a night, and give it him to eat, which done, turn him loose, and he shall not only follow you, but also hunt and seek you out, when he has lost you, and when he comes to you, spit in his mouth, anoint his tongue with your spittle, and thus doing, he will never forsake you.

The Complete Horseman or
Country Gentleman's Recreation, 1795

Mounting for Ladies

If she be very timid, she may practice mounting indoors, with her right hand on the top of an upright piano, and her left on a gentleman's shoulder…

Alice M. Hayes, *The Horsewoman,* 1903

On Toothache

'…the horse rarely suffers from toothache; the nerve does not approach so near the crown of the tooth as in man.'

Lieut-General Sir F. Fitzwygram, Bart.,
Horses and Stables, 1911

On Grooming

…curry him well under his belly, near his fore-bowles, and in a word, all over very well, his legs under the knees and cambrels only excepted; and as you dress his left side, so must you the right also…

This currying is only to raise the dust, therefore, after the horse has been thus curried, take either an horse-tail nailed to a handle, or a clean dusting cloth of cotton, and with it strike off the loose dust that the curry comb has raised.

Then dress him all over with the French brush, both head, body, and legs, to the very fetlocks, observing always to cleanse the brush from the filth it gathers from the bottom of the hair, by rubbing it on the curry-comb; then dust the horse again the second time.

Then having wetted your hand in water, rub his body all over, and as near as you can, leave no loose hairs behind, and with your hands, wet, pick, and cleanse his eyes, ears and nostrils, sheath, cods, and tuel, and so rub him till he is as dry as at first.

Then take a hair patch and rub his body all over, but especially his fore-bowles, under his belly, his flank, and between his hinder thighs; and in the last place, wipe him over with a fine white linnen rubber.

When you have thus dressed him, take a large saddle cloth (made on purpose) that may reach down to the spuring-place, and lap it about his body: then clap on his saddle, and throw a cloth over him, that he may not catch cold…

The Complete Horseman or
Country Gentleman's Recreation, 1795

Recipe for Hoof Oil

Take 4 ounces of Venice turpentine, 3 ounces of the best rosin, of bees-wax 2 ounces, 1 pound of dog's grease and a half a pint of train oil; melt all these ingredients together, except the turpentine; then take them off the fire, and put in the turpentine, stirring it till it be well incorporated; then pour it out into an earthen gallipot, and keep it for use, but do not cover it till it is cold.

(Anoint his hoofs round from the coronet to the toe with this ointment. After this, stop his feet with cow-dung.)

The Complete Horseman or
Country Gentleman's Recreation, 1795

The Neglect of Carriages

A carriage requires as much care as a sofa, and is often treated like a wheelbarrow, thrust after use into a damp shed, to encourage the decay of the silk, velvet, or leather linings, and cause violent colds to the ladies who sit in it without the slightest precaution, when within doors they carefully dry and warm everything, from a pair of stockings to a pocket-handkerchief.

Samuel Sidney, *The Book of the Horse,* c.1880

Coaching Etiquette

The usual hour for driving in the summer is from four o'clock to seven, and in the winter from three o'clock to five, or even a little earlier. Ladies driving themselves, in either a Victoria or a pony carriage, would drive in the morning or afternoon, according to choice, although the morning hours from twelve o'clock to two are the most fashionable hours. In town or at watering-places ladies would not drive unattended by a groom, neither would they ride in town unattended by a groom, unless accompanied by a male relative, when a groom's attendance might be dispensed with. A gentleman would always ride on the off or right-hand side of a lady. In the country, ladies frequently ride out alone when they are particularly good horsewomen, but ladies would not ride to hounds unaccompanied or unattended.

In driving in an open or close carriage no particular place is reserved for the owner of the carriage when accompanied by her friends. A guest or guests would always enter the carriage before the hostess; were there two guests present, and either of them were a young lady, she would naturally seat herself with her back to the horses, leaving the two married ladies to occupy the opposite seat; but this would be a matter of courtesy on her part, and not of etiquette.

A gentleman would sit with his back to the horses if a

second lady were present; a gentleman also would be the first to descend from the carriage, with a view to assisting the ladies to alight, whether he purposed re-entering it or not. As a rule, the hostess would descend after her guest, and not before her, unless it were more convenient to do otherwise, when she could make some polite remark before alighting; but if a lady were merely calling on an acquaintance to take her for a drive, she would not descend from her carriage for the purpose of allowing her to enter it before her.

From *Manners and Tone of GOOD SOCIETY* by *A Member of the Aristocracy*, c.1880

Coaching Characters

There were some quaint characters amongst the coachmen. Ned Mountain drove the Exeter Defiance. He left Basingstoke at ten at night, drove down till he met the up-coach, when the coachmen changed coaches, and he got back to Basingstoke at eight in the morning, driving from eighty to ninety miles every night. He was once unwell and sent for the doctor, who cross-examined him as to his habits. He said he always had a pipe and a glass at eight o'clock every morning, upon which the doctor expressed astonishment that he was alive after drinking in the morning. 'It may be morning to you,' said Ned, 'but it's my bed-time, and I can't leave it off.'

Saunders wore the most correct coaching costume; a low-crown flat-brimmed white hat, and spotted shawl round his neck, which he wore on the hottest day of summer, declaring that if he left it off 'he always got the chop-ache'. He also wore what some call overalls (otherwise knee-caps) of drab cloth that buttoned up from his ankles to the top of his thighs – generally over top-boots – in the hottest weather, declaring he got rheumatism if he did not. His top coat was the thick drab West of England cloth. It was necessary to make the sleeves very large on account of the stiffness and thickness of the cloth, and the consequence was that in wet weather the rain drove up them and wetted him. To obviate this he used to make Bill Emery get some clean straw out of the stables to fill them up, and to do this effectually Bill kept a short strong stick to ram the straw tight. One day whilst they were changing horses Bill purposely left the stick up his right-hand sleeve. They had not gone far when they came to a sharp hill. Wanting to hit his leaders with his whip, Saunders was perplexed and pained to find that he could not bend his arm, and was unable to use his whip, so he called to the guard to jump down and touch up the leaders, declaring that his arm was quite stiff from rheumatism. He did not discover the stick up his sleeve till he got to the next change…'

His Grace The Duke of Beaufort, *Driving*, 1890

Gypsies

Gypsies have a fine faculty of evasion, catch them who can in the same place or story twice! Take them; teach them the comforts of civilisation; confine them in warm rooms, with thick carpets and down beds; and they will fly out of the window – like the bird, described by Chaucer, out of its golden cage.'

William Hazlitt

To make a horse look young

Take a crooked iron, no bigger than a wheat corn, and having made it red hot, burn a little black hole in the tops of the two outermost teeth of each side of the nether chap before next to the tushes where the mark is worn out then pick it with an awl blade, and make the shell fine and thin; then with a sharp scraping-iron make all his teeth white and clean; this done, take a fine lancet, and about the hollows of the horse's eyes which are shrunk down, make a little hole only through the skin, and put in the quill of a raven or crow, and blow the skin full of wind; then take the quill out, lay your finger on the hole a little while, and the wind will stay in, and he will look as youthful as if he were but five years old.

The Complete Horseman or Country Gentleman's Recreation, 1795

When to Mate Mares

February is the best time to put the mare to the horse. If in hard condition she should have a dose of physic and cooling diet, and then if she shows no signs of being stinted, a few quarts of blood may be taken. But it is a much better plan to reduce the mare to a soft condition by degrees, with soft food and slow light work at drilling and harrowing, if she is not turned out to grass. *She should on no account be allowed to see the horse again under three weeks*. Many mares are rendered barren from allowing them to see the stallion frequently, to ascertain whether they are really stinted.

Samuel Sidney, *The Book of the Horse*, c.1880

A Good Man

'Wanted a man to attend to horses of a Christian character.'

Advertisement quoted in '*A Lincolnshire Glossary*' written by Jabez Good, the village barber at Burgh le Marsh, Lincolnshire, c.1900

Tidal Wave

On 9th September, 1899, a fissure opened up in the tow path at Dudley Port. A tidal wave of water from the canal gushed through the opening and into the marl pit of a nearby brickworks.

Two boatmen were caught in the rush of water. One saved himself, his boat and horse, by quickly securing his towrope round a telegraph pole. The other, not so lucky, lost his boat but by cutting the towrope, managed to save himself and the horse.

Rough Justice

During the depression of the 1930s times were tough. Caggie Stevens, who features in the book, remembers how he and his father dealt with potential violence: 'There was only me and me father and as many as six big men would come along the towpath to raid our coal boat.'

But he used to prepare for such occasions. He looped a shortish piece of rope into a noose and got the boat horse to pull the noose up into a tight, hard knot. 'A blow on the back with that would fell a man.'

Lampass

Occasionally the gums or bars become congested, swell, and protrude beyond the wearing surface of the incisor teeth, rendering the mouth so tender the horse cannot eat. It is commonly owing to the teething process. This is called lampass; and the old race of farriers were in the habit of treating it with their favourite remedy – the application of a red hot iron – a brutal piece of ignorant folly. Gentle laxative and mash diet will generally reduce the congestion and relieve the animal. Sometimes it may be advisable to lance the gums, but in this affection it is seldom necessary.

Samuel Sidney, *The Book of the Horse*, c.1880

Hunting by Rail

There is no more luxurious conveyance than a railway carriage. Hunting-season tickets have long been an established system…

The railway directors of the best hunting lines run specials, and put on drop carriages to express trains, for the accommodation of hunting-men. A party of from half a dozen to a dozen can engage a saloon carriage, provided with a dressing-room and even cooking arrangements. The finishing stroke has been put to the luxuries of hunting by the addition of American sleeping cars – dressing-rooms by day, bed-rooms by night – so that you may breakfast going down, dine, or take tea, and sleep or play whist returning. The Midland and London and North-Western Companies have found it worth while to make direct extensions for the accommodation of hunting-men; and all over the kingdom the locomotive has become a hunting machine.

Samuel Sidney, *The Book of the Horse*, c.1880

Of Stables

As to the situation of a stable, it should be in a good air, and upon hard, firm, and dry ground, that in the winter the horse may come and go clean in and out; and if it may be, it will be best if it be situated upon an ascent, that the urine, foul water, or any wet, may be conveyed away by trenches or sinks cut out for that purpose.

By no means let there be any hen-roosts, hog-sties, or houses of easement, or any other filthy smells near it, for hen-dung or feathers swallowed, oftentimes prove mortal and the ill air of a jakes sometimes causes blindness; and the smell of swine is apt to breed the farcin; and there is no animal that delights more in cleanliness, nor is more offended at unwholesome favours than a horse.

The Complete Horseman or Country Gentleman's Recreation, 1795

The 'Blues and Buffs'

Scarlet is the uniform of every established fox-hunting club in the kingdom, except one – the Badminton – an hereditary pack in the family of the Duke of Beaufort through four generations, since, in the time of the fifth duke, a pack of fine staghounds was converted into foxhounds. Curiously enough, although the Somersets were among the stoutest friends of the first Charles and the last James, and have since the Georgian era been distinguished for the stiffness of their Tory politics, the uniform of their hunt has always been the blue and buff of Charles James Fox, of his Whig followers, and of their organ, the Edinburgh Review. The best thing that can be said about it is that, made double-breasted, it is a very becoming riding-habit when worn by the ladies of the hunt.

Samuel Sidney, *The Book of the Horse*, c.1880

Of hunting Horses

You may furnish yourself with a horse for hunting at some of our fairs, which should as near as can be, the following shapes.

A head lean, large, and long; a chaul thin and open, ears small, and pricked, or, if they be somewhat long, provided they stand upright, like those of a fox, it is usually a sign of mettle and toughness.

His forehead long and broad, not flat, and as it is usually termed hard-faced, rising in the midst, like that of a hare, the feather being placed above the top of his eye; the contrary being thought by some to be a token of blindness.

His eyes full, large, and bright; his nostrils wide and red within, for an open nostril is a sign of good wind.

His mouth large, deep in the wikes, and hairy; his thropple, weasand or wind-pipe-bag, loose and straight, when he is reined in with the bridle; for if when he bridles, it bends like a bow, (which is called cock-throppled) it very much hinders the free passage of his wind…

…and some do not scruple to affirm, that wherever you meet with a horse that has no white about him, especially in his forehead, though he be otherwise of the best reputed colours, as bay, black, sorrel, he is of a dogged and sullen disposition, especially if he have a small pink eye, and a narrow face, with a nose bending like a hawk's bill.

The Complete Horseman or Country Gentleman's Recreation, 1795

A CANAL BOATMAN

Alan 'Caggy' Stevens, Tipton, Birmingham

1 boat loaded: one horse, 2 miles an hour
1 boat empty: one horse, 3 miles an hour
2 boats loaded: one horse, 1$\frac{1}{2}$ miles an hour
2 boats empty: one horse, 2$\frac{1}{2}$ miles an hour*

In the first half of the nineteenth century canals were the arteries which supplied towns with goods, which fuelled industries and transported their manufactured items away for sale. Horses walked along towing paths beside the canals and pulled working boats through the water by long boat-ropes attached to their harness.

When railways began to be built, often following the line of the canals, the bulk of canal trade passed into railway trucks and many canals became neglected. The notable exception to this, however, was the Birmingham Canal Navigations. These stretches of water in the industrial heartland of England *did* come under the control of a railway company, but for a number of reasons – not least being that local industries situated near the waterside were geared towards canal transportation – the BCN continued to function. In fact, the railway merged into the system and built basins where freight passed from train to boat.

Of the many men who worked horse-drawn narrow boats on the BCN, perhaps only one carried on the skill into comparatively recent times. His name is Alan Arthur Stevens, although to many he is known simply as 'Caggy'. He has a boatyard on the canal at a spot between Dudley and West Bromwich. Trains on the busy main railway line to London thunder along the rim of the yard, and shops, businesses, pubs and housing estates stretch around it.

On the canal side of the yard there is a colourful handpainted sign saying 'A. STEVENS Boat Yard', nailed to the dark bricks which continue from the canal bridge to the yard wall.

*These are the speeds at which one horse could pull a narrow boat or boats empty and full on a canal.

I was contemplating this spot when a man walking his dog along the tow-path stopped; nodding at the sign, he said, 'He's in.' I explained my presence: 'I've come to talk to Mr Stevens about the days of horse-drawn working boats.'

The dog-walker pointed to the opposite side of the canal where a brown-and-white horse was skilfully extracting a hoof from a loop of chain hobble which had wrapped round its legs. 'He's still got a horse you know, that's his.'

I found Caggy on board his boat, a big-built man with presence, and I guessed his identity at once; but had there been any doubt, the boat's two name plates – first 'Caggy', then alongside that 'A. Stevens Canal Contractors, Tipton' – would have dispelled it. After greeting Caggy, I asked him how he'd come by his nickname.

'It's because I'm left-handed, cag-handed, same as my father – he was also known as "Caggy". A lot of canal men had nicknames. "Stabbit" was one; I don't know what he was adoing, but the clock went off one morning before he reckoned it should have done and he got out of bed and stabbed it with a knife. Then there was one named "Pinwire", though I don't know how he got his 'un; he was a Tipton man. And there was a chap called "Silver Tongue" because he could rattle, see?'

Caggy stepped off the boat and we walked to the canal bridge to cross over to his horse. The bridge floor was made of brick, and every fourth course was followed by a line of partially raised bricks which ran across like bars. Caggy explained that these helped a horse get a grip in wet weather.

Tosh, the horse, looked up expectantly. The canal-side grass wasn't exactly prime pasture, but he looked well, and a box of greengrocery left-overs by his stable proved suburban living had its perks. He was eight years old and half Shire, which was why he had a moustache. Tosh's job wasn't to pull loads of freight, but trippers on a 72ft (22m) long pleasure boat called The Rye. 'A half-inch longer and the boat wouldn't have worked the locks,' Caggy remarked.

With a bar on the boat if needed, the three-hour canal trips had proved popular. Unfortunately, however, this enterprise had recently foundered because Caggy's three partners had dropped out of the scheme; one had died and the other two were busy with other work. Tosh, after four years at Caggy's yard, and the boat were up for sale.

Tosh

We walked back to Caggy's boat; sitting room was minimal, but it was comfortable because he stoked up the glowing coals in the stove. Caggy's father was also a boatman:

'He was born in 1881; when he started work it was for a steerage contractor called Saddler at Oldbury near here, whose horses used to haul boatloads of coal and bricks. Father was a good boatman, but one day he met with a very unfortunate accident: they were at Birmingham, and it had been snowing quietly all day, and he was moving his horse from one side of the canal to the other by taking it over a bridge, at the same time swinging the tow line which still attached the horse to the wooden boat, over the boat. Unfortunately the line dropped under the boat and got caught up on a loose plate on it, making it suddenly pull tight. It whipped the horse over the side of the bridge and onto the tow-path; it broke its back and they had to put it down. He had the sack for that; eventually he went to work for his brother who had a business supplying horses to haul boats for a firm called R.W. Ratcliffe & Co.

'I left school at fourteen and started work with my father and his mate right away. That was in 1932. Father's brother had died but father looked after the job for his brother's wife, my Aunt Lily. Ratcliffe's produced the best iron from scrap and this went to make high quality chains. We used their boats and our horses to take coal to their furnaces. We went to fetch it from several collieries, all mostly on the Cannock Chase extension of the canal. We were day-boat men, that is, we went home at night, although we did have odd nights out in cabins. The local name for day-boat men was "Joeys".

'We lived in Oldbury, not far from the canal, but my aunt kept her horses the other side of Oldbury and so I used to have to walk a mile to fetch the horse we were using, and the same journey back with it at night. If we were going to Cannock Chase I'd have to be up at one o'clock in the morning. Mother used to get up and make us a bacon sandwich before we left the house. I used to go and fetch the horse while me father got the boat ready to start.

'When I got to my aunt's stable I'd give all the horses a feed of corn apiece. We called it corn, but in fact it was mostly chaff, oats and bran mixed together. It was put ready by a man who used to do a bit of work for me aunt; he used to cut the chaff with a little petrol machine which was belt-driven, and mix it. When I was small I remember a man

Jack Taylor working Thomas Clayton's loaded butty Mole *up the Farmers Bridge flight of thirteen locks through the heart of Birmingham in August 1958. Some of the buildings on the left have been demolished and the site today is occupied by the Museum of Science and Industry. (Photo: The Bob May Canal Collection)*

used to come round from the country with bales of greenstuff, and Aunt Lily used to buy some of this, too, for her horses.

'The horse I usually took out was a black one called Bob. The others would probably be fetched about an hour after we'd gone. Bob fed whilst I was a tackling him and he'd also eat a feed of corn from his nose tin when I was walking him through Oldbury.

'Back at the boat my father would have made up a fire in the stove and put the boat's mast up. He'd loop one end of the boat-line round the beam in the middle of the boat – there were about five beams which held the boat together – and then put the end of it, which was a noose, onto the top of the mast. He did that because an empty boat doesn't need so much line as a full one – you see, a horse could pull it comfortably without straining, and so if there was a long line it would go slack and sag. With a full boat the horse needed the whole length to pull comfortably, and so then the line went straight to the top of the mast. He'd tie the other end of the line into a double knot which we called "the pegging noose"; when I arrived with the horse he'd secure the pegging noose on the line made by two short pieces of rope which came down from either side of the spreader. The spreader was the wooden bar on the back of the horse harness, which hung above the horse's hocks.

'The spreader had a "tug", or hook, on each end, and from these a rope went either side of the horse and up to the hames on the collar. These side ropes or traces had big oval beads called "spowles" threaded along them so that the rope didn't rub the sides of the horse. On average there'd be fifteen or sixteen spowles on each side, might be less to make a neat job of it, and it was important to leave enough room for the horse to work his legs, and not draw the traces up too tight. The spowles were painted bright colours – we used to paint them when we did the tackle up in the summer.

'The hames on a boat horse's collar were shorter than those you'd see on a farm horse; if they weren't, they'd catch on the bridge arches as they went underneath. They used to have a little brass bit on top.

'We never used to lead a horse, we always drove from behind. On his tackle you'd got two ropes each with a snap hook on, and these went on his bridle, one each side of his mouth – like that you could guide him from behind, and it was only in bad places that you might get to his head. The commands to guide him were simple, you'd say "Come up" for "go", and "Whoah" to stop.

'The boat-line which connected the horse to the boat was 32 yards long, that's about 96ft. The thickness varied, you could get a 5lb line or a 6lb one, and there was a few 7lb. Some firms would give their chaps a boat-line every three weeks, some every month, it was according to what work they was on; some which had a horse which pulled heavy, they only lasted a fortnight. It was a cotton boat-line, cotton so that it would float, because if one boat passed another, the man on the inside boat stopped his horse and the line would lie on the top of the water for the overtaking boat to go over. But sometimes the chap on the boat you were overtaking would shout "Heave it up!", and then you had to heave your line over their boat and their horse. Some horses wouldn't have it over them, no, they'd rear up, but some would take no notice.

'Often a horse would walk along on his own while you'd both be on the boat, and this was known as "baccering". Some boatmen trained their horses to a baccering whip, a great big whip which they'd swing and crack. But the whip we used to drive with, and touch the horse with now and again, was only a small one. I had one which I used to carry in me belt, but only if I was driving a fresh horse or anything like that; but I considered a horse wasn't very good if you had to drive it with a whip. I didn't believe in having to knock 'em about like that – none of mine wanted it, you could drive 'em by just dropping your hand on their back, if you was in a hurry.

'The problem with baccering was that when there was a lot of trade about, your horse might meet another, and one horse could pull the other into the canal if

George Arnold and Betty hauling a Central Electricity Authority butty in the narrows at Bromford Stop toll house on the New Main Line, Oldbury in 1959 (Photo: Graham Guest/Bob May Canal Collection)

69

there wasn't a driver to hold them. Also when the spring grass was about you'd have to put a wire muzzle on your horse to prevent him stopping to graze. Everyone liked a good baccering horse. If you bought a horse you'd ask "Is he a good baccering horse?" because although he might be a good horse, you might have to walk him all day.

'We'd go down Tividale Locks to get to Cannock Chase Colliery, a journey of about seven hours. We used to take our "chuff", or food, in a "frail", that's like a bag made out of the same stuff that straw hats are made of; it had a folding piece over the top with two handles on so that you could throw it over your shoulder and onto your back. On the boat we used to carry a pan and a kettle to use on the stove. The stove was like the one I've got here, a bottle stove – there was hundreds of them used. I've had lots pinched off me over me life. This one's gone at the bottom now, and they cost £300 or £400 new!

'The advantage to these stoves is that you can dismantle them, take off the pipe and the collar and lift out the firebox, and that's what we used to do when we got to the colliery. We'd whip the stove out of our empty boat and into the loaded one that was ready to come back, and the bigger you had the fire, the quicker you changed it!

'We'd swop the mast from the empty to the full boat, too, because with Joeys boats you use a mast you can change to any boat. And we'd also transfer the helm, tiller, cabin tools and the boat shaft. Boat shafts had wooden handles with a steel hook on the end. The handles could be from fourteen to sixteen feet long, and you used a boat shaft to reach across a distance – say, to the dock side – and lever your boat along. You're lost without a shaft, 'specially with a horse, because you guide an empty boat into a lock with a shaft while the horse is pulling it. Cabin boat people steered all the time, but our boats were lighter, so we shafted.

'On the return journey we'd have about twenty-five or twenty-six ton of coal on the boat and it would take nine hours to come back to Oldbury – that's over two hours longer than going with an empty boat. And it could be more than nine hours if you had some boats afore you at the locks, see; there was twenty locks each way to Cannock Chase from Oldbury.

'You used to feed your horse in all the locks you was in, because he had more time to eat it then. You carried a bag of corn on board and you'd put the nose tin on as soon as he got in the lock. We used to try and feed the horse at practically $2^1/_2$-hourly intervals, because without a feed of corn every $2^1/_2$ hours, they'd be no good.

'The best boat horses were about seven to eight years old because their bones would be "set" – heavy work before that age could pull 'em off their legs, 'specially hauling a loaded boat, because there's no downhill on canals. A good horse was not too heavy; if it was heavy-legged it would get what we called "leg-tired", because some days we'd work up to eighteen hours. It was better to have half-bred hosses, say half Shires, ones with spirit and not much more than 16hh so that they could go under saddle-backed bridges.

'They didn't really get much training to start the job; some firms would have an extra man with them to train the horse for a week, or sometimes you'd only have someone with you for a day. They supposed it was a boat horse without you went in the canal!

'Horses *did* go into the canal. I remember it was two days afore I was nineteen and I'd been driving this horse all morning. He was an awkward character we hadn't had long, and he took a lot of breaking in, and he just walked into the cut and never got out. He didn't really try to jump out. It wasn't far from home, so father and I walked home.

'If a horse was frightened by a train or something it'd jump in the canal, you know – then they was generally in 4ft of water, and they couldn't get out; as a rule then other boatmen would come and help. If the horse had a nose tin on you'd unbuckle it and get it off sharp because that could drown him. Then you'd try and get the tackle off in case it got caught up. Someone would get a plank and you'd tie two ropes, one to the fore part of the horse and one to the back, and put the plank under his belly; then about three or four men would bear down on the plank and then they'd pull up on the ropes and roll him on. A horse would soon jump up if it could when it was rolled out. It was a tricky job, you know, planking 'em out – nowadays the fire engine would come and lift 'em out.

'Father liked keeping the brasses and the tackle clean – looked after, a good set would last about thirty year. If we got a new set or needed repairs, we'd go to Mr Fisher's harness place at Oldbury. Father would clean the leather first, then soap it with saddle soap, and he'd black it afterwards with boot polish. He had brass hames, brasses on the martingale, a nameplate on the headcollar and brasses on the tackle running down the straps. He used to clean the brass with ordinary metal polish, and in winter if it was raining he'd get a bit of engine oil and smear it over them – then when the rain stopped, he'd get an oily rag and rub 'em up again.

'Some boatmen didn't agree with too many brasses because they said it put a lot of weight on the horse's tackle, which no doubt it did. However, at one time, when I was only a kid, there was a fellow on the Cannock Chase run who every May Day used to give half a quid to what he thought was the best dressed-up hoss that day. They'd come back the same day from Cannock or Walsall as a rule, see. Course in them days, half a quid would be as much as you'd get for a good day's work.'

A train goes noisily past on the track above Caggy's boatyard. As it speeds into the distance, we hear and feel the revving of engines as the traffic draws away from the level crossing. In the boatyard itself an engine throbs, powering grinding and metal-cutting machinery. Caggy continues:

'When my aunt died, we moved the stables closer to home. We had three horses on regular and one spare, and we used to employ four men as well as there was father and meself. The boats used to belong to Ratcliffe's although we did have one we owned. We bought it off my aunt's daughter. It was built like a cabin boat and we had it for taking tap cinder from Ratcliffe's to Johnson's Forge at West Bromwich and to Gadd's Forge at Tipton. You see, they lined the bottom of the furnace with the best tap cinder, and we took a boatload a week to each forge. This was heavy work for a boat, and we used to have to find a special boat for that job.

'I didn't get many days off. I can remember when I was seventeen I had two days off at Christmas, one at Easter, one at Whitsun and two in August – that's six days, ain't it? Though before the war we didn't work on Sundays, and I'll tell you for why.

'There were canal companies then, not like the British Waterways, and the BCN in this area controlled up to 250 mile, summat like that, of canal. Well, they used to lock the canal up twelve o'clock on a Saturday night until twelve o'clock on a Sunday morning. The lock keeper used to do it, on Saturday night he'd have a lock on a chain in the ground and bring it up to the gate, go through a staple, put the lock on and lock it. That was so you couldn't work the canal without paying tolls. It was tolls then, boat licenses now, but then you worked on a toll on how much the boat had got on.

'They could gauge the size of the load you'd get on because when you first had a boat you

had to take it to what they called a "test". If you had a wooden boat you'd have a load or two in afore you took it to be tested, because this sort does incline to get a bit waterlogged. You'd go to this place, and they'd put a table marked with inches down the side of the boat in four places; then they'd have an old steam crane – this is about sixty or seventy years ago... I'm seventy-eight now – and they'd put four 1 ton weights in; they'd wait for the water to settle, then a fellow would come out of the office and check how far down the boat was in the water with that 4 ton in it. Then they'd put another 4 ton in to make it 8 ton, then 12, then 16, 20, 24, 28. My big boat would carry 36 ton. Then they'd work the table out, and they could gauge whatever coal that boat had got in it to within 5cwt, it was that accurate. The figures went round to all the toll offices, and each trip you'd have a canal ticket with the weight you were carrying on it, and then you'd have to pay tolls on that at the end of the month. Of course Ratcliffe's owning their boats, they paid the tolls. I was always better than father at the writing in the business; he had to let me take charge on it when I was eighteen.

'I was told that when they built Netherton Tunnel they put $4\frac{1}{2}$d a ton on the toll until the tunnel was paid for – but they never took it off, and it was on until boats became licensed! Netherton Tunnel is about a mile and a half from here. It's 3,027 yards long, that's just under $1\frac{3}{4}$ mile, and it had electric lights in it, the electricity generated by running water. The lights were down the middle, but when the tunnel was heavily engaged, smoke used to collect in the top of it and there'd be hardly any light at all from the electric lights – and really, these needed to be over the horse's head. So we used to do what we did in all dark tunnels, and that

Leonard Leigh's iced-in butties are shown at Pelsall Common on the Wyrley and Essington Canal during the winter of 1940. An icebreaker and crew (on the far side) are ready with the horses to keep a channel open. (Photo: The Bob May Canal Collection)

was have a big can with a fire in it – we had plenty of coal, fetching it all the time – and we'd put the can on the front of the boat and have the horse right by the front end, by having a short line on the middle beam (if the boat was empty). On a loaded boat the horse had a full length line and had to find its way in the dark. They got used to it. In fact our horse Bob used to go back through the tunnel on his own, baccering along the tow-path with no light. Being a black horse you wouldn't see him 'till we came out the other end. We'd be steering the boat which on a return journey was loaded.

'In the early days there would sometimes be an unexpected hazard in the tunnel in the shape of a runaway horse! There was an LMS stable at the top of the nine locks at Brierley Hill, and the railway horses from it used to pull station boats, holding about 10 to 16 ton; one of the boats used to go to Albion Station at West Bromwich, then back again via Netherton Tunnel, loaded both ways, and generally the horse used on this boat would go on his own. However, sometimes on the journey going away from home he would decide to go back to his stable, and all of a sudden they'd yell, "Look out, our horse has turned round and he's running to meet you!" You had to get off and run in front of your horse and back him out of the way. There's not much space in the tunnel on a tow-path – I think they'm 5ft wide in Netherton: the width of the canal itself is 17ft and taking the two tow-paths in, the total width is just 27ft; so for each tow-path that's 5ft wide ain't it? Well, that railway horse used to sit on his bum agin the wall and swing his legs over the rail and turn round like that.

'Course, I'd have to go and make him turn round the other way when he was coming to meet me! Well, someone had to stop him or else there'd have been a collision, because one horse couldn't really get by another. There *was* what they call "horse holes" in the wall, five of them, and for example if an empty boat pulled up to a loaded one, the loaded boat's horse would get in this hole and the empty boat could go by it. But it must have been tricky because horses will kick at one another when they're close up. The holes were still there in Netherton, but they were never used in my day.

'If there weren't tow-paths in a tunnel, one of you took the horse over the road above and your mate legged the boat through. I've legged boats through Dudley Tunnel.

'When the war started in 1939 I was twenty-one, and I had to join up. At the time, boatmen became exempt from service at twenty-five, but I'd only done three months in the regulars when they were made exempt altogether, and so they had to allow me home.

'I remember father told me that in World War I, boating wasn't recognised as a trade at all. What they did was send all the boatmen into the army, and then send out fourth-grade army rejects to do the boating. But that was a disaster, and they generally drowned the horse, drowned themselves and sank the boat!

'We were pretty busy while the war was on because Ratcliffe's were contracted by appointment to the Admiralty to make the best chain iron. Then my father died in September 1943, halfway through the war. I took over, and I was just twenty-five. They called me in the office and said "Alan, you're a captain from today; we've got seventeen boats, and being appointed to the Admiralty we've got to have a captain for them." And that still works today, that does – on me cards from when I was twenty-five to when I was sixty-five it was "Captain Alan Arthur Stevens".

'During those war years Ratcliffe's used to keep a week's supply of boatloads in hand before they started up, and they used to burn about thirteen boatloads a week. There was

25 to 26 ton in a boat, so it worked out at about 325 ton a week. But not long after the war I had to look for other work because there was an "anti-smoke campaign", and by 1948 Ratcliffe's had converted to oil. I took the last boat of coal there in October 1952.

'I went to work for contractors. I had one or two boats of me own then, but some of the firms I worked for found their own; I was still working with my own horses. Then the big freeze-up in 1947 as good as stopped the canal. We measured the ice under the bridge here at Tipton and it was 18in thick, solid ice, and it don't freeze so hard under a bridge as in the open.

'I'd got four horses at the time, and they were on ice-boats cutting a path through the ice for fifteen or sixteen weeks. There used to be twenty horses on an ice-boat, nine one side and eleven the other, and we came from Smethwick like that right through to Tipton with forty men, twenty driving the horses and twenty rocking the boat. During that time they paid out the most money they'd ever paid for having a horse on a boat that year – £20 each horse, and forty-nine years ago that *was* money. So I got £80 a week, and you could keep a horse well for about £5 a week. Mind you, they didn't pay me 'til the 10th August that year; but when they did, I bought my first motor boat.

'In 1949, however, I still had as many as six horses. You see, it was quicker to take a horse-drawn boat through locks than it was to take a motor tug and butty, and there was a good many locks. There was thirteen at Farmers' Bridge, and then down Asted was another six. With a horse you could take the boat through at once, but if you took a tug you'd got to work every lock twice to get the tug, and then the butty through.

'Occasionally I used to buy my horses from what they call 'The Block' at Birmingham, under auction. They used to come direct from a farm. But mostly I used to buy horses that had been condemned on the road, say they'd run away and busted up a cart or a van, and the authorities wouldn't let 'em work on the road no more. They'd even run away with a boat if they could, but they made the best boat horses once they'd settled down.

'One mare which I bought in about 1955, as horses were going off the canal, kicked and pulled me right into the water once. She was a milk-round horse with Midland Counties Dairy when I knowed her first, but I didn't know much about her until I actually bought her – and then I found out her kicked. It turned out that she'd been at one of their Birmingham depots at first, and then she got transferred to Polsworth, and the stables there had only bales between the horses and she came on heat and started kicking and didn't stop. She busted three drays up in a week.

'They sent for the vet, and he said "Have her ovaries out, have her shot or sell her." They sold her to a dealer called Shakespeare, and I bought her from him. One day when I was in Birmingham I spoke to the chap who used to drive her for the dairy. He said, "You got that mare I used to have, her could beat the electric truck an hour a day. You see, when you'd delivered one house, you'd take a crateful of milk with you and she'd move on to each house on her own – but with an electric truck you had to go back and fetch it!"

'In 1965 I bought a horse called Mac off Brummidgon (Birmingham) Corporation. They used to buy their horses as four-year-olds, in batches from Ireland. Mac was due to be a police horse, but they couldn't break him on the road and so they had to send him to pull the salvage boats which used to take rubbish out of Birmingham to a tip.

'Mac was a game horse: he'd start the rubbish boat off on his own at Lock 13, and he'd get right to the edge of the canal to do it too, so that he could get under the bridge to start.

George Bodley and Mac

He wasn't quite six when I bought him and he was sold to me because the Corporation stopped operating their own salvage boats.

'He was a big horse, too, 17hh and weighing 16cwt. He used to fill the bridges up round Birmingham; he used to work out exactly where to tread by rubbing his off-side ear, the one near to the canal, along the wall – he'd got to be very near the edge of the canal with a saddle-back bridge or he couldn't get through. Yes, he was as game as an old shoe – but if you took him on the road you couldn't hold him. And he was spooky; like, on the canal when he went through a bridge, he'd look round the corner to see if there was anything to shy at, and if there was, he'd jump.

'Once he did a spectacular leap. He was out with one of my chaps, George Bodley: the Bodleys are a well known family on the canal – they used to be on the Birmingham-to-London run when I was young. Well, it was a moonlit night and George was driving Mac beneath a railway arch; I was on the boat, and I could see what was coming. When I was driving I always used to hurry the horse on if I heard a train approaching. Anyway, George didn't, the train went over the bridge, and its reflection fell in the water in front of Mac. He thought the train *was* in front of him, and swerved so violently that he swung George, who was holding his bridle – and George was 18 stone – completely over the cut, a distance of 17ft, and brought him back again to the spot he'd taken off from!

'I had Mac nearly ten year, and then he died of colic in the stable. It's surprising the number of horses what die with that, you know. I had one brown horse, a blood horse called Nobby, which went on 'til he was nearly thirty-five year old. He got very long in the tooth.'

At this point Caggy started to stir himself and to make safe the fire in the stove. A sociable being, he was due to go out with friends. They usually go to one of the local pubs. Caggy's favourite tipple is a pint of Guinness laced with port, followed by a whisky. And if there's a football match on television they will often watch it in the pub; Caggie has always supported West Bromwich, which is not far from Oldbury, and used to attend their matches, too. He also explained to me that some years ago it was always the custom amongst boatmen to go to the pub every Sunday dinner time; and the picture house was another favourite outing, especially amongst the cabin-boat men. On a Sunday they'd tie up in various places (perhaps at Sutton Stop, Coventry which is on the Southern Oxford canal), "click together" and go to the pictures in the afternoon or evening with a girlfriend.

When the canals closed down, many of the men went to work in factories where they earned more money for half the hours they'd done on the canal. However, some weren't as happy as they had been on the canal: as Caggy put it, 'Canals always seemed to have a pull with 'em. With boating they were their own gaffer, they got their orders night or morning and might not see their boss all day – not like factories!' Before I left he sang me a plaintive old song about a lady giving a home to a street urchin.

'It's called "Everybody's Loved by Someone",' he said 'And I've never heard nobody else sing it, only boatmen. Father used to sing it when he went through tunnels.'

The next time I met Caggie, one of his friends, Tom Micklewright, was at the boatyard. Both Tom's grandfather and his father had been boatmen. 'It's in your blood,' he explained

– which is why obviously, although he's retired, he comes to the yard to help Caggie.

Tom took me to the part of the yard where Caggie stores the harness he uses on Tosh. In the centre of each blinker is a brass oval bearing the initials T. & S.E., evidence that at some time in the past the bridle had been worn by a boat horse owned by the haulage firm T. & S. Element. Many years ago Tom had worked for the Elements: 'You were very much your own boss. You'd come to the stable in the morning and find a note from the gaffer pinned onto the stable post saying something like "Cannock Chase tomorrow"; we wouldn't see him for days together, he'd be out getting work. I worked with a mate: one of us would get the boat ready and the other the horse, but we often helped one another.'

Tom recalls earlier work: 'I can remember scraping the inside of a horse's collar with a penny to get the dried sweat and scurf off. The first animal I drove on the canal was a white mule for a man named Mr Bough. When I was a lad, every boat took two days to do a journey.'

We pick up Caggy from his boat, and set off for a nearby public house, one of two locals which Caggy frequents at lunchtime. On the slope up from the yard, Caggy points to the new retirement bungalows built on the opposite bank: 'There used to be a foundry called Chatwins there,' he says. We peer over the wall and look at a few wooden living boats on the canal below, one of which had recently been repaired. Caggy remarks: 'The best thing to stop a leak on a wooden boat, both years ago *and* now, is chelico, that's a mixture of tar, horse dung and cow hair. You make it up yourself, seal the leak, then cover it with a good

Caggy in the Teme Valley, 1990

piece of plate and nail it round the edges. One of the boats I had not long ago was made of iron; it was 106 years old and I sold it for a good price.'

Inside the pub there's a regular clientèle of retired locals, men who knew Caggy and the canal well. The pub seems to stay open all day, and dominoes games and drinking go on apace.

I ask Caggy about the reputation that Joey boatmen had for fighting. He admits that he could throw a fair punch in his day, and says 'I was like a big Viking.' It seems that Joey boatmen used to get somewhat quarrelsome when they were waiting to go through locks, especially when, as Caggy explains: 'One of them might have whipped by up in front and got there first, a bit like barging to the front at a set of traffic lights; and there also used to be a great deal of taunting about having a better horse than someone else.'

Tom talks about the time he worked for a canal carrier called Ernie Thomas. He recalls that during the boatmen's annual week's holiday, Mr Thomas used to turn his horses out into a grass field near Pleck Bridge in Gower Street, a spot that has since been built on. 'The horses would come off the grass dopey, and some had "lumpus" [lampas] which is a sore mouth and ulcers on the gums. To help them feed you'd put water in with their food in the feed can. The cure for lumpus in those days was to put a twitch on the horse's jaw, put some bars in his mouth to hold it open, and then use a shiny horse-shoe nail or knife to release the pus and blood from the ulcers.'

Caggy, however, remembers a different remedy: 'Rub with salt or a pummy stone to cure ulcers and harden the mouth again.'

I ask what secrets they had for keeping their horses in condition. Caggy continues: 'I remember a man who had the best horse on the cut, but when he died and the horse was taken over by another, it was never as good. There was an old boater called "Cuffs 'n' Collars" who used to make up different herb remedies. He gave me instructions on how to make some, but I don't know what I've done with them.' Tom recollects one: 'One pick-me-up for a horse was to bake a horse radish in the oven, then grate it over his corn.'

We talk about how hard the boat horses worked. Tom admits that some didn't get much rest, usually only two or three minutes going through a lock, or if they had to wait, half an hour; and it was always a twelve- or thirteen- hour trip. 'Sometimes you had to be tough on them to get home at all – and it was just as hard on us.' He himself used to get so tired with starting at five o'clock in the morning that one night travelling home on the 9.30pm bus, he'd fallen asleep and rolled all down its aisle. Regarding the horses, Tom adds one more sad fact: 'Some old boatmen used to give their horses vitriol in their water to make 'em go – used to burn their insides out.'

We talk about the decline in the use of horse-drawn boats, and how stables alongside the canal fell into disuse. Some have now become canoe stores, or in the case of one near the city centre, a jazz club. Caggy was probably the last commercial contractor to use horses. He'd kept a few right up intil 1976 although their use in the latter days hadn't been without problems. For example, when a new bridge was put over the Fazeley Canal it blocked the tow-path, and this path was on the route Caggy's men took to Camp Hill locks with an empty rubbish boat. When they got to the bridge they had to tie up the horse and pull the boat down to the factory through six locks, then pull a loaded boat back to the horse. Caggy sued the Waterways who owned the tow-path for the money he had to pay to get an extra man to help handle the boat.

Nowadays the main problem concerning tow-paths is barriers put up to stop motorbikes – although Caggy admits he was given a key to unlock these barriers for Tosh when she pulled his pleasure-trip boat.

In 1978, Caggy had sixty-four working boats, half at West Bromich and half at Oldbury. He still has a few. But commercial boating is not what it was: as Tom says, 'After the war the gaffers couldn't afford to pay what factories did, and so it became a dying trade, with no young ones coming up.'

Caggy nodded in agreement: 'There were sub-contractors on the canals at the end. They didn't really look after the boats, most were sunk and the waterways had 'em dragged out. A few of the iron boats became pleasure boats. A lot of the collieries had closed, and any boat-freight trade there was, passed to lorries.'

But even today, road transport doesn't rule totally supreme. I left Caggy and Tom discussing taking one of Caggy's boats loaded with scaffolding bars to Smethwick. Caggy had got the job because the work site, near the canal, just wasn't accessible to a lorry.

Note Caggy died in early 1997. Some of his friends attributed his demise to the soaking he had received a few days earlier while working. A few months previously he had sold Tosh back to the dealer from whom he'd bought him; Tosh was then sold on to a farmer.

Crowds line the street to watch a circus procession, circa 1880

A CIRCUS ARTISTE

Emmie Fossett, Skegness, Lincolnshire

It is said that the first circus ring was built from the proceeds of the sale of a diamond ring. Philip Astley, a retired cavalry instructor who had taken to attracting whole audiences with his displays of riding skills and tricks, found the piece of jewellery after one of his 'Equine Exhibitions'. As no one claimed it, he sold it, and in 1769 used the money to build a circular arena sited in Westminster Bridge Road, London, near to the present-day location of Waterloo Station.

Astley made his show place circular because he had discovered that if you stood on a horse's back whilst it was galloping, it was easier to stay on if the horse went in a circle. In this way Astley's Amphitheatre was born, and with it the beginnings of a long tradition of circus horsemanship.

One particular circus family, the Fossetts, have always been noted for their horse acts. They came to prominence through Robert Fossett; like another famous circus owner, 'Lord' George Sanger, Robert took it upon himself to assume a title and call himself 'Sir' Robert Fossett. The title was not, however, without credence, because on several occasions Queen Victoria asked 'Sir' Robert to take his circus to perform at Windsor. When Robert died in 1922 his wife Mary arranged for a white marble statue of a horse to be shipped over from Italy and placed on his tomb. The horse presides over a touching inscription to him. It begins: 'He is pulled in for his last rest... .'

This memorial is still in very good condition in a Northampton cemetery; it commemorates other members of the Fossett family too. 'Sir' Robert had eleven children, all of whom married into circus families, and all usually distinguishable by their good looks and red hair.

Emmie (Emmiline) Yelding is one of 'Sir' Robert's grandchildren. Aged seventy-six, she has retired from circus performing and lives in a charming bungalow in Skegness, a seaside resort which seems to attract retired entertainers because Emmie's cousin Jacko the Clown (son of Jacko the Clown, and just as famous) lives round the corner.

Emmie's bungalow is filled with circus memorabilia, and her conversation is sprinkled with Fossetts: she talks not only of Jacko, but Fossetts who through marriage have become Roberts, Yeldings and Cottles and members of several other circus dynasties. It becomes even more confusing when she explains that she had two mothers, both Fossetts! Her natural mother, also called Emmiline, was the daughter of 'Sir' Robert. She married Ellis Cook, and the couple had Emmie. Emmie explains about her father:

'My Dadda wasn't originally from the circus world. He'd run away from home, and eventually joined granddad Fossett's circus when he was about eighteen; and that's where he met and married my Mum. She was a high school rider – it's like riding a dancing horse, all dressage and dancing.'

We pause to study photographs of Emmie's mother, who looks very beautiful in her old-fashioned riding costume. Emmie admits: 'My Mamma was very clever and lovely – they all were, the Fossetts, a very clever family, and they were noted for riding. Sadly she died when I was four, and my Daddy married Sarah Fossett, Mamma's sister, the youngest of the eleven Fossett children. She was a ballerina rider. She and Daddy had four boys, so I had step brothers, Alec, Gordon, Robert and Tommy who was the baby.'

Sir Robert Fossett's memorial

Emmie produces a battered and much loved copy of *British Circus Life*, written in 1948 by Lady Eleanor Smith, a great circus enthusiast and one-time president of the British Circus Fans' Association (now known as the Circus Friends Association). Lady Eleanor's book follows a year in the life of a small circus called Reco's, and the proprietor's wife, Mrs May Reco had been a Fossett and was aunt to Emmie's aunt-cum-stepmother. Thus the colour photographs are of special interest to Emmie, and one in particular: of her father Ellis, at that time ringmaster for Reco and in charge of the circus's horses. He looks most elegant with his shiny top hat, waxed moustache and pink carnation pinned to the lapel of his black tail-coat.

Emmie with her natural mother

Another photo shows Emmie's brother Gordon, riding on the road alongside a group of loose ponies as the circus cavalcade moves from one town to another. At the time, Gordon was sixteen: big, handsome, and auburn-haired, a rider, clown and acrobat. Emmie takes up the tale of her family:

'Two of my other brothers, Alec and Robert, were left behind to go to school, one at Bradford and the other at Manchester, and I'm sorry to say we've lost all trace of them. I was in touch with Alec, but couldn't go to his wedding because we were with Harry Bennett's circus at the time – and I've never heard from him since.

'I wasn't left behind, because I had to work for a living – but that's life, isn't it? I wasn't actually born on the circus but at Wandsworth at my Mum's friend's shop, but I came straight into circus and grew up with it; the ponies, the horses and the dogs were our life.

'Mammy's circus name was Isabel, and she did a very pretty act known as the "ballerina on horseback"; it was also known as the "trick act". She wore a ballerina dress and skipped on the horse's back using a hooped cane. The act also involved a dance called the "pummell", and then she did what we call the "throw-off" – standing on the horse as it goes round and fetching one leg up and back behind her. I can't do it now because I have a bad hip, but I could at one time.'

Emmie is due to go into hospital for a hip operation, a legacy from her circus riding. She observes that a great many circus people end up with bad hips, '. . . me cousins, everybody. I think it's wear and tear, all the running about and the dancing.'

She continues with her life experiences:

'Another part of the "ballerina act" was known as the "garters" and the "balloons". The "balloons" were in fact paper hoops held up one on each side of the ring, and Mamma had to go through them. The "garter" is actually a ribbon, or two ribbons, each pulled out opposite each other from the pole in the middle of the ring, and the ends held by two ring doormen; nowadays you don't usually have ring doormen – you have, in circus language, someone who knows how to "pass the garter", that is, knows how to pass it under the rider

Emmie's natural mother with her brother Jim Fossett (youngest of eleven Fossett children), the Performing Dog and Pony Act. The pony is Lipton who appears, 'kissing' Emmie's mother, in the photograph on the opposite page

as she approaches and jumps it, otherwise she catches her foot in it.

'My act was voltige rider and wire walker, and I was known as Renee. I had a little horse called Sultan, and he was spotted, he was just smothered in spots. In fact spot horses are rare – my uncle Bob Fossett, Mummy's brother, used to breed them, although father and mother bought Sultan from Sangers for me. He was cob size. Then, you could buy horses for £20; nowadays you couldn't touch one for a thousand.

' "Voltige" is vaulting at the side of the horse; the horse must move along very quickly and then you perform all the different tricks. You lie over the horse, over his neck, and you finish with picking up handkerchieves, hanging over the horse and picking up the hand-kerchieves from the ground.

'I started practising when I was six years old. My father used to say "We're not going to run the little horse round until you can do the routine using a bale of straw." On the bale we went through the different knee positions, and how to point my toes – but then you had to get on the horse to learn voltige. My father had a belt like a thin washing line attached to me, and that went under the roller which I held to do the vaulting; he held the lunge in the middle of the ring, and these were the only safety precautions we had. Mummy taught me to have style: she had lovely style and presence and grace herself – and then Daddy took over my teaching.

'We were with G.B. Chapman's circus at the time, and that was a big circus name. Mr Chapman had a shop in Tottenham Court Road and he started a circus and beast show and had all wild animals. Anyway, mother and father had a contract with G. B. Chapman, and father was ringmaster.

'G. B. Chapman had a wonderful little voltige rider called Sylvia Dash, but when I was eleven years old she was expecting her first baby, and Mr Chapman, knowing that my Dad was practising me and that I was getting on very well, asked if I would be ready to stand in. And that was my first engagement, at the Grand Theatre in Birmingham.

'I got clothes and pocket money. I had an extra special pair of shoes and suit, and I had to keep that to wear to agents when we went for bookings.

'My riding costume when I was very young was short little pants, tied round the back and neck. Later when I did the voltige act I wore a ballerina frock like my mother did in her ballerina act. We used to have these dresses made, but we made our own head-dresses. Mammy had a very pretty one for her "trick act", a wide diamontee; she had ringlets in those days. We'd buy flowers for me, and I'd put them on the side of my head and put glitter on them – we'd buy the glitter. On our feet we wore little satin pumps like ballet shoes, but without the hard toe. Mummy used to cut them out using a brown paper pattern. The sole was soft calico and they were tied on with ribbons round your ankles.

'Riding is a very difficult act in the business, because you depend not only on yourself but on the horse, and on the public. Also the horse for the ballerina act had to be of a different tem-

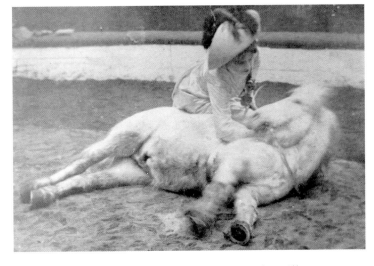

perament from the one in the voltige act; Mummy's horse was called Peggy, and she'd go round at a steady tempo, but for voltige you have to have a fast horse. Dad used to groom the horses. He'd start with a brush, then use a curry comb, and then wipe them down with a soft cloth to make their coats shine.

'To help you balance, you always put rosin on your horse's back. It's like a dark brown powder, but you have to knock it to make sure it's really fallen as powder; I used to put it in a little piece of sack and bang it over the horse's rump. Rosin is still used in circuses, and you'll see trapeze artistes wipe their feet in it in a box at the side of the ring before they do their act.

'If I faulted in a trick, Dad would discuss it with me, but always "in the waggon", never in the ring because that was considered very wrong. I practised a lot when I was very young, but I did improve as I got older. Mind you, it wasn't all plain sailing, and I had a very nasty accident when we were with G. B. Chapman at the Drill Hall in Oxford. I was coming up out of the handkerchief and the horse stumbled and I was dragged from the stirrup. That was a buster – bad accidents are known as busters.

'In riding you can hurt yourself with the simplest trick. When we were with Harry Benet's circus at Bournemouth Winter Gardens, my mother – my second Mum – broke her ankle just before coming out of the ring. She was doing what we call "the cuts", which you do when the act is finished – you jump up and clap your hands. On that day, however, a lady was sat knitting in one of the ringside seats. Now, there's a circus superstition that this is unlucky, and if it happens you usually go up to the person and ask if they'd kindly put

Emmie, then just twelve, performing at Southport with other members of the Fossett family

their knitting away.' Tom, a long-standing family friend who has been kindly supplying us with coffee during Emmie's interview, intercedes with an interesting bit of knowledge: 'That knitting superstition comes from the guillotine days of the French Revolution I think you'll find.' Emmie nods and continues:

'Birds coming into the tent are another bad omen, and we were also brought up, like people outside circus, to believe that thirteen was unlucky. Another thing, my nanna would never work in green, and my cousins the Roberts Brothers don't like green either. In fact Mummy *was* wearing green, her green trick-act dress, at a performance at Waverley Market, Edinburgh when she fell and knocked her leg up completely.

'G. B. Chapman performances were one-day stands. The rest of the circus had mechanical transport, but Uncle Jack and his family travelled by waggon and three horses, and so did we. The horses were our own, not circus ones, three piebalds. Chapman's put up a stable, and when we were on the circus ground the horses stayed in there.

'If it was a very big journey we used to travel overnight, otherwise we went by day. As we travelled along, Mummy would cook our meals in the waggon on an old-fashioned stove called a "Hostess" stove, all polished up with black lead, and with the fire on inside it. We weren't galloping or anything. Dad used to drive and he used to take his time. We'd pull up into a by-way, put nosebags on the horses, and then give them their little drinks and have our own dinner.

'On Good Friday Mum would cook fish, the old-fashioned way you know, and I used to have to go and buy them. Although you was circus, in those days you were brought up in lovely ways. We'd never sew on Sundays, although we'd clean the knives and forks. I remember as a little girl sitting with her doing this, and we'd have a bar of chocolate because she used to sell the chocolate in the circus.

'When we travelled along, our riding horses, including Mum's black-and-white ballerina horse Peggy, and a mule, were tethered behind the caravan. The mule was a "kicking mule" because in the circus he kicked, you see – the clowns tried to ride him first of all, and then they used to have a couple or three people from the audience, and no one could get near him. One day, when he was getting on, our little mule was ill, and so we pulled in at Little Paxton outside St Neots and put him in a stable and asked a vet to come. He came, and in the end had to take the mule away. It broke our hearts, me Mam pulled the blind down and we were both in tears; we so loved our animals.

'Mammy had her ring horse Peggy for several years. She was always stabled, either under canvas or in a building, and never kept out. Circus horses shown in the arena don't go out. Mum used always to have her rugged to keep her coat nice. In the winter, when Peggy was stabled at G. B. Chapman's farm, we used to pick clover together and give it to her.

'When we were travelling, the circus agent who'd made all the location bookings would go on ahead and mark an arrow on the road in whitewash to show the way. The whitewash eventually wore off; we didn't dare use paint!

'At G. B. Chapman's the elephants used to travel by walking along the road. Horses are frightened of elephants, and even though they were stabled in the same tent, if the elephants had to pass the horses on the road you'd cover their eyes by putting a little wad over their heads until they had gone by. Many a time I've seen a milk float with the milk gone

*Emmie, Sammy Freeman and John Yelding with Charlie Barth
in the tails at Sanger's circus*

flying because the milkman's horse has taken fright at the elephants!

'In the old days, the circus girls used to sit on the footboards of the living waggon. When the horses went uphill at a trot they'd hang on like grim death, and as the hill got steeper and the horses eased up, they'd jump off and push a block under the wheel to stop the waggon rolling back. It also gave the horses a break. In fact Daddy used to say "We'll pull up and give them a rest." There used to be piles of gravel on the verges, and if the road got a bit slippery we'd put buckets of this down to give the horses a better grip.

'Coming down steep hills we had a man put a pole in the wheel spokes to stop the waggon coming down too fast. The wheels had wooden spokes and iron rims. My cousin Emmie, one of Uncle Jack's girls, used to sit inside their waggon and sew, and one day she got out too quick, before the horses pulled up, and she put her foot under a wheel. She had to go to hospital, even though in those days we were made to wear brogues to keep our feet good and safe; so if she hadn't have been wearing hers, goodness knows what would have happened.'

At this point Emmie and I talk about the hardships of circus life, and the wear and tear it causes. Emmie admits, perhaps thinking of her arthritic hip: 'If I had me life over again I wouldn't change it, though to be frank, I think I'd be a bit more studying for myself; you know, in those days you'd rush about in the rain, you'd been brought up like that. For example when we got into a ground, Mammy'd say "Just go and get some milk," and in those days, unlike now, it used to be difficult to find a place open, and you'd say to her, "Where?" and she'd say "Well, you can speak, can't you, so just ask!" '

I ask Emmie if circuses had their own blacksmiths: 'Sometimes, but if not, in those days there were plenty outside. The horses were always shod for tenting, that is travelling and performing in a circus ring during the summer months; but in the winter when we went on the halls and the theatres, you'd have perhaps a week at a time at different theatres, and the shoes were always taken off. The halls had ring mats, you see, and the shoe studs could catch in them.'

In 1941 Emmie's family's yearly pattern of summer tenting and winter halls was broken by an interesting interlude: Emmie explains: 'We were hired for eight weeks to work on a film being made at Boreham Wood. It was called *Old Mother Riley At the Circus*, and the star was Arthur Lucan – it was a "big" picture then. Part of it was about a circus, and my Mum, Daddy, myself and the man I later married, John Yelding, did a sequence; this was filmed in a wide shot, and when it came to the close-ups they put the stars in!

'John's stage name was "Speedy", and he was an all-rounder he did a cowboy act doing rope spinning, and as well as riding he did the trapeze and tight wire and a famous clown act.'

Emmie and her family's brush with the big screen continued, because when *Old Mother Riley* was complete, they went back to the studios to take part in a circus film starring George Formby. Back in the real world, they were working on a new riding act, as Emmie describes:

'Involved in this new act were John, his two brothers Claude and Tony, and Mammy and me. But to get the act up we needed to practise somewhere, and as we didn't have our own circus we didn't have a practice ring. Anyway, a certain Lady Docker helped us – her husband was the director of Rolls Royce and he had night clubs and restaurants, and they were very good friends with the Mills circus family; they just loved the circus. Lady Docker had a beautiful home at Wallingford in Oxfordshire, and in the buildings there was a full circus ring with mirrors all the way round. We got in touch with her, and she let us practise in the ring for six or seven weeks.

'When it was time to leave, it was just before Christmas and it was snowing. We were due to go to perform with a circus at the Crystal Palace in London, but it had just burnt down! The venue had been hastily changed to a drill hall in Bristol and that's where we headed. We had a horse-drawn waggon, but I was riding a little cream mare called Dillia, bare-back, no saddle. I was wrapped up, but it was *so* cold that I used to sit on one hand and then the other.

'We travelled bit by bit; with horses you can only go so far, you can't wear them out. Before nightfall I'd knock on a farmhouse door and ask the farmer if we could pull in, and

Emmie performing at Sanger's circus

if he'd kindly find us some stables; the farmers were always very helpful in those days. I'd explain what we were doing, and where we were going – the correct way to do it. We were brought up to be polite to people, and kind, and I think that you will find in life that if you're like that, it gets you along.'

The vagaries of horse-drawn travel temporarily ceased in the mid-1940s when Emmie, her brothers and mother and father travelled with Reco's circus. They left their waggon and horses at Reco's farm, and took over a 'Tilling' bus belonging to Reco. It was painted red and yellow, and on the outside had posters advertising the circus. One half of the bus was living quarters, and the other section the circus box office. This bit also doubled as a dressing-room, and at the end of the day as a bedroom. The bus, kept spotlessly clean, obviously had the advantages that mechanical horse power can have over real horsepower, but it proved far more dangerous – it went on fire twice! Emmie recalls the second conflagration:

'We were at Lowestoft. It was one morning, and we were dressed in the oldest glad rags, our work clothes. After doing our work we'd change to sell programmes, and then again into our ring costumes – but first thing, you don't put on your best. We were just starting to get on the road when one of the circus men, poor old Tommy Ross (Rosaire), came to fill

up the petrol tank; he had a cigarette in his mouth, and suddenly the whole thing went up! We used a pick-axe to get into the side of the bus to get Mummy's jewellery out, she had it in a bag in the wardrobe, but we lost everything else, all our beautiful costumes, everything. And the bus was a write-off.

'We had just what we stood up in, and to make matters worse it was wartime then, and clothes were all on stamps. Reco sent away for stamps, but they were late coming and we had to move on. However, we were lucky because lots of people from the shops were very helpful, and a circus friend called Emily – sister to Clara Paulo who is well known as a circus rider – came along when she heard we'd had a fire, and brought a wooden case with little ring dresses in; this was a nice turn for me, although for my Mum there wasn't anything.

Emmie's late husband John in the costume he wore for their cowboy act

'A sort of tea tent was put up for us, and I remember that we'd got our little performing dogs in boxes; we exercised them, but otherwise they lived in these boxes; I ended up ironing our bits and pieces on these boxes. I had to go round to find digs for Mum and Dad and my brother Gordon. I stayed with Miriam in her bus – she was half of a rope spinning act called the Chico's.

'I was about twenty-five or twenty-six when this happened. After we finished with Recos in 1948 Mammy finished riding, although she went on with her dogs. I did a double riding act with John Yelding, that is using two horses; it involved jumping up from the floor onto the horses, and fork jumps, and I used to mount on John's shoulder and do a *pas-de-deux*. We also did a cowboy act together, and joined Charlie Barth and Sammy Freeman for another riding act.

'After a while, and after my parents had died, John and I went on to work for Sangers and Stringers circus; and then we went on a stage show with Morecambe and Wise, doing the wire act, the cowboy act and with John's performing pony.'

I ask Emmie if she had a favourite horse: 'I think they were all favourites. Dinky, the Shetland that appeared in *Old Mother Riley At the Circus*, was an outstanding pony. He was with us when we did a London review called *Exquisite*. The taxi men used to know as soon as we turned up in London because Dinky used to come in the cab with us, you know, the old-fashioned hackney cabs. It was the talk of the town!' Emmie laughs at the memory.

'Lion, John's horse, was wonderful, too. We were doing a show which was supposed to be in the open, but it poured with rain at the gala and so the show was put on a stage. It was a difficult stage to get to, and we put a plank supported by two blocks over the musicals, the band you know, and walked Lion over that. He just stood there while we blocked him up, and then walked over the board – and that was wonderful, really, because it was asking a lot for him to go over like that.'

In the latter part of their careers Emmie and John Yelding ran a circus and zoo for Leslie Sanger of Brighton Circus; but as Emmie said, 'You can't do two things' and so they concentrated on the zoo. For twenty-five years they ran Yelding's Empire Zoo in Peter Pan's Playground at Southend. Finally, because of John's failing health, they sold their animals to a zoo in Basildon, Essex, and retired to Lincolnshire; since, when, sadly, John has died.

Emmie introduces some young visitors to one of the young chimps at Yelding's Empire Zoo

Emmie still goes to the circus whenever she can. She says: 'It means as much to me as ever, I love it. And it's encouraging to see the young people, because they're the ones that are going to keep it going. Sometimes they have a tough time with animal rights supporters, but a lot of those really haven't a clue; if they went up and asked, they'd find out that circus people genuinely love their animals.'

I ask about circus riding now, and whether the old acts still exist. Emmie considers:

'The ballerina act you probably wouldn't see today, although it was done in Gerry Cottles' about seven years ago. Another riding act which Clara Paulo's sister, June Whitney, revived, was the jockey act. Traditionally in it the rider dresses up as a jockey in silks, does jump-ups from the floor and all tricks imaginable, and ends up standing on the horse with the saddle on their shoulder.

'My cousin Robbie did a good jockey act, and his father Uncle Bob, he did the jockey act with what we call the "baskets". For this he was blindfolded and had a sack over his head, and a basket strapped over each boot, and he jumped on and off the horse like this.

'When Uncle Bob died, his brother Bailey and sister Mary – and she was a noted horse-woman – ran Fossett's Circus, right up until about nine years ago. One day when they'd come back from tenting, a gentleman from America who'd contacted them previously, rang to say he was staying in a hotel in London and asked to come to their farm at Tiffield. He wanted to see Grandad's old parade waggons, which we used to call "tableaux" – in the days before I was born, performers would ride on them, the circus owner sitting in front with a lion on each side, and they'd be drawn through the town the afternoon before the show. The American gentleman had come from the Circus World Museum at Baraboo, Wisconsin, and he took a couple of tableaux back to Wisconsin. In fact, I think all our names, the Fossett names, are now in the museum.'

This last story seemed a fitting end to my talk with Emmie, for it seemed a truly honourable tribute to the Fossetts, the famous circus riders.

start, because in those days it wasn't so easy to initiate a business as it is today. The railings are there to this day – there are some you might have seen as you crossed over the railway en route to the church.'

Edward went on to explain that his great-grandfather married a daughter or niece of a blacksmith already working in Closeburn, adding 'To that extent on that side of the family we go back a long time as blacksmiths.'

I expressed surprise that Closeburn, being a fairly small hamlet, should have had sufficient work to support two separate blacksmith businesses. However, I was soon put right. As Edward related:

'There were in fact *three* blacksmiths, because at that time Closeburn was very much at the forefront of industry. It all started through the efforts of a man called Stuart Menteith who bought the local big estate in 1783. He was a very progressive man and initiated a great many enterprises; amongst these was expanding a lime works, because he wanted the locals to see the benefits of lime for sweetening the soil and for killing heather. Menteith eventually sold out the works to a very wealthy quarry- and mine-owning family called Baird, and they carried on the good works. Water was brought from over about a dozen mile distance to the lime works, and that was a tremendous thing because it drove a saw mill which provided employment, and a watermill in the blacksmith's shop, and a turbine in the joiner's shop, and a 40ft diameter wheel which provided motive power in the quarry. Finally the water entered the River Nith about three miles down the road from here – but before doing so it drove a wheel in a very big blanket mill, and this, too, provided a lot of employment.

Hooping a wheel a generation ago

Dumfries Farriers' Association photographed at Waverley Works, Coatbridge in 1927

'There's no question about it, we were way ahead of the few you know – although this wasn't entirely by chance: this parish has been very lucky over *many* generations in that a school was established here as early as 1723. It was called Wallace Hall Academy, and it was the second oldest academy in Scotland.'

Edward speaks so warmly of Wallace Hall Academy, I asked if he attended it.

'I did, and I had a good education. Men who through circumstance never went to university were given a grounding that provided for bigger and better things. So my grandfather's generation was pretty well informed simply because they'd had a fundamental education at Wallace Hall Academy. But in the beginning I was the most reluctant pupil! My sole ambition in life was to work with horses, and I didn't want to be bothered with school.

'However, when I was about ten years old I had a teacher called Mrs Alexander. She'd come back to teaching because of some family misfortune, but I was at least one that benefited from that, in so far as she came to teach our class. She was'na long there before she said that she didn't want to do any more lessons but to have a discussion; she said she'd just come past the blacksmith shop where my grandfather had been hooping wheels, that is putting the iron tyres round them, and asked us: "You all know how to measure iron on the flat, but does anyone know how to measure it in the round?"

'Of course we didn't, and then she went on to tell us how to arrive at a length, you know, multiply the diameter by $3^1/_7$ – and all of a sudden I was one of a number that could see there was virtue and value in learning, that it had a practical application; and I said to myself "boy, I'd better listen here, because if I'm going to work after I leave school, as I'll have to, then the more I know about this the better".

'Mrs Alexander taught us about heat convection, how sound travels and about all aspects

96

of anatomy and biology – and there I found a subject really close to my heart.

'When I reached thirteen I had the problem of whether to carry on at school, or to leave. My grandfather was very anxious that I should go on, and I harboured secret ambitions to be a surgeon. However, by that time my father had suffered rheumatic fever. He's made quite a good recovery, but he had a dicky heart and he couldn't do the hard, hard physical work he'd done previously. There was a big family of us – I was one o' ten – and so finally, I decided to try and become a blacksmith, because there was no guarantees.'

I inquire whether working for his father had been hard.

'Oh, gee, that's for sure, but you know I look back on it as very happy times because I knew nothing else; but it was hard work, make no mistake. This was during the war years mind, when it was even more so: we used to start at six o'clock in the morning and have breakfast at about 8am, then work through until midday when we had dinner; this was the main meal of the day. Sometimes if the blacksmith's shop was full of horses, if you got quarter of an hour for dinner you were lucky. Then maybe you'd work through to five or six o'clock, depending on how many horses you had, or even later; and only then did you have tea, which was a fork and knife job. Then you went back again and worked to maybe half past nine or ten o'clock at night – twelve or fourteen hours a day and more was commonplace, six days a week; but there was no work done on the Sabbath day.

'There'd been a workman with my father and grandfather before I started work, but when I joined he left, and so there was just the three of us. Shoeing horses represented about 75 per cent of our work because there was'na a tractor in this whole area.

'My grandfather, he used to do a lot of hard manual work; he was a fast, experienced workman. But I used to be sorry for him, even in those days, because I thought it was a gross injustice that a man should reach his time o' life and have to work so hard. But in the war years everybody was making an effort. Boy, I've seen him with not a dry stitch on his body from the time he started in the morning until the time he finished at night. That was customary, however: sweat, and I *mean* sweat, would run out of the soles of your boots; when you went for your boots in the morning they were all grey round where the laces were. Every day practically.

'But I was taught to be clean, because personal hygiene was one thing my father and grandfather were very strict on. You know, when you got to the age when you needed to shave, you were expected to do so; and at night we'd wash ourselves in a bucket in the [blacksmith's] shop and "take the rough off" before we went home, because the facilities we had in our house in those days were pretty primitive, I can assure you. Looking back on it I don't know how my mother coped, but she did.

'There was also the question of footwear. In those days we wore clogs in the winter-time because they were tremendous for keeping your feet warm – you never had cold feet. They were invariably made from a pair of boots which had worn down. The local shoemaker was a first-class tradesman, and he could cut the uppers off the boots and put them onto a pair of clog bottoms, wooden soles. Then there was the "caulkus", as it was known in this part of the world, the steel which went round the edge of the bottom, just like a miniature horse-shoe; I made the caulkus myself.

'There was no such thing as protective toe-caps in those days. It just happened the same as it happens today, people got their toes tramped and one thing and another, but it was just a chance you took. The same with eye protection; one in every thirty or forty thousand might have lost an eye, I've no way o' telling, but there was no protective eye wear or any o' that sort. Strangely enough, today I would'na a worn it anyway, and nor would the men years ago, because it creates too big an impediment; and the volume of work they had to get through in a day would never have allowed that sort of luxury.

'When I first started work I wasn't paid very much, in fact the first seven years I didn't have a wage at all. I was an apprentice and an improver, and I got my meat and my keep and the odd penny or two if I was lucky. There was no fixed wage. I remember asking my grandfather one day, whilst we were busy working – and I chose the most inopportune time – I said to him, "Is there any chance of getting a wage?" And he looked at me, and said "A what?"; and I said "Is there any chance of getting a wage?" – and he then asked me the most silly question (at least, I thought it was that silly I hanna an answer), he said "What do you want a wage for?" I said, for the want of something else to say, "I just want to be like other young fellows when I go out at night and have something to spend."

'He looked at me in a disdainful way in front of everybody – and you know, those guys could reduce you in very quick time – and he says to me, "You want to be like other folk, you *want* to be like other folk?" and by this time the shoe he was making was half cold and he looked at it in disgust and flung it in the back of the fire, and he says to me, "My young man, you're being given a *trade*. Don't you know that sheep flock together, eagles fly alone?" And that was me, "sheep flock together, eagles fly alone". But I knew within myself that at the end of the day, if I was in any way inclined, they were going to make me a tradesman and I had to content myself with that.'

I ask if his first job was to hold the horses which came in to be shod.

'Oh no, no, in those days a man was sent to the shop with two horses, and it was his job to hold them, and it had to be in such a fashion that the blacksmith was not held up in the least bit timewise. The horse had to stand properly in anticipation of a hot shoe or whatever was to be fitted, otherwise the man was told about it.

'And we knew all the sizes of the horses of regular customers – the size, shape and everything about their shoes we carried in our head. In the winter time we used to have a day of making shoes, and the day before my father and I cut off lengths of bars for this. For an average workhorse this started at about 16in and then we went $16\frac{1}{2}$, then 17, $17\frac{1}{2}$, 18, $18\frac{1}{2}$. We made ten pair of each, hind and front.

'On a big day – and I mean a *big* day, boy, I'll tell you – my father and I used to make seventy-two pair o' shoes; and that, believe you me, was really hard work – it was relentless. You didn't need anybody to sing you to sleep that night!

'We used to hang the shoes on nails that were spaced along the roof joists, and when a horse came in, either a strange one or one we knew, you'd think "Oh, that horse takes an $18\frac{1}{2}$ in shoe", and pull a pair off the hook. When we made the shoes we always left the heels to be turned and a clip in the front, which meant that by the time your shoe was sufficiently hot to fit, you did the whole operation in one.

'Today, things are completely different. Now, the majority of horses are not for draught purposes, but for leisure and pleasure; they have smallish feet, and the factory-made shoe is commonplace. These are greatly improved from what factory-made shoes *used* to be, but I don't think it does much for the young person who wants to get practice as a shoe-maker.'

I ask if horseshoe nails have changed.

'Oh yes, going far enough back my grandfather used to buy a special rod of iron with which to make them; it invariably came from Scandinavia. My grandfather made the nails from this, but he didn't point them, they were just cut off to a given length and that was it. Now, it was the job of an old blacksmith, a man getting infirm – well, at least that's what happened in Closeburn smithy – to sit striddled on a special stool and to make nails with an instrument known as a tinman's stick. This had a small sort of angle, and he used it to sharpen the nails, putting a point on them with a wee hammer. It was a very exacting job, because a lot depended on the pitch of the point as to how your nail behaved when it was being driven through the foot. If it hadn't the necessary lead in it, instead of coming out of the foot as it should do, it'd go straight up – so it needed an experienced hand to point nails.

'It's a long time since country blacksmiths made their own nails. Nowadays they are all machine-made, beautiful polished nails, and the majority are imported.'

As we talked, Edward aided his concentration by passing a miniature pair of silver pliers from one hand to another; they had been lying amongst the papers on his desk. When we began to discuss the blacksmith's task of correcting defects in horses' feet, he held the tiny pliers aloft.

'This is a pair of model hoof testers; the real sort are massive, not heavy but big, because you've got to be able to get a grip of the foot and squeeze. They're still used today, to bring pressure to bear on certain places in the foot to find the sensitive spot, which should help to indicate what is making the horse lame.

'Obviously, when the horse comes into the shop and there is lameness, then the person that's with the horse draws your attention to it and the first thing you do is walk the horse out and then maybe trot it to establish what the cause of the lameness might be.

'I was always told, "If it's lame of its head, look at its foot", because horses will nod as they step on the lame foot. If it was thought that the trouble was in a foot, then the horse would come back inside, the shoe would be taken off, and then you used the hoof testers. If you got a reaction to them, showing that you'd struck a sore point, you'd take your knife and dig into the foot – and invariably you'd find an ulcer or abscess, and so you'd let the pus out as best you could.

'What used to be done was that the foot was wrapped in a bran poultice – bran with invariably a wee drop o' washing soda in it; this had a tremendous ability to draw the pus. We used to tell the farmer or ploughman to apply that three times a day for two days. If all went well, they then brought the horse back for us to put the shoe back on. But before you did that, if you were satisfied the wound was absolutely clear, you took the horse's shoe and had a piece of leather cut to exactly the same shape as the shoe. Then you took what used to be known as Archangel tar, now known as Stockholm tar, you spat on your fingers because this tar would stick like glue to them if you didn't, then rubbed the tar right round the hoof. The tar had an iodine base and it would keep the foot right whilst it was covered. Then on top of the tar you'd put gun tow: this is fibrous and not unlike cotton wool, and it was used in guns when they were fired with black powder and it stemmed the powder. And whilst you were putting the gun tow on the hoof, you'd hope and pray that the horse didn't pull his foot away and put it down and stand on the floor, because if it got covered with dirt you had to start all over again! Then you put the leather on the underside of the shoe and nailed the shoe on.

'Maybe a week later when the wound had had time to heal, the ploughman or the farmer would take a knife and just cut round the inside rim of the shoe. Any fragments of the dressing beneath the shoe itself remained there until the next shoeing and did no harm.'

Edward went on to explain about corrective and therapeutic shoeing, which has always been part of a blacksmith's work: 'Because of the work they did, many heavy horses used to develop unsoundnesses like sidebone or ringbone, which they'd carry to the grave. However, we could make a shoe which could accommodate the disability and give the horse some comfort. It wasn't a task of trial and error – you had to know what you were doing, and if the horse didn't walk away sound or near enough sound, you were pretty disappointed.'

I asked what he considered to be the most difficult job in shoeing, and he replied, 'Och it's not difficult, once you're a competent tradesman. You seldom encounter anything that's really difficult, except a difficult horse.'

I wondered what he did about that, but it was obviously not a problem: 'Well, an experienced man like myself, and I'm one of a big, big number, I've never come to a foot I couldn't put a shoe on, one way and another.'

I say that I've seen old photographs showing difficult horses secured in wooden stocks in order to be shod. Edward considered before he replied, then: 'Well, you get quite a bit of that on the Continent. The Ardennes breed in France is a short-legged, stocky horse and often the only way to do these is to secure them in a set of stocks; in that way the farrier is not at risk, and at the end of the day you're not fighting with the horse. But the only blacksmith's shop I know in this locality to have a set of stocks for really unruly horses was up at Drumlanrig Mains, the Duke of Buccleuch's estate, where my great uncle was foreman blacksmith for forty-two years.'

I mention that when I'd been down at Closeburn parish church I'd seen this great uncle's grave, and Edward looks pleased. 'You saw his gravestone, did you? Thomas Martin, a great blacksmith I can tell you, one o' the best that ever stood behind an anvil, I would say. He was a superior workman. First of all he was a first-class horse shoer, and like his father before him he was an implement-maker, a plough-maker. He had tremendous enthusiasm for his work and he was *meticulous*. I can let you see work that he's done, that he travelled the length and breadth of the country to do, and you'd find it very hard indeed to duplicate it.'

The high principles of workmanship maintained in times past also carried into the day-to-day business dealings of the smithy, because Edward went on: 'Each blacksmith had his district and his customers. And if, for instance, a customer arrived at Closeburn and he'd come from Thornhill or Carron Bridge up the road, questions were asked before we ever shod the horse. We'd say "What's wrong with your own blacksmith?"; and if he said "Well, I'm not happy with him", or words to that effect. we'd say, "Well, we suggest you go back and have a word with him to see if you can put it to rights." Because you would never try to poach – there was no way you'd take away another man's work. In days past they were high-principled men, and they would rather have gone hungry than do that. But this is something which has gone by the board, and I think we're the poorer for it.'

I enquire if blacksmith's tools have changed over the years, and Edward replies: 'I've tools in the shop that I've used for years. One which springs to mind, it'll be two hundred years old, is a 70lb block called a cress block. This has many uses; you can place stakes in it and bend them, or forge on it and keep round edges. One of my forebears would get people to wager that he couldn't lift this cress block in one hand – it was usually for half a mutchkin

The Duke of Buccleuch's carriage and horses

102

– a liquid measure equal to an English pint – of whisky. He used to win because he'd place his thumb in an indentation in the block and lift it!'

Continuing to think about old tools, Edward admits that his smithy fire is no longer fanned by hand-worked bellows; but even in the days when it had been, that particular task had been no hardship, and he explained why:

The 70lb cress block

'We had tremendous coal in those days, tremendous. All his working life my grandfather bought coal from one or other of two pits, one Bannockburn and the other Plean, near Stirling. These two pits produced the finest coal for blacksmiths in Scotland. As regards shoes, my grandfather had the belief, and my father as well, that if you couldn't heat 'em you couldn't make 'em; also if you spent half a day in heating your iron or steel, you weren't going to get a lot done in the day – so it was essential to produce good, clean heat fast. This coal was wonderful, and we used to put on big, big fires. My father and I continued to buy from the two pits for as long as we could.

'That coal is no longer available now. I don't know if the seams are worked out, or whether it's just not viable to mine, because the coal would come from a seam which may be only 18in deep, and men would have to hew it out lying on their backs. These days, unless the coal face is 6ft deep which a coal-cutting machine can rip off, they just shut the pit. It's a shame, because I tell you, if I could get good smithy coal, that would be a tremendous thing nowadays, because the coke we've got to work with is *not* good – even the best you can get, it isn't good.'

We talk about the gas-fired forge, an appliance where there have been big advances, but Edward would still prefer a good coal furnace: 'This isn't a figment of my imagination, but a piece heated in a "normal" coal fire will last longer and work more easily than one on the gas fire. It's marginal, but nevertheless, it's there.' Edward then returns to reminiscences of his apprenticeship days:

'I remember my father when we were having a heavy day, he used to joke "Come on now, come on, this job's a question of mind over matter, I don't mind and you don't matter"! And he and my grandfather were also not above quoting the bible to you. I recall I wanted away to play football on a Saturday, and I was obliged to ask my grandfather if this was going to be possible – a team up in Ayrshire wanted me to play for them, and I thought that this was a real step up in the right direction, who knows, I might have become a professional player. I was keen to go, and I asked him and he said, "You want to go and play *football*? Don't you know young man, that it's written in the scriptures 'When a child act as a child, think as a child and reason as a child, but when a man throw away childish things' – and that's what you've got to do, learn your trade, never mind football!" And he really meant that, I can assure you.

'I never went, and it was a hard life, but my father would also say to me, "If you've made your bed, boy, you're going to lie in it", meaning that I had chosen to learn to be a blacksmith, and not a footballer, and that it couldn't be both. That was their reasoning, and they meant it; but they were also firmly of the conviction that once you'd become accomplished in what you were doing, then that in itself brought a certain amount of happiness and joy.'

It was obvious from our conversation that the three generations of Martin blacksmiths were dedicated craftsmen. I ask Edward what mementoes he has of his family's skills, and he replies: 'It's very difficult to talk about your background and your family without being boastful. Other people will just have to judge how good we are.' He then rose from his seat, went into an adjoining room and returned with a framed card:

'This may interest you. In 1893 my grandfather went back to Longtown in Cumberland, his father's home town, and took part in a horse shoeing competition. He won this card as first prize. It was the junior section, and his brother Tom won the seniors, and then they came home. It was a great achievement.

Three generations of horseshoe-making. Each shoe bears the distinctive family mark on the outside branch of the shoe. (clockwise from top left) A shoe made by Edward's father in 1910; a shoe made by Edward; a 'one-heat' shoe made by an apprentice called Marchbank in the 1890s; a pair of donkey shoes made by Edward's father in the 1940s; and a shoe made by Edward's great uncle Tom in 1920 for one of the Duke of Buccleuch's carriage horses. In the centre is a shoe for a hackney foal made by Edward's grandfather in 1900

'My grandfather's name was Edward, and so was my father's. I have a medal in my possession won by my great-grandfather in 1870 at the Royal Highland Agricultural Society of Scotland Show. My grandfather won it, too, and my father, and I've won it at different times, but I was especially pleased in 1970 because I won the gold. That meant that there'd been a hundred years that Edward Martins had left their names in the annals of the Royal Highland Society, and you know I'm particularly proud o' that because I think it would be true to say that I don't know of any other family in the whole of Great Britain that can say that.'

I ask Edward if he still competes. 'No, no, I'm within two or three days of my seventieth birthday, and there comes a time when every man has got to accept *anno domini*. Well, it's not that final, but nevertheless I'm not the man I used to be, that's for sure.'

Edward has also given up taking apprentices, explaining that: 'If you're going to teach a boy a trade it's hard work and a big responsibility.' He has, however, had many apprentices over the years, and was one of the founder members of the Farriers Registration

Council, serving on it for eighteen years. When he first became a member, the business of training young people came up, and a superior training scheme was initiated whereby youngsters apprentice themselves to experienced farriers for four years, spending about twenty-seven weeks of the first three and a half years at college. They then take an examination, the Diploma of the Worshipful Company of Farriers, which if they pass, allows them to operate on their own. First, however, they must go back to their 'master' to complete the remaining six months of their four years' apprenticeships. 'If the truth be told,' Edward remarks, 'this scheme is the envy of every other country, although some will not admit it.'

At this juncture we leave the office and walk back to the smithy. Once there, Edward steps up onto a side bench and lifts down various horseshoes from hooks, then places them on the floor for me to look at. One was made in 1910 by his father; another is his own handiwork; a third was made in the 1920s by his great-uncle Tom for the Duke of Buccleuch's carriage horse. A smaller shoe was made in 1900 by his grandfather for a hackney foal, and Edward explains that this shoe was fashioned out of the back of a scythe which is the best iron possible. A fifth shoe had earned its place in the line-up because, one day in the 1890s, it had been made by an apprentice called Marchband in 'one heat'. Finally there is a pair of dainty donkey shoes which Edward's father made in the 1940s.

Edward points out a tiny mark on the outside branch of the shoes: it's a sort of family trademark. He adds, 'In fact the shoe that I make is not a lot different to the shoe that my father and grandfather made, since I worked under their influence for years. My grandfather died in 1948 and my father in 1972. Also, strangely enough I have a shoe here in the smithy which a cousin of my father's made in 1920 before he went to Canada as a

Mr Homes
To James Townsend

		£	s	d
1896				
Feby 1	4 new shoes		2	6
	piecing coulter		1	0
3	1 link in timber chain			2
	new shear & slade to digger plough		4	0
	piecing coulter & 2 handles + new asetrys + repairing plough		5	0
4	4 new shoes to nag		2	6
6	new bar for fire place & 6 new stays + nails for Stanley Hill		1	6
	1 new hinge & nails & 4 hooks for door		1	10
	new hinges & 3 fastenments for gates		2	6
10	4 new shoes		2	6
15	1 new shoe & 4 removes & 3 links in traces		1	1½
17	2 new shoes & 6 false links		1	9
18	new clip for scuffle		1	0
21	3 new shoes		1	10⅓
	new hooks & hinges for door Stanley Hill		1	4
22	4 removes to nag		1	0
	3 new shoes to pony		1	6
24	2 new shoes & 2 spring hooks		1	11
Mar 3	1 new shoe & new rubber		1	1⅓
9	1 shoe & 1 remove & 12 false links		1	9
	mending handle for winnowing machine			4
13	2 new shoes		1	3
14	4 new shoes to pony		2	0
24	2 new shoes & 2 removes		1	9
	new bolt & staple & ring & 1 link in hames		1	4
25	3 new stays for cottage		1	6
28	mending steel pike			8
		2	6	8½

Page from a turn-of-the-century blacksmith's account book

young man. He worked with my grandfather and his name was Edward Martin as well, and you can see that it's a Martin shoe!'

We look at the donkey shoes his father made. Edward has also made donkey shoes in his career, and he believes that donkeys 'properly educated' are quiet, civil animals. Moreover he advocates that parents, instead of buying their child a first pony, should buy a donkey instead. 'It's an ideal animal for a kiddy you know, and seldom, if ever, does anyone think of it.'

Edward has also shod an ox, and is probably one of only a handful of farriers alive today to have done so. He'd learned how to do it by watching his father shoe cows which had problems through walking on the road. On the occasion he shod the ox it was filmed, because the animal was starring in a television programme which retraced the steps of an old drover who walked his bullocks from Galloway to Smithfield Market in London.

'Do you know, it was only when I'd done this that I understood how Smithfield had acquired its name in those far-off days – it was because it was the place where the animals' shoes were removed.'

He turned to help his American pupil, who in our absence had made several credible attempts to fashion a crozier. And the thought came to me that this Edward Martin, the boy who'd followed his family's trade and become a blacksmith and not a surgeon, had mastered his craft so well that a surgeon, envying his skill, had come to learn from *him*.

PIT HAULIERS

Norman Barnes, Ely, Cambridgeshire and
Len Cox, Blaenafon, South Wales

Horses have been used in coal mines probably as long as there have been coal mines. The first record of them being employed underground dates from the mid-1700s, and it is likely that in 1842, when women and children were prohibited from working underground, the number of horses used for haulage increased.

An act of 1887 gave inspectors the right to visit mines and check on the treatment horses received, but it proved to be insufficient to prevent cases of cruelty and neglect. In 1911, prompted by protests from, amongst others, the National Equine Defence League, a Royal Commission report was made, and this brought about legislation which helped to improve the lot of pit ponies. It was known as 'The Pit Ponies Charter', and it was timely, because in 1913 the number of horses at work underground reached an all-time high of 70,000.

Over the years, mechanisation meant that the number of ponies required steadily decreased, so that by the 1930s there were in the region of 32,000. Norman Barnes, now living at Ely in Cambridgeshire, worked from 1932 until 1936 at Horden Colliery on the coast east of Durham. North Shaft was sunk in November 1900, the first of the three shafts at the colliery; at 1,247ft it was for many years the deepest in Britain, and Horden itself the largest mine. Horden Colliery closed in February 1986, although water is still being pumped out of it. Norman recalls his days at Horden:

'I was fourteen when I started work. I was a driver delivering underground, and drove a pony which pulled a tub. Horden was a big colliery, and there was a stable for each district in it and a horsekeeper for each stable. The stables were on the main landing.

'Although the Galloway breed of horse I believe died out years ago, we still used to call

108

the pit ponies "Galloways", and if it was a Durham man, he'd talk about "drawing a Gallow'a". The horsekeeper looked after the ponies, and he'd put your name on a board and what pony you had that day. They were all prepared ready for you. They wore eye shields, solid leather things, to protect their eyes.

'I used to take the empty tub to a man called a putter; he served the hewers at the coal face. There was only a tub's width of rail from the landing down to the coal face and back, so you couldn't walk beside the tub. Instead, putters and drivers used to crouch on what we called the "limber", and would drive with long reins. The limber is the same as the shafts on a dray, but whereas such shafts have a platform where a man can sit, the limber on the tub ended in a bow which had a single piece of steel which became a hook; this fitted onto the pony's swingle tree.

'Away from the electric light near the coal face, you had to rely on Davy lamps for light. The horses were sensitive animals, and their instinct was marvellous; for instance they knew exactly when a roof was "working", that is, putting pressure on the timbers, and they'd dig their heels in and stop.

'I would take the full tubs to the landing, and the horse was so well trained it knew how to stop and turn round when it got there. On the landing, empty tubs ran on what was known as an "endless way" that is, they were trundling round on a big return wheel. The cable which powered the wheel went back to an engine at a junction at the shaft; the engine supplied all the various districts, and it had two drums, one going one way and one the other – that's why it was called "endless". On the cable there would be a set of six to eight tubs joined together like a train: empties came in, full ones went out.

'I would clip the front and end of a full tub on, and the tubs were then pulled out to the main landing – and that operation could be dangerous, because when a full tub was taken off the horse, as soon as you dropped the limber the pony was trained to swing itself round in front of an empty tub which would be on the other side of the cable. But sometimes the limber could be dropped too soon, and the hook on the swingle tree would get caught in

Shoeing the ponies

Pit ponies usually slept standing up

the moving hawser and then the pony would get dragged along. If that happened you had to run to the top of the landing to press the bell for the line to stop, but sometimes you couldn't be quick enough and I've seen ponies killed or injured that way. In the days before the humane killer, if a pony was injured underground it was put down by hammering a spike into its forehead.

'Pit ponies went to a lot of shows – well, carnivals – that's what we had up in the north. I remember two very small Shetlands called Samson and Delilah – they worked three foot seams – going to shows. We didn't get involved in that, however, it was the horsekeeper who did that.'

Norman's cousin, George Harker of Horden, County Durham, was a miner all his working life at Shotton, a neighbouring colliery to Horden. He, too has clear memories concerning pit ponies:

'Some pit ponies had a thin black line the length of their spine, and a line across their withers forming a cross, as you see on donkeys and asses. These ponies were always regarded as very docile and easy to work with.

'After completing their underground training, each pony's mane and tail were cut, then clipped at regular intervals after that. Indeed, I remember their tails felt like a scrubbing brush rubbing against my left arm and shoulder as I sat behind them on the limbers. I also remember that the ponies were shod with cold shoes underground, their hooves shaped to fit the shoes, with a knife.

'Contrary to the "pit pony's prayer" in which the pony asks for a "clean dry bed and a stall wide enough to lie down in comfort", I remember that pit ponies always slept standing up.'

THE PIT PONY'S PRAYER

This was sent to the Yorkshire Mining Museum, Claphouse Colliery, Overton, Wakefield, by a lady who recalls her father reciting it to her.

To thee, my master, I offer my prayer. Feed me with food clear of dust, properly mixed with bran and rolled oats, so that I can digest my food; also water and care for me, and when the day's work is done, provide me with shelter, a clean dry bed and a stall wide enough for me to lie down in comfort. Talk to me. Your voice often means as much to me as the reins. Pet me sometimes, that I may serve you the more gladly and learn to love you. Do not jerk the reins, and do not whip me when going uphill. Never strike, beat or kick me when I do not understand what you mean, but give me a chance to understand you. Watch me, and if I fail to do your bidding, see if something is not wrong with my harness or feet. Examine my teeth when I do not eat, I may have an ulcerated tooth, and that you know is very painful. Do not tie my head in an unnatural position, or take away my best defence against flies and mosquitoes by cutting off my tail. Finally, oh my master, when my useful strength is gone, do not turn me out to some cruel owner to be slowly tortured and starved to death, but do thou master take my life in the kindest way and your God will reward you here and hereafter. You may not consider me irreverent if I ask this in the name of him who was born in a stable. Amen

Len Cox of Llanelly Hill, near Blaenafon, South Wales is a miner now retired, but one who worked with pit ponies in more recent times. Len started work at Big Pit, Blaenafon in 1950 when he was fifteen years old. The pit closed in 1980 because the workable reserves were exhausted; however, in 1983 it opened to the public as a mining museum, and Len is one of a group of knowledgeable miners who act as guides.

The underground stables at the pit are always popular with visitors. Each small stall has an iron manger and the name of its one-time occupant tacked to the wall: Patch, Tiger, Essex, Albert, Victor and Welsh. A conveyor belt from the coal face to the surface finally made the ponies redundant; the last two, Victor and Welsh, left in the early 1970s.

When Len Cox left school and went to work at Big Pit there were seventy-two horses at work there. He recalls: 'One man, the ostler, fed them, washed them and cleaned them out. It seems a lot of horses for one person to look after, but that was his sole job. He fed them in the morning before they went out to work, and he fed them when they came back in. Then the afternoon shift went out. There was only a couple working on the night shifts.'

Len admits that in his early years at Big Pit he didn't have a lot to do with the ponies, apart from driving them a bit in the part of the mine known as Kay's Slope. 'It wasn't driving really, because the horse was only pulling a couple of drams of timber a day.' Len says 'drams', not 'trams', because they say 'drams' in the South Wales coalfield and Len comes from mining stock; his father and grandfather both worked at South Wales collieries. He continues:

'My job at Big Pit was as a collier; it was when I left and went into a private mine, Griffin's, that I worked with a horse full-time as a haulier. There was only five horses there, and twenty colliers, so you was talking about driving. They were on the run almost, because of the number of drams they had to pull in 7¼ hours. Each horse hauled twenty-five to thirty drams of coal a day. In actual fact they wasn't working *all* the time, because you'd pull to a collier and then perhaps you'd have to wait five to ten minutes for him to fill the dram; so you wasn't going in and straight out.

'We hauliers were paid a weekly wage, and the colliers would give us a tip, I think in those days it used to be 10s to share between us. We'd be at the mine at 7.30am for an 8 o'clock start, and finish at 3.15pm. We were supposed to have about twenty minutes' food time, but in a private mine you wouldn't of course, because the colliers would be waiting for drams and you'd have to give 'em.

'Griffin's, like Big Pit, had an ostler to look after the horses, but at Griffin's he did other work as well. The stables were above ground because it was a drift mine, so you'd walk down a slope to work in the morning. I was there for about ten years, and nearly all the time drove one horse, a Welsh cob of about 14hh. I called him Gypsy because he was brown and white.'

I ask Len if Gypsy wore a leather head-shield like the ones I'd seen in a discarded pile of tack at Big Pit.

'No, just a bridle with little blinkers so he wouldn't turn his head. There was nothing to stop him bumping his head or knocking his face. We used to take a nosebag underground for him, which the ostler made up; he'd drink when he came up at the end of the shift – I've never seen a pony drinking water underground.' Len then goes on to explain his work as a haulier:

'Down the road to the coal face there were rails, and the wheels of the dram ran along these; the horse went between the rails. I should imagine you were driving almost 200 yards to the face. I had one road to a collier which was about 1 in 7, so you see how steep that was, and the other side of the colliery you was going uphill 1 in 7. However, it was very rare that a horse would give up; he would go down on his belly pulling a dram of coal before he would give in, they *wouldn't* give in. I've seen that horse o' mine come off the road about 3in with a full load, which is just over a ton in weight. I'd put my back underneath the dram to get him up a little bit, and he'd pull and get the dram on the road again, that's how good the horse was.

'The different commands went like this: come here, to turn left; see, to turn right; stand back, to come towards you; git up, for him to go forwards; stop!, to halt.

'A chap once came to Big Pit and said he had drove a horse, and I said to him, "What do you say when you turn left?" – he had no idea. You see, in big mines there wasn't any turning roads, they were just straight, so the only command was *whoah*, for the pony to stop. In private mines there were different roads to go to, and you couldn't go in front to lead, because you were going too fast. You'd stand between the dram and the horse on the gun, which was a sort of horseshoe piece going down from the shaft to the dram.'

Thinking about certain tales I'd heard about pit ponies, I say to Len:

'I've heard it said that ponies wouldn't let you pass if they didn't want you to, and you had to give them a titbit: is that true?'

'No, no, they'd let you pass, you wouldn't have to give 'em a titbit. The hauliers used to bring them in an apple or a lump of sugar, but I've never seen anybody else.'

'What about the stories that pit ponies knew when it was time to knock off, and wouldn't draw another load?'

Pit pony at Baldwin's 'Clog and legging' in 1910

'That's a lot of rubbish, although once you took the shaft and gun off a pony he knew, of course, that it was his time. Mind you, you worked hard if you were a haulier, I believe it was harder work than a collier because it was wet and mucky, so by the time you finished the day you and the horse were just soaked through. Up at Griffin's we used to wash our horses when we came up, cold water through a hose – but it was warm in the stable, so they'd soon get dry.'

I asked Len if the horses suffered any ill effects from the work.

Well, they used to have what we called bad feet; you'd see a horse stamping [he demonstrates by stamping his own foot]…he'd stamp like that. I think it was the water and the muck that they were walking through all the time. But a vet would come at intervals and he'd inspect them, and I've never seen any real trouble. The owner of the ponies, he wouldn't let you damage them. If it was a bit low underground you wouldn't work 'em, you would get the colliers to repair that.'

'Did you ever come to grief?'

'Well, one day when my horse lost a shoe I had to drive another. It was a mare. We were going down a 1 in 5 hill when she knocked off the clamp which had been holding the blast pipes, and she bolted, and pulled the dram over the top of me; put me in hospital for about three weeks. A mare underground is very dangerous because they do come into use every so often. It's rare you see them underground, it's usually just geldings.'

'How long was a pit pony's working life – until they were about fourteen?' I ask.

'No, some would go on a little bit longer – not too long, because they was working hard, of course; but in Big Pit or in the other big mines they went on longer because they wasn't working hard.'

After being at Griffin's for nine or ten years, Len left and went into a factory for a couple of years. He then went back underground to work as a collier. Today he is retired, apart from his duties at Big Pit Museum, but he still has an interest in horses: he keeps a little pony of 12hh on the mountain as a pet; it's of the pit pony type. Len believes that in private mines there might be one or two horses still working, but he considers they'd be rarities.

In British coal mines there are certainly no pit ponies. Amidst a blaze of publicity, the last four – Tom, Carl, Alan and Flax, of Ellington Pit, Northumberland – were brought to the surface and retirement in 1993.

TIMBER HORSEMEN

The Croasdales and the Reads of Cumbria and
The Horsemen of Ardentinny, Argyll

The number of rings on a tree stump tell its age, the inner rings being its earliest years and the outer, its latest. The following history concerning men and timber hauling can be gauged on the same sort of dial: the first part is at the heart of the stump, the second could be said to represent the middle, and the epilogue, the outer rings.

THE CROASDALES OF HAVERTHWAITE

The parish of Haverthwaite was given its name in Viking times. A 'thwaite' is a forest clearing in which the Vikings grew their oats to make their haverbread. Located north-west of Ulveston in Cumbria, Haverthwaite is still a wooded area, and it is easy to understand how it became home to a timber-merchanting dynasty by the name of Croasdale.

A few years ago, Jack Croasdale, now aged sixty-eight developed the family business from being solely timber merchants, to becoming makers of high quality timber playground equipment. The firm was asked to help refurbish the local playground, and the idea grew from this; the firm even supplies overseas customers. Nowadays Jack takes a less active role in the business, and his sons carry it forward; so he found time to spend an afternoon showing me old photographs and telling me of the early days when Croasdales relied on horse power and horsemen.

The first Croasdale to settle in the area was Henry. He arrived in a neighbouring village, Finsthwaite, in 1723, and he and his wife Eleanor prospered. They had four sons, and one worked as a cooper, that is a barrel-maker, for a local gunpowder works; some of Jack's present-day factories are on the site of the old gunpowder works. The next two generations also included coopers; and the youngest son of the last couple, born in 1794, was called Isaac: he was Jack's great-great-grandfather. Jack takes up the tale:

'Isaac bought Bridge End in Haverthwaite, where I now live, in about 1830. I believe that initially he was a coppice-wood merchant looking for the type of wood that would split and rive to make hoops for gunpowder barrels. These barrels couldn't have any iron hoops or nails: they were made of thin wooden hoops that were hammered down with an iron ring to bring the staves together, and then they were fitted with copper nails, because copper never causes any sparks to fly.

'Isaac also supplied ships' fenders to Liverpool docks. The fenders were made of bundles of wooden rods, twelve rods to a bundle, and were hung over a ship's side when it was docking. From Haverthwaite to Liverpool Docks was eighty miles and they used to sail from the River Leven here, which runs out of Windermere into Morecambe Bay. A main part of the business was crate wood which he also sent to Liverpool docks, and it would eventually find its way down through the canals to the potteries. You see, there was a big export business in crockery, and the potteries wanted crates made out of riven coppice so that if a crate landed on the ground, or was rolled, it was fairly flexible. In fact, we continued to send crate wood right up to the 1950s, mostly alder, birch, ash and sycamore, anything that would split and rive.

'Isaac had several sons, but the only one surviving to carry on the business was James. He was a character. At one time in about 1860, he sent his men up a hillside to extract timber

Jack Croasdale

with their horses and carts; to do this they had to go along a right of way which ran through a neighbour's yard. The neighbour, a man named Hunter, came flying out one night and said "When you get back home you can tell your boss that it's the last time he comes through here making such a mire and mess. If anyone lands up here tomorrow I'll be out with my shotgun!"

'Now James weighed about twenty stone and was nearly six foot tall and when the men told him what the neighbour had said, he said "We'll see about that, I'll go myself". Next day James came clip-clopping up the hill. Hunter was shouting and screaming that he'd shoot him if he came through his yard, but James wound his reins up, laid them across the flank of his horse, got into a trot and swept towards him. Hunter's small son, fearing his father would be trampled, shouted "Shut, father, shut!" which means "shoot" in any other language. Anyhow, his father didn't "shut" and James drove on. For ever after the little boy was called "Shut" Hunter. James' photograph hangs on the wall in the Croasdale offices, and he studied us gravely as we studied him. In the sitting-room of Jack's home, laid out on the table, there were more photographs and records of the past: for example Jack's grandfather's daybook with notes of his piecework and timber terms, such as bobbin wood, smarts, brooms, swill wood and coals. Jack could explain some terms: 'Swill wood is very, very straight-grained oak for making a "swill" which is a basket; these had little handles on and were used in the docks for refuelling with coal, or on the land for potato picking. "Brooms" are the birch brooms which went up to Motherwell for the iron industry: they were thrown onto the molten iron as it came out of the furnace to oxidise and extract impurities. "Coals" were rather long sticks and they were sold for putting under the oven in the old kitchen ranges. Every house had what they called "stick houses" for storing their firewood, and the size of the wood went down to small sticks for kindling.'

Jack sorts through his collection of old photographs and extracts one: 'Here's a photograph of my father with a load of firewood – that load would fetch about 7s 6d and he's delivering in the village of Cartmel. He'd worked since he was a boy. When he was thirteen he'd come home from school, and my grandfather would have a pony and trap ready and send him in it to Barrow-in-Furness, which is fifteen miles [24km] away. He'd have to take charcoal bags into the coppice woods at Barrow. We employed charcoal burners because there was a ready market for charcoal; the gunpowder works needed vast amounts of it, and there was also an iron company which used it for smelting.'

Jack has clear and detailed memories of the work and the life-style that being woodmen involved:

'My father was brought up to be a horseman, and he always gave his horses short names which they knew. When I was small there were three teams of horses going out in the mornings, probably nine horses with the waggons. At night after I'd been put to bed I used to creep back down and sit on the stairs to listen to the four waggoners who lived in. They had their own staircase with two double beds in their room, iron bedsteads covered with big, heavy red quilts. These men would be up at six o'clock to groom and feed the horses, then they would come in for their own breakfast. When they went back out they'd take their "tommy" or "baite box" with them; it would hang from the waggon shafts and was big enough to hold a baby. They needed lots of big thick slices of bread, and they would take slices of beef on Monday and Tuesday because enough had been cooked on Sunday to last for those two days. My mother also baked fiddle-fruit pasties for them. They were called "fiddle" I suppose because they were folded over and crimped round like a half moon or like an old fiddle. These were cut in two and put on end so the juice wouldn't run out, and they took custards, too.

'One of the men used to clear his box out at about 9.30am when they settled down to have their drink, and he used to slam his lid shut and say "Now then, that'll not be to hanker after" – in other words, he hadn't got to worry about it for the rest of the day, as he'd had it all!

'One of the waggoners was called Ted, but everyone called him "Dad". He wasn't married, but he was "Daddy" of them all because he was on top of the job, master of it. He'd do his horses at night, wash and maybe shave once a week whether he wanted it or not, and go to the local pub, the Anglers' Arms. When he came back he'd slip his clogs off, take the straw out of them and put it across my mother's kitchen range to dry out ready for the morning. Bits would be left lying around and my mother was always fed up with it, but couldn't sort him out!

'Waggoners worked with the horse-drawn waggons, carters had a horse and cart and horsemen worked in the woods extracting timber. The men would each have two or three horses to groom, and their harness to keep clean and the brasses polished up.

'The horses were never true Clydesdale or Shire, but crosses, though they always had a lot of feather on them. My grandfather and father usually bought them as five-year-olds from farmers. I haven't got any receipts for purchases because it was always done by a spit in the palm and a clap of the hand. Sometimes they got ten bob of the purchase price back from the seller as "luck money".

'Timber hauling was hard work for horses, and fourteen was about their top age for working. My uncle was employed by Silcocks, the animal feed company, and we used to get a special horse feed from them. This used to come in large quantities. A horse ate a hundredweight of it a week, and I don't know how much chop was mixed with that.

'When the horses were out working in wintertime the men would always put rugs on them whilst they were stood still, because they'd generally sweat a lot when they were working and would risk catching a chill.

'The horsemen in the wood were on day work, and they'd use their horses to pull logs by chains to a fairly handy loading place. The job was called snigging. A horse could pull 10 to 15cwt, although 7 to 10cwt was enough, and they'd have two horses to drag a log which was a ton. To start off they'd round the log at the bottom, make it more pencil-shaped so that it didn't cut the ground so much. As the chain straightened up and the horse started pulling, the log would roll over and get some momentum to start it, though it would almost come sideways at first, not straight forwards.

'I was a horseman myself for a few months when I first left school, but I was pretty green. It takes years to become an accomplished horseman. I was just sent to get in little bits of firewood, but twice I got into trouble. On one occasion I hit this boggy ground and wasn't alert enough to stop the horse and back off; the horse went in up to his hocks, then keeled over, and its legs were fast amongst the birch roots. I had to sit on its head for a while and calm it, then scream for the woodcutters to get us out. On the other occasion I took the horse amongst some big rocks to some larch logs. I hooked one up onto its chain and then led it out, but the log got jammed between the rocks. Instead of backing off which might have released it, I gave the horse another go and it responded – but the tree locked, and its end came round like a bow and sprang back and pulled the horse over – it was lying there amongst the rocks and might easily have rolled right over the top and been a gonner. Those are the sort of situations you do get into in the Lake District woods, and experience certainly counts.

'The waggoners would collect the timber drawn out for them by the horsemen. They'd go out at about 7.30am in the morning, with each horse's provender in a woven, hessian-type bag which was hung from the waggon shafts. When the waggons picked up from the Brocklebank estate at Grisedale, which is about eight miles from here, it would take them the best part of three hours to get there; say, three waggons would leave here, and another two would leave Greenodd where we had another sawmill, and they'd all get up to that area.

'When they arrived they always loaded the timber by erecting a tripod known as "three legs and blocks": two legs of about 20ft each went over the waggon, and a longer leg of about 22ft went over the timber lying down on the far side of the waggon. The "blocks" were two pulleys suspended on chain beneath the top of the tripod; the bottom block had a shackle on the end of it called a "dog", which was fixed round the log to be lifted – when it tightened, the spikes on it went into the trunk. Five vertical ropes ran between the "blocks", eventually leading to one which was attached to a horse; the procedure of fixing it to the horse was called "blocking on".

'The tripod achieved a reduction of weight by one-fifth, because the horse had to walk out five metres to lift a log a metre – or fifty feet to lift it ten feet. The tail end, the thin end of the log went up first, and the waggoner who was loading the waggon guided it up and then

A tripod, known as 'three legs and blocks', used for loading timber

A four-horsepower team handled with the skill that only came with experience

leaned on it, and his extra weight brought the butt up; and if the butt end was very heavy they helped raise it by putting a chain on it. The log was pushed into position on the waggon as the horse reversed off.

'In most cases there was a man leading the horse, but quite often a clever animal would go on word command alone – you know "ahoy", "go back" and "back off" – and it wouldn't get its feet across the ropes when it came back towards the tripod. Maybe four or five tons would be put on each waggon, and it would take about fifteen minutes to load it; it would take three or four hours to load the lot.

'In the team of horses used for pulling the loaded waggon, the lead horse was always the clever, steady one; a fiery horse, one that always tore and drove itself, went behind the lead – he'd quieten down eventually; and the shaft horse was always pretty heavy, and stockier than the others. If you look at some of these old photographs you'll see that the chain between the horses goes up in a straight line; but if you had the smaller horse at the front, the chain would go up and down again.

'The places the waggons came down from were quite steep and narrow, just woodland tracks. The rear wheels cut in quite a lot on corners and they had to hold the horses right out on the corner, otherwise they'd cut in and roll over. They had some excitement at times!

Haverthwaite Station

'The journey back was much slower, because every time they came to a hill they had to stop and borrow some horses from the waggon behind. They might take two horses from the waggon behind and finish up with five going up the hill. Five horses could tow five tons. Once one waggon was up, they'd uncouple the horses and take another one up; they'd come down in the same sort of convoy. It would take four hours to travel the eight miles back.

'Often they went to the railway station yard and unloaded, either onto the ground or directly onto a railway set, a long waggon with maybe a smaller one at the end. There's a story that one day they were unloading in the station yard with a hand-operated crane when a passing chappie looked over the wall and said "Excuse me . . ." A little waggoner with bandy legs went across to him and the bloke said, "Can you tell me where Haverthwaite station is?" The waggoner said "Aye, this is it, this is the station." The fellow said "Oh, I thought it was further round the corner, down the hill," and the waggoner said, "Aye it was, but we carted it up here"; and the man looked down at his little bandy legs and said, "Yes, my word, and you had the heaviest corner!"

Jack relishes this story and then continues:

'By the time they got back from unloading and had fed and groomed their horses, it would be six o'clock and they'd come in for their evening meal. At seven o'clock they'd go back to the horses, "doing them up" as we say, and bedding down, and then one or two of the fellows would start wrestling in the field. It was a great local sport, Cumberland wrestling!'

I express surprise that after such a strenuous day the men had sufficient energy left to wrestle. Jack laughs, 'Well, a lot of the time they would have been sitting on the waggon shafts,

122

although coming back they'd be running up and down encouraging the horses. But there wasn't a lot of heavy lifting, not for the waggoners.'

We look at a few more photographs. There's Jack's dad, George Croasdale, leading a team of six horses which is dragging a waggon from the lake shore at Lakeside. The oak tree on the waggon was floated down the lake from Wray Castle, Ambleside.

'My father told me that they had the trees pulled into the edge of the lake on the Saturday morning; there was heavy rain over the weekend, and when they went back on the Monday morning, they'd all disappeared and were found floating round the north end of the lake. They had to go out in a rowing boat and drive a spike into them and tow them back to the bank again, and it took quite some time to do that.'

Jack points out that his father's right hand is on the lead horse's collar and his left hand is leading. 'He's pushing his feet away from the horse. I was never a horseman, but my father was possibly one of the finest, and particularly for getting a team of horses to work. With six or seven horses somebody had to be in charge – you couldn't have everyone shouting – and he was the one on those occasions with a bit of persuasion, and sometimes bad language, but the horses responded because they knew him, knew his voice and that he was in command.'

Croasdales bought their first lorry in 1934. However, they carried on using horses in the firewood industry during World War II. In 1950 they started estate thinning operations for the Forestry Commission, and had seven or eight horses doing this work up until the 1960s when they were replaced by a mechanical winch system.

Jack's father George, with a team of six horses dragging a waggon, loaded with an oak tree, from the lake shore

THE HORSEMEN OF ARDENTINNY

Ower the hills to Ardenteenie
Just to see my bonnie Jeanie
Just to get one o' her smiles
I would walk a hunder miles

Sir Harry Lauder (1870–1950), the music-hall entertainer and songwriter (he wrote 'Roamin' in the Gloamin'), made the above verse famous; he lived near Ardentinny, in Argyll. Well, I was driving to Ardentinny, but to hear the stories of two retired horsemen, Alaister McLean and Werner Cameron. In the 1950s both had worked for the Forestry Commission dragging 'thinnings' from the woodland on the hills around Ardentinny.

The Forestry Commission had started work in Ardentinny in 1919, and in 1926 expanded by buying the big local estate called Glenfinart. They established a tree nursery, and planted the hillsides with seedling trees. They had also created smallholdings for forest workers who came home from work and tilled them in the evenings. It was a close-knit community, and still is, for Ardentinny – bounded on three sides by the hills and on one side by the sea – is only accessible by two routes: a long, looping road around Loch Lomond, and a ferry which runs from Gourock (west of Glasgow) to Dunoon, the town below Ardentinny.

Alaister McLean lives in the centre of Ardentinny, Werner Cameron on the outskirts near to the ruins of the once stately mansion 'Glenfinart'. Alaister has lived in Ardentinny for longer than anyone else. He was born in 1923, and came to the village in 1925 when his father began work as a ploughman on a farm on the Glenfinart estate. In the following year when Major Leschallas sold the estate to the Forestry Commission, Alaister's father, Sandy McLean, became their first horseman in the glen.

Alaister took me out to Barnacabber Hill, one of the hills bordering the village; 'cabber', he explained, means 'home of the deer' and it was certainly appropriate because there were deer on its lower slopes. Pointing up the hill, Alaister told how his father took his horse, Polly 1,500ft up the hill carrying fencing materials, because trees were going to be planted up to 1,000ft, and beyond that a farmer grazed his sheep. As well as doing the fencing, his father took up the seedling trees for planting; these were carried in panniers on Polly's back.

Alaister's forestry work with a horse began in 1955. Previous to that he had been a forest worker, but it was in that year that Mr Angus, the local forester, told him and some of his mates that if they got a horse each and dragged timber thinnings they would get piece-work, which was extra money. Alaister explained:

'The area from Stronchullin Farm right up over the Larach as we call it, was at the age to be thinned. The deal was, that we would get money for a week's piecework, and they would also give us each week one of those big white five-pound notes for the horse. So my mate and I went to a farmer up on Loch Fyneside and bought two horses at £35 each. Mine was called Billy, a cross between a Highland Arran and a Clydesdale with a black stripe down his back, a fairly heavy horse. My mate Jock's was a little lighter.

Alaister's father holding Polly with Alaister riding

'At that time I was living up the glen in a cottage just below the deer farm. It had a red-tiled roof – and still has – and four or five acres of land. Jock was living the other side of the house I now live at, and he had two or three acres. Every field was used on these smallholdings – on five acres there would be, say six drills of potatoes, six of turnip and cut hay for feeding cattle and horses.

'Billy was about seven or eight when I first had him. He was diligent, and on the whole quite obedient – in fact, when I bought him the farmer said "Alaister, you could sleep with him!" Jock's horse was flighty.

'Jock, a chap called Harry and I usually worked together. We kept our horses at our homes. In the morning I'd feed Billy at seven o'clock and get my own breakfast; then I'd put together my "piece" that is, dinner – six slices of bread and cheese and jam mostly, anything like that, and a flask of tea. Billy's food of oats and hay was put onto his hames, and then we'd be away. The glen was quite an area for dragging in; it would be, say, a mile or two miles at the most on the main road until you got to the hill.

'The logs were cut by the boys in the cutters and just left; they weren't stacked or anything, and you used the horse to pull them to each other and then just hitched on another. You had a long chain and all you needed to do was loop it round and do it that way. Sometimes the forestry boys would cut a road line through the trees and one of us, that is Jock, Harry or myself, would go off on his own for a couple of weeks to drag the trees from this; but we were never parted very much.

'The difficulty of the work was the terrain. If it got very, very steep the horse was slower at walking up, and coming down – the drag – it would seem to only just manage to keep in front of the load. Sometimes the logs would catch up on the swingle tree and slacken the chains a bit, but when a horse was experienced and well trained, it went a bit quicker to stop this happening. You could get into some tight corners, too. Whereas larch wood is easy because it is more open, usually planted on a bit of reasonable ground, a bracken face or something, sitka is tight in places and you are working under a canopy.

'Unfortunately Billy got caught up in the glen: his foot went down between two roots, a muddy bit it was – he put his foot down and then tried to get it back out, and he pulled the

Billy

shoe clean off, which shows you how he pulled, and he was never the same again. I worked him for a wee while, but I was advised by the local blacksmith who used to come down from Dunoon to shoe the horses, who said, "He'll never get better". Billy used to come home at night when I was working him in the summer time, and I'd give him his tea, but he'd just go and lie down; so I had to put him away to the knackers in Glasgow. I'll never forget that day I had to walk him down the road to the lorry, it was a terrible day.

'I got another horse called Meg for a short while after that; and then the winches came in, and the horses were finished in Glenfinart Forest.'

I met Ardentinny's other retired horseman, Werner Cameron, in his garden. It is probably the grandest garden for miles: roughly two acres in extent and walled, it was once the kitchen garden to Glenfinart House. Werner, looking like a dot in the centre of this vast expanse, tends his cabbages and strawberry plants; but he doesn't mind the solitude, because unlike Alaister, he spent his horseman days working on his own.

He came to Britain as a German prisoner-of-war in 1946 when he was twenty-five years old, and chose to stay. He took a ten-acre Forestry Commission holding in 1953, and he adopted his wife Betty's surname 'Cameron', fearing that their children might meet anti-German prejudice when they started school. Werner's holding was a field of five acres and five acres of grazing. His forest dragging area was Glenbranter, north of the woodland where Alaister had worked.

At first he worked a forestry horse because it was his intention to spend his money on a cow for his holding, but that horse met with misfortune: 'We were on steep ground, too steep to come straight down, so I cut a slant across; but the horse stopped and the "tack" – which is what we called the trees that it pulled – went past the horse and pulled it on top of them, and it slid along the trees and must have damaged its spine.'

After that he bought a small Clydesdale horse, but it was really too old, and after two years when it was finding the work difficult he bought Kate. Werner said of Kate: 'She was a very large Clydesdale, really too heavy for timber because here the hills are quite steep – but she did very well. Horses had to adapt themselves because the hills are criss-crossed with small ditches or burns. At the beginning she could not get the hang of stepping over a ditch, which was only a foot – she would step into it and stumble; but after a few weeks she learned to jump or step over some of them.'

I ask Werner to describe other problems.

'The most difficult bit was to stay in front of the tack in steep places when the tack would slide of its own accord and catch up with the horse, which had to run on in front of it. The

Alaister with Meg, and mate Harry with his horse Peggy. Loch Long can be seen in the background

steep bits were only short snaps, however, maybe thirty yards [27m], then the ground would level out again, then maybe there would be another steep snap; so it was never really a long distance where she had to run.'

Werner then admitted that he had been responsible for spoiling Kate, not in her work but over her food:

'I fed green oats to her. I grew the oats myself, and it was a very wet winter and summer, and the oats wouldn't dry in stooks so we strung wires along and put the sheaves against the wire to dry them. Every night I took one of these green sheaves and fed it to the horse, and after a fortnight she started to go lame. I had to get the vet and he told me that I should not have fed green oats to her and it had actually poisoned her, given her laminitis. Her shoes had to be removed because the pain was in her hooves, and twice a day I put her for half an hour in very cold water to cool her down.

'I had to stop working with her. Now just at that time in October there was a cattle sale at Strachur and there were horses for sale there, too. In fact I wasn't looking for a horse, but a dealer had bought one at the sale and was told afterwards that it was a kicker, a spoiled horse and a very bad one, so he tried to get rid of it. He had heard that my mare was ill, so after the sale he approached me and asked if I would swop my horse for the one he had bought if I would give him an extra £10. At the beginning I didn't want to do it, because I knew the other horse and knew it had a bad reputation – but he talked me into it.

'My new horse, Danny, looked more like a polo pony, he was an Irish cob. On the first day he wouldn't pull anything, not even a light load, and kicked the chains. But I hit him with a stick and finally he settled down, and you know he didn't kick again and turned out to be the most marvellous worker.'

I asked Werner how he had known of Danny's bad reputation.

'The horse had belonged to my neighbour who had sold him to some forestry contractors. They had been doing the same sort of work, but they spoilt him because they were cruel – basically they didn't understand how to treat horses, and the Forestry Commission had no interest whatsoever in how things were run. The contractors had hit him and things like that. Lots of horses if the load was too heavy, they would start to run because that was the only way to keep moving – but some men used to think that if a horse ran they needed to put a heavier load on to slow him down; but that was quite wrong, and then they would start to hit the horse with a stick, and *that's* when it would start to kick.

'But once I had trained Danny he was marvellous; I didn't need to lead him at all, and he would go up and down the hill on his own. Going uphill I hung onto his tail and it was he pulled me up mostly! His only foible was that sometimes he would not go through boggy, wet ground, and that's the only time I might have to go in front of him. He would follow me anywhere, but he wouldn't go on his own through it.'

I ask Werner to describe exactly his work with Danny.

'The Forestry Commission had large areas which they called "compartments", and you would have one of these for two or three months and have to extract up to nine thousand logs. It was mostly thinnings, smaller trees, so one load could consist of five or six trees. If it was a bigger tree, what we called a saw-log, we would just put that one on.

'We worked up what we called a tack road. You started at the bottom, and then the trees were cut sometimes two or three hundred yards up the hill so you stuck to one road and came down it for two or three weeks. After so many loads the top soil was pushed away and your road got deeper and deeper, so sometimes you hit a tree root and other times you hit rocks, and that's when the trouble started because the load would stick and stop. The horse had to learn to relax when the chain came down – but at the beginning it didn't know to do that and it would keep pulling, and the strain might break the chain or swingle tree and the horse would disappear for maybe half a mile, and you'd have to go after it!

'I would make my own swingle tree from a piece of oak, just shape it and then take it to the blacksmith, and he would put all the mountings on it. It was safer to have the swingle tree break, than not, because otherwise it was quite a force into the horse's legs and could damage them.

'To free a stuck load I carried a steel pin with me, about four feet long, and I'd lever the load away from the obstacle. If it was a small rock or a root I cut it out with an axe. You'd also take the horse out at right-angles and over to the opposite side of the track and just take one heave, and that generally freed the load and the horse would straighten up again and go on. After about a year Danny got so smart that whenever he hit a snag he would go to one side like this on his own, but of course he didn't know which side to go to, so sometimes he made it worse because he pulled it tighter into the wrong side. When this happened he went to the opposite side, and many times I didn't even see him do this; it was only when I came down afterwards and realised that he had actually made it worse, and then better. He would only do it twice, once to one side and then to the other side, and if it didn't work he would stop and wait for me.

'One time the drag hit something, and to save himself he spread his hind legs; in doing this he put them against a tree and a hoof got caught in the tree roots – Sitka spruce has very shallow roots. He couldn't get his foot out, so he just stood there, half hanging, waiting for me to come and cut the root away. That is when a horse might pull a shoe off, trying to free its foot.

'If his load was stuck in a steep bit he would sit down because his head would be lower than his back – he would sit down like a dog on his hindlegs and wait for me to rescue him!'

The rescuing was not always a one-way process, because Danny sometimes came to Werner's aid, too. Werner recalls one such time:

'The Forestry Commission were putting out experimental plots right on top of the hills and I had to take up fencing material. It was a marvellous May day, but at the top just after lunchtime the mist came down and I couldn't see anything, it was so dense. Up there you had gullies, and I was scared to move; even crawling, your hands might reach nothing and you could overbalance. Also there were no landmarks, so I could have just gone round in circles.

'I didn't know what to do, but I couldn't wait up there indefinitely, so I said to Danny 'You have to lead!, and I hung onto his tail and let him go; and he took me off that hill and down, and with never any risk of falling into a gully because he could sense where they were.

'I enjoyed being on my own with Danny. I could follow my own line of thought, and the only thing we'd see was sometimes a deer.

'Each day we worked mostly until four o'clock. Animals are far better time-keepers than us human beings, and sometimes when it came to 3.45pm and I wanted to go up again, Danny would not, because he knew the time all right! That's the only time I had to pull him up.

'At home I had cows, and in the summer when they were out grazing at the top of the field all I needed to do was to shout out Danny's name and he would round them up and chase them down in front of him. Sometimes I was scared stiff one of them would break a leg. I didn't teach him to do this, he just did it for devilment!'

Werner kept Danny for four years and then the Forestry Commission brought in Ferguson tractors with winches. Werner couldn't afford to keep Danny on his five-acre field, and so he sold him to a dealer.

Werner was taken on by the Forestry Commission as a chokerman, doing similar work to that which he'd done before with a horse, putting loads together and putting them on ropes, called slings, but for a winch to take out. He recalls wryly: 'Many times the ropes broke because the tractor driver misjudged how much to tighten the tension so that the drag would rise just a wee bit over a hump. He had to judge it the same as the horse had – and sometimes the load scattered everywhere!'

EPILOGUE

Although several decades have passed since the introduction of winches and tractors into timber extraction, there is a renewed interest in using horse power for this sort of work. Enthusiasts say that horses are less destructive to woodland habitat, and that they can get up very steep slopes and into places which tractors cannot; these advantages help to outweigh the argument that a horse's output is limited, and that it needs constant attention.

About five years ago the British Horse Loggers' Association was started, specifically to promote the use of draught horses in woodland. Its headquarters are at Holme Lacy College near Hereford, and people wishing to acquire the skills of logging with horses can attend courses at the college. Pupils seriously interested can become competent enough to set up in business as horse loggers, others simply enjoy the skill for occasional use and the fact that it is a good way to maintain interest in heavy horses and to preserve the breed.

The association holds displays at shows, demonstrating the traditional method of dragging

Kevin with Velvet at work in the woods around Witherslack

timber with chains, and the more recent Scandinavian method of carrying the logs on a small trolley with wheels and solid shafts; these shafts reduce the risk of a log slipping forward into the horse as the load comes downhill. They also stage horse logging competitions, and it was at one of these that I met George Read and his family; they had travelled south from Witherslack in Cumbria. George and his son Kevin were competing, and these two men and their horses stood out from the other loggers. Their horses were smaller and rougher, and their harness was old and well used; and George and Kevin were not wearing smart breeches, but working clothes.

Kevin told me that he was twenty-six, and that this was his first logging competition. He thought that probably he and his father were amongst only a handful of loggers present who pulled timber full-time for a living. I stood by the rope which marked the boundary of the competition course and waited for Kevin's father, George, to complete his turn so that I could snatch a few moments of his time. George's horse was also a 'Danny', a Dales cross, as was Kevin's horse, Velvet.

Eventually George, leading Danny, came across to talk. He told me that he'd been 'in timber' since leaving school at fifteen years of age: first, five years with the Forestry and then five years working at Croasdales with horses; he remembered Croasdales loading timber on their waggons with the 'three legs'. For the last twenty years or so he had been self-employed and nowadays he and Kevin work together.

Danny had belonged to a man called John Watson who, George informed me, 'had pulled timber all his life'. He'd been John's last horse, but John had got to an age where he had found it too much to break Danny in – and so he had given him to George. 'John used to come with me and Danny in the woods,' George explained, 'and the deal was that I could have Danny,

130

George Read

The Read family at a competition organised by the British Horse Loggers' Association

but on the condition that I'd never sell him, even when he was too old to pull timber. He's nineteen now, and I reckon he'll work until he's twenty-three or twenty-four.'

George likes small horses: 'Big horses went out when the felling and dragging of big hard-woods finished, because they get tired going uphill. Small horses, half their weight, are better on steep conditions. Get a small cob if you want to make a living because you can make more money with that sort.'

I ask George if he *did* make a living using just horses. He replies:

'We refuse three-quarters of the work we're offered, and we operate full time, fifty-two weeks a year – and in summer we can work fourteen hours a day. We can compete with other timber extractors because we buy good quality timber on bad ground, ground which is so steep it's impossible to use tractors on it.

'During the winter months, say eight weeks, we don't make anything, but just break even and cover wage costs; we usually work from 9am to 3.30pm because working under the cover of spruce makes it dark. However, in one particularly good year we extracted five or six thousand tons of timber with three horses. So you *can* make a living without machines.

Also machinery can cost £50,000 or more, and you have to shift a lot of timber to get that

The photographs on these pages show competitors at a British Horse Loggers' Association show

money back. Danny won't owe me a penny even if I don't do any more work with him at all.'

George talked about horses in forestry in the 1950s and 1960s: 'It was the practice to thin out woodland, and the horses pulled away the thinnings. Then it became policy to cut timber when it was relatively young and to replant completely. But with this method, the trees don't grow straight and tall – they think they will, but they don't.'

George and Kevin work their horses with the traditional chain and swingle tree, because their terrain is too steep for the Scandinavian wheeled 'bogies'. George remarks: 'Nine months of the year the loggers in Norway don't use bogies anyway, they use sledges on ice; they can pull five ton a trip with two horses that way.'

Kevin joins us. He admits that his father is a hard taskmaster: 'He used to come and watch me train a horse, but he didn't use to say anything because he thinks you have to learn by your mistakes. When I got home he'd just say "You're daft, doing that".'

George laughs: 'You never stop learning about horses – though having said that, not everyone has that ability. I can tell a horse is having foot trouble before he's lame, but some people would look a lifetime and would never see it at all!'

AN ALL-ROUND HOROSEWOMAN

Diana Coaker, Dartmoor, Devon

If you go to Sherberton Farm to ride at Diana Coaker's trekking centre, you may be put on a startlingly blue-eyed horse from Russia, or a solid-limbed product of France. However, these more unusual equines are delightful exceptions in a place where the tradition of Dartmoor pony-keeping is as solid and enduring as the lichen-covered boulders on the surrounding moorland.

I met Diana in her kitchen, hastily grabbing a sandwich having been out with a party of ten eleven-year-old children, and she confirmed the long association between the farm and Dartmoor ponies: 'There have been pedigree Dartmoors here for six generations; moreover Anthony, my youngest son, is the sixth generation to farm Sherberton.' The farm is right in the heart of Dartmoor. To get to it you cross several grey stone bridges huddled over clear, tumbling water, the surrounding fields bordered by walls made of rounded boulders.

Diana keeps her riding ponies in an old Devon longhouse. Her Dartmoor ponies are visible from the farmhouse, in fields called 'new-takes' – or 'newtechs' as they are known locally. Dartmoor farmers acquired new-takes through an old tradition whereby every fifteen to twenty years they were allowed to take in a new piece of the moor. Usually the new piece was very rough ground and the rocks out of it were used to make the boundary. This is a custom which is no longer permitted; however, existing new-takes have been the subject of a specific project in recent years, something which Diana's late husband, John, initiated with the Duchy of Cornwall and which other farmers have now taken up: that is, to keep so many Dartmoor ponies in a new-take, liaising with the Duchy in a scheme which helps farmers improve their pony progeny. Diana explains: 'You have a pedigree stallion running with about fifteen mares in the area of a new-take. The owner of the mares gets paid so much to run their mare there, and the owner of the new-take also gets money. The idea is to produce registered stock.'

Improving the Dartmoor pony's lot in life is something else which concerns Diana. Under a National Parks scheme, each January Diana, plus another breeder-cum-farmer, a vet and a National Park representative go out to farms all over Dartmoor and inspect ponies: if their condition is good, the farmer will continue to receive a subsidy for them.

Dartmoor ponies are also very much part of the life of Diana's children. Her daughter Susan is the Registration Secretary of the Dartmoor Pony Society; like her mother, she is a well known judge at shows. She and Anthony are on the Commoners' Council, and one of the rulings it has implemented is to have what is called a 'clear day' for the ponies. This day is in October, and on it, all ponies are taken off the moor and members of the Commons' Council go round and count them. If a farmer has too many he is told to get rid of the surplus: this prevents overgrazing, and as a consequence, hungry ponies straying in search of forage.

Diana's present personal campaign is to redress the situation whereby Dartmoor has no control over its stallions; it is the only common that she knows of in England which allows any old colt to run around: 'I'm trying to get it that the stallions which run on the moor are inspected and are of a good standard of either Dartmoor or Shetland. At present the problem lies with one- to three-year-old half-bred colts. You see, an older stallion keeps together the more mature mares he likes, and will not have a young mare in his herd. So these young mares then take up with these young colts and they breed awful nondescript things which make two guineas in the market. If stallions were licensed these colts would have to be cut or taken off the moor.'

It is obvious that Diana becomes deeply concerned about matters when it comes to horses. She confirms this by commenting: 'A few years ago people *rode*, but they can't ride now – they're taught to ride with their knees stuck out and their hands

Diana organises a day's trek

up in the air, and it doesn't work. I think that's why there are so many accidents. If you watch any of the good riders, *they* don't ride in this current lackadaisical fashion!'

I ask Diana if she teaches riding to the people who hire her ponies for trekking; she says, 'I teach them as they go along. When I have a party of children they must all learn to shorten their reins before they go on, and they hold on to the front of the saddle until they can rise to the trot.'

Riding at Sherberton goes back a long way. Diana's sister-in-law had riding ponies in 1933, and Diana believes there were probably ponies there before that. She herself came to

Diana's aunt, Dorothy Brooke, founder of the Brooke Hospital for Animals in Cairo

Sherberton and brought her own ponies when she married in 1951. That was the beginning of a fresh chapter in her life, which to that date had had much to do with horses. She remembered clearly her early days before Sherberton:

'I lived in a house called Kenbury six miles outside Exeter and which today is under the motorway. My mother hunted, and my father showjumped and hunted, and also played polo at the army polo club at Exeter. He'd been in the army, and during his army days he'd had a horse called Glad-Eye, which he later wrote a book about.

'Glad-Eye was a short-tailed cob which went right through World War I with father – it even went to Egypt with him, and *came back*, which a lot of cavalry horses didn't, because the army sold them to Egyptian buyers. I believe they sold over 20,000. In 1930 my Aunt Dorothy, the wife of father's brother who was Major General Brooke, went to Cairo and was shocked at the condition of the surviving cavalry horses. She wrote a letter to the *Morning Post* about them, and it raised over £20,000. She bought the 5,000 horses still working out there; the ones that were very bad were put down, and in 1934 she set up the Brooke Hospital for Animals in Cairo; as many will tell you, it still exists today and has gone from strength to strength. In fact they have now moved into India too, which I understand is absolutely terrible, with horses still working in mines.

'Anyway, about Glad-Eye – in 1934 or 1936 there was a parade of twenty-four veterans at Olympia, and my father took Glad-Eye – and Princess Elizabeth (the present Queen) gave him twenty-five lumps of sugar! Father had met the princess at an officers' garden party, and had talked to her about Glad-Eye and the forthcoming veterans' parade; and she had promised to come to it and give Glad-Eye twenty-five lumps of sugar. So she kept her word, and afterwards wrote letters to Glad-Eye and sent him sugar.

'I once took a horse by train to a London show; there was another horse on the train, and when we arrived at Paddington it transferred to a really posh horsebox – but I had just my father in his car to meet me. It was early morning and I set off to ride from Paddington to White City, and I shall always remember that when I asked directions of the first two people I met, neither knew the way!'

The phone in Diana's kitchen rings. It is to be the first of several phone calls, all enquiries for puppies she has had advertised for sale. The caller is unlucky, because all of them except one have been sold, and that one is to stay at Sherberton. Black and white and called Fly, she is the fifth generation down from a Sherberton collie called Peach. Fly lives in a cardboard box by the kitchen range, and during our talk had crawled out to do some exploring. Diana put the phone down and continued:

'My father used to work his horses on the farm at Kenbury, because when he wasn't playing soldiers he was playing farming! They pulled the mowing machine, the plough and did everything. We had a cowman to help with our herd of thirty cows, and their milk was taken to Exeter by pony and trap; in the winter the hunters took it, and in summer, the polo ponies. At first it went to a little dairy in Alphington Street, and when that closed, Hammet's Dairies took it – but they were the far side of Exeter so then it had to go by car instead of horse and trap.

'When World War II started we moved from Kenbury to a small house at Lympstone. The milking herd was sold, but we still kept the horses. I was fourteen then. I left school at sixteen and went to work for our milkman on a farm, and I worked there all through the war and then continued afterwards; it was hand milking in those days, too! My main mode of transport was either horse and cart or my bicycle. Sometimes I'd drive off to some dance in my horse and cart. I remember going to Sidmouth once, which is quite a long drive, to a hunt dance. I left my horse at a hunt member's stable, then drove it home afterwards, lit by candles on the cart – but of course there wasn't much traffic about in those days! On the occasions I reached home in the early hours I used to leave the cart at the bottom of the drive and walk the horse up the side of the drive so no one heard me come back. Of course, despite coming in so late, I still had to be milking cows at 7.30 in the morning, and sometimes I'd drop off to sleep during afternoon milking – I'll always remember the vet catching me asleep against a cow!'

Diana then explained that at home at this time she looked after her parents' horses, and in the evening used to take children out riding. By degrees the riding stable grew, until in about 1946 she had eight ponies. She also found she was doing a lot for the local Pony Club, so decided to stop working at the farm and concentrate on her horses. Weekends were usually taken up with going to gymkhanas:

'In those days you had open events, and everything was always round a ring. There was no stopping and starting, and it was far more competitive than it is today; you had to have a fast

Diana was once National Hunt point-to-point champion lady jockey

pony and be really quick.' John Coaker, who was to become Diana's husband, was also a regular competitor at the gymkhanas, and Diana recalled those days:

'He was absolutely unbeatable, really incredible; 'I had two good gymkhana ponies, and as I obviously couldn't ride both, he used to ride one. It was quite usual for us both to go to a gymkhana and win every event. We had this one pony which was very good at musical poles because it could canter on the spot – in fact it was so good we used to take it in turns to ride it.

'However, I think I really got to know John after I'd bought a Dartmoor pony in Exeter market for four guineas. I took it to Exmouth Show where the Coakers were showing their Dartmoors, and John's father said "Oh, look! There's my Two Tails!" They recognised it from its brand, and remembered that it had been reared on a mare which had lost her foal, and they'd skinned the foal and put it on this one and so for a few days it had two tails. That's how it became "Two Tails". Well, you see, Two Tails wanted a husband so I put her on the train to come here. In those days it was easy to put horses on the train at Exmouth and someone met her at Princetown and led her over. I suppose things grew from there with John.'

In the early 1950s Diana and John were amongst the first owners and breeders to export their ponies to the Continent: 'In those days there were no roll-on, roll-off ferries, you had

to ship them. They went into a little crate which a crane lifted on board, and then they were put in a pen.'

It was also at about this time that they started another venture:

'A chap from the Fells called Jack Williams came to see us. He used to buy ponies and organised pony trekking, and suggested we did this, too. Then an organisation which ran recreational holidays asked us if we'd be interested in doing pony trekking and said they'd send five or six people a week. That's how the trekking began. We advertised through horse magazines, and also *Farmer's Weekly* used to bring fifty children every year.

'For a time we had a hundred horses each summer, but as it was impossible to keep that number during the winter, we lent some out and sold the rest. We had an annual horse sale on the third Saturday in September. We still hold the sale – we're coming up to our thirty-fourth – but now it's collective and other people can enter horses for sale. However, all the horses are sold under very strict warranty and if you've got a pony that's just been broken you have to sell it on a week's trial. A lot of people don't like that.'

In addition to the trekking business Diana used to fit in riding at point-to-points, and often took part in, once fell off in, and won several times, the annual hunt race which took place on

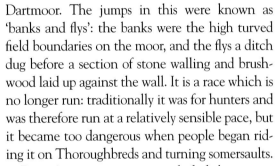

Dartmoor. The jumps in this were known as 'banks and flys': the banks were the high turved field boundaries on the moor, and the flys a ditch dug before a section of stone walling and brushwood laid up against the wall. It is a race which is no longer run: traditionally it was for hunters and was therefore run at a relatively sensible pace, but it became too dangerous when people began riding it on Thoroughbreds and turning somersaults.

Diana's racing career included becoming National Hunt point-to-point champion lady jockey. She cannot remember the exact year of this achievement, but says: 'It was in the days when ladies only rode once at a meeting and in a separate race from the men!'

Sherberton ponies continued to find owners abroad. Diana generally accompanied the horses to their new homes, and Peter, her eldest son, when he became old enough to help out drove the delivery lorry. It wasn't all plain sailing! In the days before the Common Market they had to contend with various countries' regulations. For example, in Italy only so many horses were allowed to travel in a horsebox, the rest had to go by Italian rail or lorry. On numerous occasions Diana has found herself at foreign railway stations organising gates to act as partitions in trucks to separate herself or a helper from the ponies, and asking for hay and water in a variety of languages.

The army has a large firing range on Dartmoor and the point-to-point course ran across some of this land.
Here one of the soldiers radios back information as the competitors pass

'It's funny how you could get hay at these border stations,' she recalls.

On one memorable occasion she found herself signing onto a ship's crew list – not for her own business, but to help others:

'A vet and his wife from Tavistock were moving to South Africa, and they'd asked my husband to do the paperwork for them as they were taking twelve ponies and a Thoroughbred with its foal at foot. They also had to have someone to accompany the animals, and so John said "Take my wife."

'For insurance purposes on board I had to become able seaman Coaker, and because I was female I had to live in the officers' quarters and abide by set rules. It was very like boarding school!

'As well as looking after the horses I had to look after three bulls and two cows which were being exported for someone else. It was very hot on the equator and I had to wash these cattle down to keep them cool. Despite doing this, one of the bulls became stressed and developed transit fever, which is a lack of calcium. We were on what they call the South African rollers, where it's a bit rough. People refused to give me a hand because they were afraid that the bull would fall on them – in fact the only person who came to help me was the barman. Because of the rolls of fat on the bull I couldn't find his jugular vein, so injected the whole bottle of calcium under his skin. But it didn't do any good, and he died, very quickly actually.'

Diana still makes forays abroad, and the last time we spoke had just returned from a trip which included buying two black Freisian horses in Holland for an undertaker in Ireland.

RACING TALES

Jack Dowdeswell, Lambourn, Berkshire
and Hector Skyrme, Letcombe Regis, Oxfordshire

England has fifteen images of white horses cut out of chalky hillsides. The oldest is the one at Uffington on the northern escarpment of the Berkshire Downs. The experts hold various opinions as to the exact date of its original carving, but some believe that the 360ft long and 130ft high outlines were first cut out of the turf in the Iron Age.

It is said that if you really want something to happen you must stand in the eye of the horse and wish it. However, it is doubtful whether, had he been given this opportunity in his youth, Jack Dowdeswell would have wished his life to have been anything other than what it turned out to be. He is a former champion National Hunt jockey who has been in racing all his life.

Jack lives in one of the villages scattered beneath the White Horse. The surrounding area is renowned for its proliferation of racing stables, and the strings of horses being ridden single file along the roads or exercising on the Downs are a regular sight.

In Jack's sitting room is an oil painting of himself on 'Limb of the Law', the winner of the 1955 Queen Elizabeth Chase. After this race Jack had champagne with the Queen Mother. He takes up his tale:

'We had a long chat and she was obviously very knowledgeable – still is – about racing. She had also noticed exactly where my horse had made a bit of a mistake and how I'd gathered it up and all that sort of thing. When I came out the press were waiting and wanted to know what she had said and what she was like. So I said "She was *just* like my mother", and by that I paid them both a compliment.

'I've had a wonderful life through racing – met royalty, danced with lords and ladies, been to St James's Palace, and all from a pretty lowly start – I was a two-bob lad apprentice. If I go back even further, in the 1920s father was a huntsman with the Craven. I'd sit on the pommel of his saddle when he came back from hunting, I'd be two or three years old at the time. Lord and Lady Essex were the Masters there and they bought ponies for their son Geoffrey, but he wasn't particular about riding and so I was able to ride these ponies and used to enter them at Olympia and Richmond and many other shows.

'I left school in 1931 when I was fourteen and signed on as an apprentice jockey with a Lambourn trainer named Gwilt. Unfortunately he was no good at pushing lads on, and would always employ experienced jockeys to ride his horses. I did ride a winner, but only had the odd ride or two in those five years.

'Gwilt had several stable lads – that is, they'd served their apprenticeships to be stable lads and were known as "paid lads" because they were getting a wage, roughly 38s a week. In fact, around 1937 there was a stable lads' strike in Lambourn and they succeeded in getting an extra 5s a week. However, I was the only apprentice jockey, and although I did what the paid lads did, I only earned 2s a week plus my keep. I was treated as a lackey. I had to work in the afternoons when the "lads" finished, and I also had to be up at a quarter to six each morning and accompany the Head Man on his rounds, looking at the forty or so horses to see if they'd passed the night all right and feeding them. I carried the feed bucket and the Head Man dipped into it; that would take an hour. At about seven I'd go in and have a cup of tea and then set about looking after my two or three horses. The stable lads got up at a quarter to seven to do their horses. The routine was that you mucked your horse out and got one ready to ride out, you rode out "first lot" onto the Downs, cantered and galloped and came in at about nine. You'd do your horse up and feed it, and then go and have breakfast. Then you'd get another horse, your second lot, ready and ride it, and come in and finish say at a quarter to twelve. Then there'd normally be a third lot, and I invariably had to go out with them, finishing at 1pm. Of course, in those days there was no swimming or treadmill exercise, no monitoring of pulse, respiration or temperature to assess fitness, no endoscoping or blood tests – I suppose it's like all sports, today there are new methods in training, and certainly some of the new ones are very good.

'Being the apprentice I also had to do what was called my afternoon's work, and I did it every day for five years – I can remember it like my army number: hay, oats, carrots, wood, chaff, lucerne, mash. The hay I had to carry around into the looseboxes, the oats were 2cwt bags which I carried to the crushing machine and crushed in the feed house. Carrots I had to get washed and cleaned and quartered ready for the evening stable. Wood I had to chop and bring in to keep the copper going. Chaff I had to cut for a feed. Lucerne I went out and cut, then mixed it in as a green feed with mash.

'I would finish just in time to go to work again at five o'clock. That was grooming, cleaning out and feeding my horses plus any other stable work – and in those days you really had to *do* the horses, you sweated as you brushed them over, and everything was polished, even the headcollar and the brasses on it. Your tack had to be spotless, but then you always took a pride in being the best lad in the yard if you could.

'All that took me to seven o'clock, but I still hadn't quite finished because then I had to walk from the stables which were at Upper Lambourn into Lambourn to get the evening paper for the Governor. It was about a mile and a half each way, and I'd get back with it at half-past eight. So I worked from a quarter to six in the morning until half-past eight at night for two shillings a week. I don't think I was overpaid!'

However, Jack did admit that the trip to the paper shop produced dividends for him, because it was here that he first met, and on subsequent visits to collect the paper, came to know the local girl he'd marry in later years. At their first meeting he'd been fourteen and Betty eleven. Betty was no stranger to the racing world: her father Archie Austen was a jockey, as her great-uncle Frank Dainty had been too – he'd won many races, including a Scottish National. Jack continues:

'I bought my own clothes on the "never-never", a bob a week. A pair of jodhpurs were 30s, boots or shoes were 25s. There used to be a man come round each week with a couple of suitcases from which he'd sell cigarettes, shoes, jerseys, shirts. He'd get you measured for a pair of jodhpurs, say, and each week I'd give him a shilling and if I made a few bob I'd give him extra. I'd also buy myself a packet of five Woodbine cigarettes which cost tuppence; a box of matches, and a penny bar of chocolate. That left me with 7d to last the week – but it does you good, having to manage.

'If I could save up enough money I'd have a 2s bet on a horse. Officially you weren't supposed to – and you aren't allowed to today, but I should say 90

Jack, as a young man, out on morning exercise

per cent of jockeys do. I remember on one occasion when I'd been racing three or four years we had two horses going to Sandown and I thought they'd win, so I saved up my money – this included the 7s 6d expenses we had per day when we went racing and money I'd won previously. I put it all on the first horse: this won at 20 to 1. Then I put all the proceeds from that onto the second horse, and that won at 100 to 6 – and *I* won nearly a thousand pounds!

'Of course, I thought I knew the lot, then. One of the horses was running again a couple of weeks later at Chepstow, and I went there and put £300 of my winnings on it and it was beaten by a whisker. That taught me a lesson, and I'm pleased it did, otherwise I'd have become addicted…. I've met a lot of people who can't keep out of the bookmakers, they're there *every* day.

Trainer Captain Powell and his wife

'On the last day of my five-year apprenticeship Mr Gwilt asked me to stay on, but I said definitely "No". Instead I went to Aldbourne to a trainer who'd known me when I'd been riding in shows as a boy: Captain Powell. I hoped I'd have a ride or two, and sure enough, in a few months I was put to ride a horse at Wolverhampton, and I had a good race. Captain Powell had professional jockeys he employed: Billie Parvin was his first jockey, then Eric Brown, Dick Holland, and Fred Rimell was also having odd rides; even so, he put me up on a few steeplechase horses.

'Then at the end of my first season I came in for a ride that had some sort of chance, a horse called Lady Rowley, and it won. Everyone was delighted, and I rode it again a few weeks later, and it won again. This horse got me going, because Captain Powell then put me on other horses that had good chances and again, some of 'em won. So within some months of getting there he asked me to be first jockey. I suppose that was the end of 1936, start of 1937, and in the next season he had the best season he'd ever had.

'Things went well through 1937, 1938 and 1939, but then the war broke out. Captain Powell had been on the reserve and so was called up immediately. There weren't many jockeys riding because a lot had to join the forces, and many horses were turned out of training. The Grand National was stopped completely and didn't restart until 1946. Racing did go on in a limited fashion; in fact in 1942 it was organised on a regional basis, that is, there was flat racing at six courses. This meant that horses trained at Newmarket ran at Newmarket; horses trained in the south ran at Ascot, Salisbury and Windsor, and horses trained in the north ran at Stockton and Pontefract.

'I helped Mrs Powell train the horses that we had left, but as I was twenty-two I was soon called up, too.

'When the war in Europe ended I was in Italy and had to stay on there because my demob number was twenty-eight. It was to be a year before I could return. It so happened that my regiment had been allocated half a dozen horses, ones which the retreating Germans had pinched to pull their guns, besides from elsewhere, and my Colonel passed the word round that if anyone wanted to ride, to go down to our HQ. So eventually I did, and said to the sergeant in charge, "The Colonel has said I can come and ride, and can choose whichever horse I want". So I did, and it was the Colonel's! I said "Well, what's good for the Colonel will do me nicely" and took the horse for an hour. On my return the Colonel said "You've taken my horse!" "Yes sir," I replied: "You're a very good judge!" This cheered him up a bit, and in due course we became friendly; and soon after I went and trained the regiment's horses, and rode in the races which we held every fortnight.

'The first ride I had was at a place called Iello, which had been an aerodrome but which all the German prisoners of war had made into a racecourse. I think my being a professional

helped during the finish, and I won by a head. As I was walking round the paddock afterwards someone tapped me on the back and I turned round and it was a general. He said to me, "You *are* Jack Dowdeswell aren't you?" So I said I was. And he then inquired, "What do you think about this course that's been made? Come into the stewards room and have a chat". The generals were the stewards of racing out there, and I met them all, including General Heydeman, commander of the whole southern European Command at that time, but who in civilian life had been involved in racing.

'The following week my Colonel informed me that General Heydeman wanted to see me in Milan; a staff car was to pick me up, and I was to stay with him for the weekend. It soon went

Jack (right) with Betty (standing) and Captain Powell

round the regiment that I was friends with all the generals, and they called me *Mr* Dowdeswell, just in fun. So I stayed in the General's lovely white villa, and we chatted about racing and racing memories.

'In fact after that I went to General Heydeman's every fortnight when we weren't racing, and there was no resentment from the other soldiers as a result of this association. I rode a number of winners for the regiment, and got on well with everyone, whether they were ordinary soldiers, colonel, major or general.

*On the sands at Wittering in February 1947, when arctic conditions forced many trainers to take
their horses to the coast to continue their training*

'Once the war was over Major Powell wanted me to get back to England to ride for him.
He tried to get me back by calling me a one-man business, as I was a jockey on my own, but
they wouldn't wear it. Then one day in 1946 I had a letter from his secretary, also a friend of
mine and who'd been in the army; he wrote, "You know, the Major wants you to ride so-and-
so in the National, but as you can't get back he doesn't know what to do." My colonel was
there and I repeated this to him, and he said, "Well, we'd better do something about that."
And I was on my way home within twenty-four hours!

'Major Powell had kept the horse entered by paying forfeits for it. The first thing I did when
I got back to England was buy a paper – and to my consternation, I saw that the horse wasn't
listed in the National runners. In fact it had been taken out because they were tired of trying
to get me back, and my eventual return had been so quick I hadn't been able to let them know
I was coming. It was one of those awful things – and a horse couldn't be reinstated once it had
been taken out. As it happened, the jockey who was riding at Liverpool for Major Powell
injured himself; he'd been due to ride at Wye in Kent on the Monday, so I went to Wye in his
place and the horse won!

'By this time it was the end of the season, and after the war racing was very curtailed; but
in the four or five weeks left I rode for Powell and other people, and had perhaps forty rides,
and won nineteen of them!

'I was champion National Hunt jockey for 1946–7. The winter of 1947 was terrible, with
arctic conditions for seven weeks. Racing stopped on 21 January and didn't restart until 15
March. Because of the snow and frozen ground many trainers took their horses to the coast to

train – that gave some welcome custom to seaside landladies who let rooms to grooms and jockeys! Major Powell took his horses to Bognor and we exercised on the sands at Wittering.

'The first meeting after the big freeze was at Taunton. I remember that it snowed all through the day and then it turned to drizzle. The ground was a quagmire, but Major Powell had five winners and I was lucky enough to ride four of them.

'I was retained by Major Powell until 1947. He was starting to change to flat horses; in the past he'd had all jumping horses, but then more and more of his owners were changing to flat horses until instead of having sixty or seventy jumpers, eventually it went down to twenty-five. To ride only twenty-five horses wasn't profitable enough for me, so then I had retainers from various other people, riding for Powell if and when I could. We were always great friends, and I continued to ride for him up until the latter years.

'One particular ride for him I remember well, at Kempton in 1950 where I was to ride a 6 to 4 on chance. Just before racing started I was standing outside the paddock and a man came up to me. He said "How will you do in the three o'clock?" I replied "It must win". He said, "Get a bad start and I'll give you a monkey – that's five hundred quid." I retorted, "You must be joking!" Then before the race he came back and said "I've got a grand there for you." But I said "Well, I've got a price and that's one million, and I mean it, one million." I knew he didn't have that sort of money although he was known to be a *big* gambler.

'As it happened, the horse felt quite wrong and ran very badly, so much so that after the race I completely forgot to weigh in. I had had a fall the previous day, however, and at the inquiry the stewards said, "Well, we think you had

Jack with the National entrant Cavaliero

a heavier fall than you realised, and it probably upset you". *They* made the excuse for *me*; that must be a record, because they could have fined me £50!

'Now, that horse's odd performance at Kempton was almost fifty years ago, really before doping infiltrated the sport so we never thought about doping. Occasionally you'd see a horse being drenched with a drink of port and brandy in his box before a race to liven him up, but that was almost an open action, and not really doping. In the next twelve months I rode a lot of horses for Ray Powell and there were many which ran badly which we'd thought ought to have done well, and we couldn't make it out. Then one day at Wolverhampton, Ray Powell had a flat horse which ran badly, and the stewards pulled in Powell and the horse and had it tested. It was doped, and Ray Powell lost his licence – and he hadn't been responsible. I *know* that it wasn't Ray Powell – but in those days the trainer carried the can.'

A spectacular fall for Jack!

At this point the front door bell rings: it was Meg, the daughter of Dick Holland, the professional jockey who used to ride for Captain Powell and who was one of Jack's mentors. En route to a more distant destination she was calling on Jack to say 'Hello' and to break the journey. They talk about old times a bit; then after making sure that she has had sufficient refreshment, Jack goes out to wave her goodbye.

When he returns I ask how many winners he rode in his championship year of 1946–7. 'Oh, not many, about sixty, something like that. It doesn't sound a lot compared to today because racing wasn't as flourishing as it is now. Today they can ride afternoons and evenings, in fact they have four or five times as many rides.'

I ask what else has changed.

Jack considers: 'Well, today a jockey gets £80 a ride – I got £3, plus £5 if I won. If I went from Lambourn to Sandown and had two rides and paid my valet £2 I was in debt! Today a jockey in the top twenty-five or thirty will buy a farm or business, but in my day it took three hundred rides to earn a thousand pounds.

'You didn't get presents either, like now. I remember there were lots of promises of presents which didn't materialise. Perhaps if I'd ridden a winner I'd get a basket of mushrooms or a brace of pheasants. Today a jockey gets a percentage of the stake, so if a race is worth £1000, he gets £100. Those changes are a good thing – although in my day, even if we didn't have the perks, there was a terrific amount of camaraderie.

I had read that during his racing career Jack's many falls had earned him a clutch of nicknames in the press: for example, 'Iron Man'; 'The Fall Guy'; and as one glossy magazine put it, 'Britain's Pluckiest Steeplechase Jockey'. I remind him of those names, and he laughs:

'Yes, I was notorious for bone breaking – only when I began jumping, but from then over the years I've broken, counting fingers and thumbs, toes and ribs, collar bones, legs and arms, about fifty bones. I've got incomplete collar bones, I broke them so often I had bits of them taken out. I've a gap there – it doesn't hurt but I can't reach my arm up very far. I was the first person ever to have the collar bone operation, where a bit is taken out, leaving a gap. The first was done at Oswestry where there was a big orthopaedic hospital, by Nobby Clarke of Harley Street – and he didn't charge me a fee, which was rather nice! Then I did my other collar bone and had that one done, too, by another surgeon. Now it's an accepted operation, and a number of jockeys have had it done; it's like your appendix, you can do without part of your collar bone.

'In about 1951 I had a terrible fall. My horse fell on the flat round a bend and my arm broke off, pulled out and stuck in my ribs, it looked a hell of a mess. I was picked up and was supposed to be unconscious, they gave me morphine and things. In the ambulance room some jockeys came in and one said "How's Jack?" and the doctor, who thought I'd passed out, said quietly "He'll never race again"; but I croaked, "I bloody well will!" It took me eleven months to recover, but when I did, the doctor and I had a joke about this.

Jack on The Pills (behind) with an eighteen-year-old Lester Piggott on Tangle at Kempton Park on 28 November 1953. It was Lester's first race over hurdles

'Now I come to a lovely memory. I'd been written off by the papers – you know, "Jack will never ride again" – but had recovered, and I went to ride at Newton Abbot, my first ride after eleven months. The horse was called Cairo II and it won. And I've never in my life had a reception like it, and I've ridden winners at Liverpool – the crowd went crazy, they knew – hats were going in the air, the girls in the tea tent were throwing cups up in the air and catching them, it was wonderful!

'I've often been asked if all the injuries made me want to stop racing, but I was very fortunate in that my nerve never went. I know people to whom that has happened, and I would never denigrate anyone whose nerve goes; but for some reason, mine didn't.'

I ask Jack to tell me about his last ride as a jockey, and if he had any regrets:

'My last ride was in 1957, at Buckfastleigh in Devon; I had a bad fall and did a couple of vertebrae in my back, and I was paralysed and laid up for quite a while. The doctors warned me the accident had weakened that part and that if it happened again it would be curtains. I was riding until fairly recently, in actual fact; I used to school with John Francombe when I was seventy and I would do it today, but I had a hip operation. I was also riding for Barry Hills and John, his son, exercising on the Downs, riding gallops and thoroughly enjoying it. I was disappointed when after the hip operation doctors told me not to ride again.

'My main regret is that I'd have loved to have won the National. The nearest I got was the last National I rode in. I was riding one for Fulke Walwyn, a horse called Armorial II, but it fell with only three fences to go. He was 17.2hh, a beautiful horse, and I think I would have won – but the name of the game is clean jumping. I did a couple of ribs on that day, but that's racing, that's what life's all about.'

I ask Jack what he thinks about changes which have taken place to the National course, some prompted by Animal Rights' activists:

'Going back sixty years it *was* a tough course. However, I think it's a good thing that it's been modified – for example, Becher's is easier to jump now. I believe that people don't go to see horses fall, they go to see horses run and have a good race; so yes, it's a good thing it's been altered.'

The dinner given in honour of Jack when he was champion National Hunt jockey in 1946–7
(top left) The painting which commemorates Jack's win in the Queen Elizabeth Chase in 1955, riding Limb of the
Law and (left) in more recent times

And his feelings over protesters' views that races such as the National are cruel? 'Horses are bred to race, and steeplechase horses are taught to jump – and they have a truly wonderful life. Many of the stables are like hospitals, people don't realise how pampered the horses are.

'Yes, they break legs and necks, I agree, it's tough; but horses bred for racing love it, they follow round and jump the fences even if they've had a fall and lost their rider.'

Finally I wondered whether Jack had any advice for aspiring jockeys.

'You must like what you are doing, do what you can to do things *right*, and keep trying. But I wouldn't *advise* any lad to go into racing because only one in three hundred makes it. On that subject, and speaking as a professional, I must say that I don't agree with the present system whereby many jockeys, and particularly the jump jockeys, start their life as amateurs. They've ridden as children, they've probably been to a public school, and the difference is that they go as assistant to a trainer. Now this means that they go out to dine with the owners, are put on equal footing with them, and I think this arrangement is most unfair to the apprentice – the "lad" – it pushes him out because he usually hasn't had the education which enables him to associate on equal terms with trainers and owners.'

Jack's championing of 'lads' is reflected in a photograph taken at the dinner given in his honour when he was champion jockey. Round the room are apprentice jockeys, and this was the first time that 'lads' had ever been to such an event; and of course it was Jack who had invited them.

HECTOR SKYRME

The chalk-carved White Horse of Uffington is evidently guardian to a rich colony of racing worthies, for beneath its shadow are two other notable horsemen. One is Jack Dowdeswell's 86-year-old brother, Tom. During his career as head lad, Tom was associated with four Derby winners, the most famous being Windsor Lad, the 1934 winner. The other is Hector Skyrme, whom I met at his home in the pretty village of Letcombe Regis near Wantage. Hector is a former National Hunt jockey and head lad.

He is eighty-eight, and on telling me his birthdate, he said with a twinkle, 'I can't make it any younger; I've tried, but it doesn't work out.' Originally Hector came from Tenby in Wales, where his parents were farmers; his father also did a bit of horse dealing. Hector recalls:

'When I was twelve or thirteen father sold a cob and I had to deliver it, to Cwmynys Farm, Nantgaredig, between Carmarthen and Llandeilo. I rode it the thirty miles [48km] to the farm; there were water butts on the road in different places in the 1920s, mostly for cattle. It was usual for men to walk cattle – when my father bought our farm at Carmarthen he walked his cattle up to it from Angle in Dyfed, and it took two days and nights.

'I delivered the cob safely and had a meal at Cwmynys Farm, then carried the saddle and bridle back to Nantgaredig station to go back to Manorbier, just below Tenby. My Dad was going to meet me with the pony and trap, but I missed the train I was supposed to get and had to get the next one; so he didn't meet me, and I had to carry the saddle and bridle back home. He gave me just 3s 6d [18p] for the train fare.

'I came to Letcombe in 1928, to the trainer Jack Anthony's stables. Father knew him because Mr Anthony was also a farmer's son. There were three Anthony brothers, and they were all good trainers: Jack at Letcombe; Owen, in later years at the next village, and who trained "Golden Miller"; and Ivor at Wroughton just outside Swindon.

'Jack had about forty horses. Nowadays trainers can have a hundred or more, but in those days forty was considered a lot. I was a stable lad; my wages were £2 a week, but after stoppages for insurance and unemployment cards, I ended up with £1 18s 5d [£1.92p], out of which I paid about 22s [£1.10p] for lodgings. I used to do two horses and ride out twice a day.

'In those days if we were taking horses racing we used to walk them to Wantage Road station, four miles from here. We'd set off early in the morning in the dark, though of course there was no traffic about. If we had seven or eight runners at Liverpool there'd be a lad to each horse.

'You used to get 10s [50p] a day for travelling, but in fact you travelled free with the horse – the trains had vans which took three horses, and there was a seat in the compartment and you'd sit with the horse. Then the 10s we used to cover bed and food instead. If you went to Liverpool in those days you stayed at what they called a rough place, the Sefton Hotel, just outside Aintree racecourse. The horses would stay at the racecourse same as they do now, and there was always feed at the course for them: hay, straw, corn, bran…that's all they used to have, corn and bran, now they have nuts, it's all nuts today.

'There used to be two meetings at Liverpool. If you went to the Grand National you'd probably be there two, or maybe three days before the race sometimes. Other meetings you'd go one day, race the next and then come back the following day; so you'd be away three days.

'Jack Anthony trained for the American millionaire Jock Whitney, who was related to the Vanderbilt family. I was told that when he came to be twenty-one he inherited forty million pounds! His cousin Dorothy Paget also owned a lot of horses. Amongst Mr Whitney's horses

at the stable was a gelding called Easter Hero, by My Prince out of Easter Week. He was bred near Greenogue, Co. Dublin, by Mr Larry King. Easter Hero was as famous in his day as Desert Orchid, a good-looking horse with plenty of heart room – see in this photo how big his chest is…you could lead him round the ring on cotton. He was always a front runner from the time he jumped the first fence, two lengths in front.

'Easter Hero won the Cheltenham Gold Cup in 1929 and 1930, both times by twenty lengths. In 1929 Jack Mallony rode him in the Grand National and he came second to Gregalach, who in fact had also been sired by My Prince. 1929 was the year they had sixty-six runners, and it was a time when any horse could run in the race – any owner amateur who had a good hunter could enter it. Now you have to qualify to run in it by winning over the course and one thing and another, and they have about thirty-five to forty runners. This does, however, mean that no rubbish is entitled to run.

Hector with Easter Hero

'In 1931 we didn't run him in the Gold Cup but kept him for the National. Fred Rees rode him in it, and he made all the running until at Becher's Brook the second time Fred was unseated. However, in those days the Grand National was run on a Friday, and the Champion Chase, two miles and six furlongs was on the Saturday. Now, bear in mind that in the National he'd carried 12st 7lb to Becher's a second time, *and* he'd completed the course on his own – but the next morning he seemed fit and sound, and so we ran him in the Champion Chase! Horses, like men, were tough in those days! He dead-heated with a champion two-mile chaser, and that was his last race. He was a twelve-year-old then.

'That same year, 1931, I had to take him to America to Mr Whitney's estate. I had to take a little skewbald pony out too, about 12hh. Mr Whitney was about twenty-eight then, I think, and on his big ranch he used to turn out about 300 coloured horses on a prairie-like area, then gallop round them like a cowboy!

'We left here on a Friday morning, horsebox to Wantage Road, train from there to London Docks. The boat was called *Minniswaska*, and it had first-class passengers on board, and about twenty-three Thoroughbred horses. Easter Hero had a specially built big box on the ship, and the little skewbald a small box beside it. I'd been given £25 to go away with – it was supposed to be for six weeks, but it turned out to be longer. Just think, £25, and now I see stable lads get £29 for travelling on a Sunday if there's racing!

'On board I used to look after Easter Hero every day. He wasn't sea-sick, he enjoyed every minute. He was a horse that if anybody came with a camera, he'd always prick his ears up, do you know what I mean? He was a proper showman. He had his picture taken so many times.

He was good natured, too. When he'd come second in the National, people had pulled hairs out of his tail.

The journey to America took nine days, and we arrived at New York on the following Monday week; Mr Whitney was stood on the dock with a bunch of carrots on his arm! I'd met him before because he used to come over by boat for the racing. I brought Easter Hero out first and of course they had the *Pathe Gazette* in those days and their cameraman was there and Easter Hero enjoyed that, he stood on top of the ramp and pricked his ears, then he marched down like a champion, as if to say "I'm still a champion, you know!" The ramp was quite steep because it was a big ship, and they had coconut matting on the concrete on the docks for the horses to walk on – only a short stretch – to the horseboxes. But as soon as Easter Hero had walked down, the skewbald pony missed him, and half galloping down the ramp, he slipped under the coconut matting and emerged out of the bottom of it. [Tears of laughter fill Hector's eyes at the memory.]

'Then a horsebox took us to Manhasset, Long Island, not far out of New York where Mr Whitney had an estate – he had estates all over the place.

'In Manhasset I used to ride Easter Hero out. Mr Whitney would come occasionally, and on those days I would ride the skewbald pony out with him. The Manhasset stables were actually Mr Whitney's polo yard. He probably had about fifty polo ponies there, and a great many lads and all that – just one indication of his huge wealth and his playboy character.

'Then it came to the American Grand National, and Mr Whitney had a horse in it called Green Cheese. However, they wanted Easter Hero to lead the parade before the race, and so this is what we did – but he did pull hard! The runners cantered down, then walked past the stand; each was led by a groom on a pony, but I was on my own. A man in a red coat, a hunts-

155

Hector with Easter Hero during their trip to America

man-type man, said to me: "When you come to the bottom, they will turn in left and you will go right"; they were going onto the course, and I was to go on a track beside it. They went down and turned in, and as soon as they got level, they went.

'Soon after that a horsebox took Easter Hero, the pony and myself down to Middlesboro, Virginia, where Mr Whitney had another estate. I can remember the horsebox going past the White House in Washington. I spent a fortnight or three weeks there, showing them how to "do" Easter Hero, then started back home to England.

'Somebody drove me in a car to the airport – I think it was Washington because I was going from there to Newark. This was the first time I'd ever been on a plane, or probably ever *seen* a plane. I got on it and it ran along the runway, but it wouldn't take off; so I had to get off and get on another one. And as I sat in it – and it was a smallish plane, there'd be no more than twelve to sixteen people on board – there seemed to be like an exhaust coming back along the side of it, that got really hot, red hot.

'I got back to Manhasset, Long Island and the next day went into New York and booked my passage home; but when we docked at Southampton it was black dark and tipping down with rain, and I thought, whatever am I doing back here? I'd been away something like ten weeks. I got to the stables at about two or three o'clock in the morning; I was in digs then, and I remember I had to get up at six o'clock to ride out.

'I finished up travelling head lad and head lad over about sixteen stable lads at Jack Anthony's. I can tell you a funny story here. I remember one November we never had any runners because our horses had been coughing with some sort of bug. However, Jack's brother, Owen, had four horses running at Liverpool, so he asked Jack if I could go up with them as travelling head lad. He said to me, "If we have a winner, I'll give you a £1"; and believe it or not we did have a winner! So about a month afterwards we were up on the Downs and I reminded him about the promised pound. Do you know what he said to me? "I should bloody wait until he's finished blowing": in other words, I was asking him too quick, and I should wait until the horse had finished blowing, you know how a horse blows for say half an hour after a race!

'As time went on I had some rides and I also got married. I had twin girls born on 4 September 1939, the day after war was declared. I always said that's what started the war! I joined the RAF, which I didn't like. I was discharged early because I used to have a few rides and there was a bit of racing during the war at Cheltenham on a Saturday; I forget if there was any anywhere else.

'In those days if a race was worth up to £100 to the winner, a jockey got £3 a race. After that it was £5, and you paid your valet 10s per ride. Anyway I had a few rides at Cheltenham and I had a bad fall there, I remember the date, Saturday 2 March 1942, because I had a son born about that time.

'I left Jack Anthony's in about 1947 and did various jobs. I finished up when I was in my seventies breaking in yearlings for Jeremy Tree over at Beckhampton. My son Barry and grandson David are involved with training and riding race horses; David has ridden something like a hundred winners and he's only about thirty. When the Easter Hero Handicap Steeplechase was run at Kempton Park last year I was invited to present a cup to the winner; unfortunately I couldn't because I was ill, and David went in my place.

'Comparing the life of a stable lad years ago and now...well, *Sporting Life* was 3d in those days, today it's almost £1; but wages have risen out of all proportion, and a lad now gets more for riding out "third lot" for three-quarters of an hour than I got for being head lad for a working week! Moreover, I've watched some lads leading round, and old lads years ago wouldn't have employed them; and sometimes you'll see when they're scraping or brushing, and they've got the brush in the wrong hand! But lads are hard to get nowadays.

'We worked a lot harder than lads do now, *and* we probably had more stamina! For example in about 1930 a lad who worked with me had a horse called Talpa to do. This horse was running at Wolverhampton in a novice hurdle, so on the morning of the race the lad gets to the yard before six, feeds Talpa, mucks him out and walks (and rides him a bit) to Wantage Road Station. The train gets to Wolverhampton Station, and from there the lad leads him to the race course. The horse won.

'The lad does him up, walks him back to the station, and they get the train to Wantage and get off there in the black dark. Then he walks and part rides the horse back to the stables. In the yard he does him up and gives him a bucket of linseed mash which has been stood in a corner covered with a rug. Then the lad walks to The Sparrow pub, has a pint, and then walks down to his lodgings. He changes and gets on his bike and cycles to a dance at Wantage, probably getting there at midnight.

'Although I am telling you this tale, the man in question is in fact alive to tell it; he's about eighty-six, a bit younger than me!'

Grooms all ready for morning exercise

157

The Qualities of a Horse

A good horse should have three qualities of a woman – a broad breast, round hips, and a long mane; three of a lion – countenance, courage and fire; three of a bullock – the eye, the nostril, and joints; three of a sheep – the nose, gentleness, and patience; three of a mule – strength, constancy, and foot; three of a deer – head, legs, and short hair; three of a wolf – throat, neck, and hearing; three of a fox – ear, tail, and trot; three of a serpent – memory, sight, and turning; and three of a hare or cat – running, walking and suppleness.

> Quoted in *The Horse and How to Manage Him*, c.1894

Etiquette

When a gentleman rides in the Park or other public place, etiquette requires that he should approach a lady on the off or right side, and that in either meeting or passing, if she be alone, he should slacken his pace to a walk. When a gentleman accompanies a lady on horseback, he should ride on the right side, holding his own bridle and whip in his right hand, that he may be prepared to assist her with his left hand if needful. Nothing is so rude as for a gentleman to gallop past a lady on horseback. A gentleman should never ride between two ladies unless at their request.

> Samuel Sidney, *The Book of the Horse*, c.1880

Old sayings

Trust a cat amongst cream, but never a Yorkshire man on the back of a good horse.

Shake a bridle over a Yorkshire man's grave and he'll get up and steal a horse.

A Carnivorous Horse

Five-and-thirty years ago, the writer frequently saw a young horse which preferred roasted or boiled meat to grass and corn. His dam was killed by an unfortunate accident when the foal was five weeks old; he was fed by the dairymaid with cow's milk and soon familiarly followed her to the kitchen. He began to gnaw bones in mere playfulness, but his carnivorous taste was not suspected, but the remains of a piece of roast beef set to cool in the pantry window was carried away by him. He was afterwards offered slices of beef, mutton, veal or lamb, which he accepted like a dog; he did not like pork but all kinds of fowl or game were highly agreeable to him.

> *The Sporting Magazine*, 1819

Form and material of nails

Nails must be made of the best and toughest iron, for none other can stand the strain and jar of fast work. The quality of a nail may be easily tested by fastening it in a vice. It should not break before pointing under five bendings. The operation of 'pointing' renders nails more brittle, and they will then generally break at the third bending.

> Lieut.General Sir F. Fitzwygram, Bart., From *Horses and Stables*, 1911

White Feet in Horses

It is curious that where horses have one or more of their feet white, the white is always more liable to disease than the dark-coloured ones. The horn of a white foot is never as tough and good as that of a dark foot, and yet a white or gray horse is generally a good one. I may here remark that if there are any two colours which bespeak hardiness and general goodness more than another, black-brown and gray are those colours. I think, for choice, the former, especially when accompanied, as it often is, with a tan muzzle.

> Arthur T. Fisher, *Through The Stable and Saddle-Room*, 1906

The Galloway

In the chapter of pit hauliers, Norman Barnes tells of how he used to work with Galloways in the pits of County Durham. Here is an earlier description:

The Galloway takes its name from a useful and beautiful breed of horses, thirteen to fourteen hands high, that used formerly to be met with pretty plentifully in the south of Scotland. They are not often seen, their comparative rarity arising from the fact that the exigencies of modern husbandry have caused the farmers of that district to desire a larger and more powerful horse, the consequence being that, the old stock being crossed to a great extent by larger animals, the old breed is fast dying out.

This is somewhat to be deplored, for, like certain breeds of small cattle, the Galloway could find a sufficient support in the inferior herbage that grows upon poor lands, and on this account the breed has been endeavoured to be perpetuated more amongst the Welsh farmers, who find it an extremely useful animal for their purpose rather than upon the scene of its original habitat.

> *The Horse and How to Manage Him*, c.1894

Juniper garlands

Ray Williams of Bristol recalls the day he asked his grandfather, a timber haulier in the Forest of Dean about a large juniper bush growing by the timber horses' stable:

He claimed that this was to 'prevent the devil riding the horses at night'. Apparently, in the morning, horses were sometimes found 'in a lather'; but caused, he maintained, not by the devil but by someone introducing certain herbs overnight the smell of which upset the horses. At one time his team had refused to pass a cottage inhab-

itated by a witch; another witch he consulted told him to garland the horses with juniper, hence the bush outside the stable.

He further said that in the 1860's to 70's there was an annual service at Longhope church when 'garlanded' horses were blessed to protect them from night time rides by the devil. 'I think it unlikely that my grandfather was pulling my leg, he was not a joking man.'

Old saying

A horse which is a good walker is equally good in all his paces.

After the Race

As soon as you have rubbed your horse dry, cloth him up and ride him home, and the first thing give him the following drink to comfort him.

Beat the yolks of three eggs, and put them into a pint and a half of sweet milk, then warm it luke-warm, and put to it three pennyworth of saffron, and three spoonfuls of salad oil, and give it him in a horn.

Having done this, dress him slightly over with the curry-comb, brush, and woollen-cloth, and then bathe the place where the saddle stood with warm sack, to prevent warbles; and wash the spurring places with piss and salt, and afterwards anoint them with turpentine and powder of jet, mixed together; then litter the stable very well, clothing him up as quick as possible, and let him stand for two hours.

Then feed him with rye-bread, after that with a good mash, and give him his belly full of hay, and what corn and bread he will eat.

Then bathe his legs well with urine and salt-petre, leave him corn in his locker, and so let him rest till the next morning…

The Complete Horseman or Country Gentleman's Recreation, 1795

Riding a Steeplechase

When about seven-eights of the distance, unless a very expert hand at timing your horse's powers, do not attempt to draw it too fine, but getting on good terms with the leading horses in the race, and laying hold of your horse's head, try and leave them, riding calmly but resolutely; above all sit quite steady; if your horse is straining every nerve, let him along; if running sluggishly when getting into the straight run home, after the last fence, take tight hold of the reins in your left hand, give him a smart stroke with the whip, and two or three kicks with the spurs. But if you have reason to fear that he will swerve (as many bad-hearted ones do), continue to hold him between your hands, and give him some sharp kicks with the spurs.

Samuel Sidney, *The Book of the Horse*, c.1880

Big Gambler

A 'plunger' is a person who bets recklessly. Ernest Benzon alias the 'Jubilee Plunger' was well known for his exploits in the first quarter of this century. For example, he lost £15,000 one afternoon at a Sandown Park race meeting and £10,000 that evening during a card game. Some reports say that he lost a quarter of a million in two years and others, a million in one year!

Expenses

…a cart colt, when four years old, must be a very good looking animal to fetch £40 at a fair.

As he will not be fit to do anything like work before he is three years old, we will suppose that after that period he shall earn his keep, and will proceed to make a calculation of his expenses up to that age. They will be somewhat upon the following scale:-

	£	s.	d.
Stallion	2	2	0
Keep of mare (say for one month) prior to and after foaling	0	14	0
Keep of colt at grass and straw-yard at 3s. per week after the first six months	19	10	0
Allowance for corn during three months, while being broken-in (two quarterns per diem)	1	16	0
Man's wages for breaking	0	8	0
	24	10	0

From the *Journal of the Royal Agricultural Society*, 1845

Animal Instinct

Cavalry horses know the time better than the barrack clock, though I am free to admit that it is small blame to them if they do, since a barrack clock is generally about as bad a timekeeper as can be found. But even if the clock be wrong, they are not. When their feeding time approaches, although there may have been no indication of it given, there is such a neighing, and screaming, and kicking, as if they were all mad.

Arthur T. Fisher (late 21st Hussars), *Through The Stable and Saddle-Room*, 1906

A Reward for Services

Man has, we believe, a Divine soul, an emanation of the Deity. May not animals have, in some way of which we have no idea (for it has not been revealed to us), what I may term an animal soul – some future existence, some compensation for pain and suffering here on earth, some reward in some future state…

If any animal deserves, as a reward for services to man, and as a compensation for days, weeks, and years of abuse; if any animal deserves a tranquil future, a glorious pasturage traversed by never-failing crystal streams or water, surely that animal must be the horse.'

Lieut.General Sir F. Fitzwygram, Bart., *From Horses and Stables*, 1911

A FARM HORSEMAN

Jack Williams, Corse Lawn, Gloucestershire

If you put a cider apple – and it's not as big as an eating apple – on the 1.25000 Ordnance Survey map showing the area west of Tewkesbury in Gloucestershire, you'd cover all the places where 76-year-old Jack Williams has ever lived and worked. A farm horseman, he moved to his present small-holding – roughly the centre of the apple, and two miles as the crow flies from where he was born – when he married Flossie Voyce. Flossie, a farmer's daughter, came from Pendock, approximately one apple's width left of Jack's territory.

Jack and Flossie live in a timbered, black-and-white cottage with assorted outbuildings and an orchard which contains some ancient apple varieties. Observes Flossie, 'My favourite, Farmer's Glory, is nearly dead – that's the best on here, isn't it?' she inquires of Jack. He nods, and adds, 'It's an eater and a beautiful cider-maker; but we've still got another like that called "Peggy", and also "Tewkesbury Baron" which is a very old apple.'

Jack's horse Polly used to help make cider out of the apples by turning a stone wheel which crushed the fruit: 'she'd know how many turns to go round the mill; so you'd put in a pot of apples, and eight times round and it was done,' he remembers. He describes how he came by Polly:

'She was an unbroken four-year-old in 1947 when the butcher from Tirley bought her from gypsies; they were going to sell horses in Gloucester and she was trailing alongside of their van. After the butcher bought her she would have gone for meat because she was in a poor condition and not very safe. But I cycled over to look at her and said I'd give £35 for her – I've still got the cheque counterfoil upstairs. She used to bite pieces out of me at first, because she had a "V" shape on her side where she must have caught herself on the gypsy cart. I altered her harness so it wouldn't touch the mark.

'She turned out marvellous. Coming home I often used to let her choose the way she wanted, and she'd come the way the wind wasn't blowing in her face.

'I remember once I went for a load of poles at Forthampton estate, and the woodman put

160

on an extra few. Now, coming up Forthampton is steep and Polly had a hard job to pull it up; but she stuck to it, and had a breather and started again, and she went up that bank – her would never stop her wouldn't, her had a heart of gold. Coming down the other side the waggon started to slide, but she drew to the side on the grass and she held it with her collar, first one side, then the other. If only I'd known that was going to happen I'd have gone through Chaceley. I fixed a brake on after that.

'In 1964 this old gentleman on the hills wanted a quiet horse and kept bothering me to sell her. I did in the end, but made him promise as he would keep her and wouldn't sell her again; and she lived to be thirty-five years old.'

I asked Jack and Flossie how they'd met. Flossie replied: 'At a dance at Redmarley; we used to go all over the place two or three nights a week before we was married – but my Dad always had me up milking the next mornin' don't matter how tired I was!' And Jack said 'Yeah, I've gone home at three o'clock in the morning and changed, took mother a cup of tea and then used to go off and get the horses in. We went out for two years, I suppose a bit more. Then one day Flossie asked if I'd go over and plough her Dad's bit of spud ground.'

Flossie: 'I couldn't manage the ploughing, I could do the breaking down of the ground and the drilling with horses, but I wasn't strong enough to hold the plough.'

Jack: 'To operate with two strong young horses you have to have the strength and the knack turning.'

Flossie: 'The two horses we had were Sandy and Jumbo.'

Jack: 'I went over on the Saturday. I'd seen the horses before, I'd talked to 'em but never used 'em, and I did wonder if they'd go for me.'

Jack, his son John and fellow haymakers, with Polly pulling the haycart

Flossie: 'Sandy was quite young, he was quiet, and Jumbo…' Jack finished the sentence: 'He was a lazy customer. He wouldn't pull when I put him on first because he knew I was fresh, he just wouldn't go, he sulked; but I just pulled him one with the long plough lines a bit quick, and it went well after that. Pop, he did bring me a bottle of cider and a bottle of oil for the plough, and he enjoyed watching because he was got old you see, his wrists weren't strong any more.' Today, Jack himself wears leather straps to support his wrists which are weakened from years of pulling reins. He continued:

'We got on together well. Where I was threshing with Mr Lane on one of the Chaceley Hall farms I got some pedigree wheat for them to plant on this ground, and beans. It gave a marvellous crop, you know, fresh ground.'

Even if Flossie couldn't manage ploughing, she held her own at haymaking time: 'I used to do the horse raking, and many a night it was ten o'clock before we finished. Today it seems different – you couldn't hay-make at ten o'clock these nights, could you?' Jack took up the tale of their day's work:

'Mr Lane, who I worked for, farmed in two or three places. I used to be down in the Chaceley meadows early morning and mow, and then at eight o'clock or half past, I'd let the horses have a rest and sit under the hayrick and have a sleep!

Evacuees riding Jumbo at Grimer's Farm, where Flossie was brought up. The man holding Jumbo is Paddy the farm workman

'Our official time to be at work was quarter to seven, but we could get there earlier if we wanted. We used to go to the field to get the horses in, and generally some would come in easily and some wouldn't – but I didn't have any problem after what Dad told me to do, and that was to use aniseed. He used to have some aniseed balls in his handkerchief and put 'em in his pocket, and when he wanted the horses he'd wave and clap and they were at the gate afore you could blink, looking at his pocket.

'My father was a marvellous horseman. His nickname was "Tackler Jack". He was called that because one

Jack's son John with Polly on muck heap duty!

day everyone was frantic over a mare a foaling; she was called Bonny, and she was kicking the inside of the stable out nearly – some horses will when they foal. No one couldn't or wouldn't go in. But he said, "Just open the door a bit, I'll tackle her"; and he went in and quietened her down. Then her had the foal, but she almost killed it – but he got the foal out of the stable and my mother slipped down to the pub, the Yew Tree, and got some brandy, and they managed to bring this filly round with it.

'All that happened at Grain House Farm which belonged to Mr Spiers. They called the foal "Brandy", and she *was* a brandy colour, too! Mr Spiers gave her to his son to work down here at Lucas Farm. But one day he went to see his son and saw Brandy wasn't working but was in the field; and so he caught her and took her back behind his horse and trap, back to Grain House. When my friend Harry Peters went to work there as a ploughboy in 1943 she was still working on the farm, and I used to see her too, because I was on a neighbouring farm and I'd see old Brandy.'

They still keep in touch with Harry Peters, who was ploughboy at the Grain House in Brandy's day. Harry had worked there with a three-quarterman, so called because he worked from 9am until 4pm, then went home to look after his own cows! Harry had then gone to work for a Mr Dew at Swinley Court on the Forthampton estate; Jack was also working there at the time, and they share many memories:

'I remember the time we were at plough in Court Field at Swinley Court. Harry had a little mare as had a long tail which did use to kick, and I told him to be careful. I had three horses meself on this side in front, and said, "All right Harry, off we go" – but this mare had got her tail over the rein so Harry hadn't got a tight grip of it. She went off a bit quick and took him unaware, and we ended up nearly atop a big muck bury that was in the field!

'We'd usually have two horses on a plough if it were good going, but if you wanted to plough deeper we always put three abreast, though some used three at length all in the furrow. If you're ploughing three abreast you only wants one man, but if you've got three at length you've got to have a chap with 'em to take the fore horse, and it's longer to turn them on the headland. I prefer three abreast because with a good plough, you can plough wider and deeper.

'They used to say you could plough an acre a day if it was going well. But you've got to have a good furrow horse and one on the land. We had an old horse called Dobbin, a very light grey, which was a good furrow horse because he'd walk straight. It was the same for horse hoeing – he wouldn't let any horse pull him out of the furrow, and you know, he was so soft in the mouth, he'd have a sleek bit on 'im and it would run back and to through his mouth without getting it sore. There are some colts that reel about, go this way and that way at first, stumbling, until they get used to walking straight.

'Sometimes it was important to plough deeply as well as straight. I remember one day I was ploughing out some couch grass, and Squire York was riding over his farms and saw me. He had the bailiff with him and got him to come over and measure the depth of my furrow to see it was over ten inches. It was, and the squire said 'Well done, Williams!'

Squire York was the owner of the local big house, Forthampton Court, and Jack remembers him with affection. 'The squire' he says 'used to like mushrooms called Bluelegs. They had a little speck of greyey colour on the top and stood on a blue leg. He was also fond of medlars.'

Jack's mother had lived on the Forthampton estate: her first husband, Mr Lowe, had been the local ferryman, operating at a point on the River Severn called Lower Lode. Squire York owned the long, flat ferry which for a penny fare transported passengers, waggons and horses between Tewkesbury and Forthampton.

I ask Jack what his morning regime was with the horses when he was working on local farms.

'Put 'em into the stables to feed – rolled oats, or when we were heavy at work I used to toss sheaves into the rack; they'd hang down, and the horses would pull them through into the manger, saved threshing 'em. They'd eat the bit of straw with it, and all that didn't go on the floor. Then go and milk yer cows until half past eight – though some places didn't have any milking to do – then go round the other animals. Have our own bait, and half past nine or ten, harness up to go out.

'You didn't need two people to put harness on, you could do it yourself, although I've got some big toes to show you that! On my big toe there's only the bone left because I got tread putting on harness. It was a great big horse, 17hh, a lovely horse. I was a small lad at the time and I had to lift the pad up to put it on his back – but as you went up, he'd pick up his foot and down he'd come, wallop! I used to have to tie him across and put the harness in the manger, then get up in the manger to put it on him. He was usually a very quiet horse but I suppose it was just the cold touch of the harness on his back.

'But my toe, it's odd, our son John he had exactly the same sort of toe, naturally, when he was small.'

Flossie laughs outright: 'Well, we haven't seen his feet since he grew up and he got married!'

Jack continues to describe how a day's work used to be done with farm horses: 'After bait we'd go out with the horses and work until one o'clock, or just before. If you wanted to stop in the field longer you worked through and then finished at three, so the horses could have a breather; but if you came back for dinner you'd put them into the stables to have a feed, and when they came out they'd go to the pool and drink. Swinley Court used to have a big pool.'

'Did you ever change horses during the day?' I enquire.

Jack: 'Sometimes if it was very hot in the summer, perhaps for reaping. That was hard labour for horses, in the sweltering heat. We used to use three abreast, or some men would have them at length with a foreman's horse. Talking of hot weather, I've worked down in the meadows when it was humid and the "old maids" made the blood fly out of 'em along the bumps.'

'What's an old maid?'

'An insect, they bite and they'll fetch blood.'

Flossie: 'The sting and lump is worse than a wasp.'

Jack: 'I used to put a bunch of elen [elder] flower on the bridle to hang down, and it helps to stop them. You could put any leaf like, but elderwood's the best. My old mare always used to go and stand under an elder bush didn't she? [to Flossie]. Also before I went down there I used to treat my horses with what we called the old warble fly dressing – it's like a Stockholm tar, and the insects never like the smell o' that. Smear it along the middle of their back and down the back of the legs.'

I ask Jack if he's ever worked with any horses which had been difficult to handle. Of course, he has had many experiences.

'At Swinley Court we had a student, he was the local bank manager's son and had been put to work on the farm, to keep him out of the army, I suppose. But he didn't have *any* interest in the work. There was a horse that always got away from him. Smashed everything we had, harrows, everything, because he hadn't been properly broken and was tough in the mouth. Eventually he went as a timber-hauling horse; the horses used to work at length, and he was put in the middle – the first horse used to keep him straight, and the hind horse was always a good one like, drawing out, and he couldn't get away in the middle of the two.

'I had one run away once, but that wasn't my fault, it was this student's. The horses was frightened to death of him – he used to croon, songs like Ginger Rogers, and the horses would go frantic. So I used to carry on to *him* in same old tune! One day we were going to cut corn with the binder. The boss, Mr Dew, and his wife had gone out, and so I told him to shut the farm dogs up as we didn't want them in the corn after rabbits because we might cut their legs off. I said 'Don't let 'em out! – but he came across to me with a dog, and up gets a hare and I'm underneath the binder doing the knotter and the spanners were on top. This hare went straight through between the horses' legs, under the three of 'em. Well, afore I could get up they went down the field like bloody hell with the spanners rattling and the binder still in gear. They gradually turned as they came to the hedge, and the binder went straight into the hedge and the pole smashed off and these three horses were a-galloping along the ditch.

'I ran to the gateway which I knew they was making for and stopped 'em, but it was a bit of a tussle – they dragged me a fair ways, but I held 'em. But when I untangled them I saw that the broken pole had gone into the stomach of one of them, a four-year-old colt we'd only borrowed that morning to use. Mr Hughes, the owner, had wanted it worked on purpose to go to a show, so he'd lent it to us – but I remember I'd said to Mr Dew, "You know, that ain't very safe, I don't *like* the idea." But he'd been quiet enough until Bob the student started rattling.

'We got this injured horse back into the stable and bathed his wound, and we had to sling him up because if he got down he couldn't get up again. He was some weight, but we had a big thing on pullies to help us pull him up. He hung for a long time, and I exercised him as much as I could, let him down and then back up, just to keep his legs moving; but he didn't recover. He was a beautiful horse, worth a hundred guineas in them days.'

I ask Jack, 'Apart from injuries, did farm horses suffer many ailments?'

Jack: 'Sometimes in the very hot weather they'd get sore shoulders if the collar wouldn't fit. I used to fill old socks with sheep's wool and tie them round underneath the collar so as it didn't touch the sore patch. That was one thing about my mare, she never had a bad shoulder – but then I always used to use cold water with a bit of salt in it, and rub down on it if it was warm, that used to harden her.

'We'd make them bran mashes if a horse had trouble with sores or was poorly. In the spring we cut 'ettles [nettles] because they were good for the blood, and put 'em with the chaff.'

Flossie: 'Nobody cuts chaff now, do they?'

Jack: 'The chaff was hay, but you put a bit of straw with it to help it and added some roots, swedes or something, and a bit of treacle on it.' Still considering my question about ailments, he continued:

'Some horses used to get lumps of grease, each lump as big as a small walnut, above the hoof. One of the carthorses at Mr Lane's Sandpits Farm got it, and we think that a horse called Little Old Bob brought it in – he belonged to a neighbour but came to us to be broken in, and his owner would fetch him back when he wanted him. Bob used to pull a wide mower to cut the grass at Tewkesbury tennis courts and cricket ground in the summer, and to do it he'd wear rubber boots. We think the horse who did the mowing and wore the boots before him had this grease. Anyway, Bob developed it and so he was no good to his owner but had to stop on the farm with us, because every now and again these lumps would work up and bleed, like. Mr White the vet tried everything to treat it, even burning it down a bit, but it didn't seem to stop it.

'Horses did get the gripes, too – that is colic. They get it from too much small clover in dewy or frosty weather – they don't chew the cud like a cow you see, so it fills them and makes a blockage and they can't pass it. To avoid it with Polly, my mare, I used to bring her in as soon as I thought she'd had enough food, and she was generally happy enough to come in and

A farmworker horse-hoeing. It is believed that the photograph was taken at Bosbury, Herefordshire

stop in the stable. If I wanted to take her out for a drive I'd just let her on the long rein, and she'd fill herself and that was all. And if I was hedgelaying down the meadows, I'd tie her on a long line and she'd help herself and then go and lie down.'

I had visited Jack and Flossie on a very hot and sultry day, and the heavy weather was not conducive to too many animated trips down memory lane; there was also a cricket match on the television which Jack wanted to watch, so I arranged to meet up with them at a later date.

On my next visit Jack had kindly gone to the trouble to lay out a collection of horse bits, and an iron swingle-tree in the back garden for me to look at. He also showed me a metal rod about three feet long with a small hook on the end, used to test the quality of a hay rick: a prospective buyer would come along and push the rod into the rick, twist it, and as he pulled it back out it would bring a sample of hay with it that he could inspect. Jack admitted that this method didn't always guarantee good quality, because farmers had a tendency to hide those waggonloads of hay which thundery weather and rain had turned black, in the middle of the rick!

We talked about rick-making, and Jack explained how a horse was used to raise a tall

Haymaking

wooden pole, the jimmy pole, on a hinged base up into the air; metal claws were attached to it, and the horse then walked backwards and forwards, which turned a pulley to operate the claws to lift the hay off the waggon and onto the rick.

Also in Jack's collection of artefacts were a wooden crook and hand hook, which he called a 'hook and pig thank'; these were used to cut the corn on the outside of the field, thus making a 'road' for the horse-drawn binder so it could go round the field and cut the rest.

'We went into the house and sat down, and I asked Jack to tell me how he trained horses.

'Well, I started young. I was about thirteen at the time, and had gone to work for Mr Lane at Sandpits for 8s 3d [42p] a week, 52¹/₂ hours. He had a beautiful two-year-old which wanted breaking in, and had asked if I minded helping; and I'd say "No, not a bit", because I loved it, see. So we mouthed this colt with the bit with the middle break you've just seen, and put some jingles on it. We gave him a couple of days in a big stable, letting him walk round, then took the bit off at night to let him feed; then I'd strap it back on quite tightly, but not so as his mouth would get sore or hard, let him reach for it, like – and each day you'd loosen it a bit, but so there was still just a little bit of pressure, to let him know he'd got something to chew. By that means you let him know that you had something to control him by when he was at work.

'After about four days he was brought out and lunged round for a short while either way on a long rein with a lighter bit. We took him out in the day, too, at first without blinkers so he could see what was a coming up alongsides, because if he got over-heated he might get jibberish. So we worked him on and out like that for a bit, and that particular horse, he come ever so easy.

'I put him on dragging some old tree stumps up, and he'd stand. However, one day I'd been manure-hauling with him and I tied him to the gate when Mr Lane went into the house to do something. It was a new, thick oak gate. I was just untying him when the house door blew shut with a bang behind Mr Lane – and whhoof, he jumped off the ground and went straight over the gate so he was on the one side and I was on the other! I said to Jack, Mr Lane's son, "You run round there as quick as you can, he won't go because I got the reins on him." And I managed to get the hooks off the shafts else he'd have smashed the gate; as young Jack said, "That was a near 'un, it really was a near 'un!"

'We'd called that horse Dumbo because he was a nice little lump of a horse. He belonged to a neighbour, Mr Bellamy, but we kept him for twelve months until Mr Bellamy sold his farm and all his stock to go to another farm. At the sale Dumbo made the most money of Mr Bellamy's six horses, he made fifty-seven guineas.

'I've broken in ever so many horses since, and quite a few ponies. As mares foaled, you'd break their colts and take those you didn't want to keep to Gloucester, to sell – the selling power of them was if they were broken. The last two cart colts I took for Mr Hughes of The Mitre and Mr Ernie Butler, made over a hundred guineas.'

Flossie told me that her father had also broken in horses. Jack, thinking still about the price of horses, continued on the subject of buying and selling:

'In the early days they wasn't much money but when World War I broke out they wanted big horses. Mr Lane had four horses at the time and the army offered him 500 guineas for them. They had horses in World War II as well, and I signed up for the Gloucester Hussars – I really wanted to join the army, but they sent me back on the land.

'What happened was that Mr Bellamy and a Farmers' Union man had watched me from the hedge ploughing beans in. I didn't know they were there. Then they made a report and sent a copy to Mr Lane. There was a tribunal at Cheltenham, and I was the only one out of eight – and some of them were farmers' sons – who got sent back. One lad, about my age, was the only lad on the farm. We'd all been pals, but then their fathers actually got very bitter against me. I had to go to them threshing, and you know, I was made to feel out of place. So eventually I went out on me own, went freelance when we got married and come here, so I could go anywhere, do anything for anyone.'

I ask Jack if there is any tip worthy of mention that he'd learned in his farm horseman days. He replies immediately, 'There's nothing any more foolin' than going up hill with a load and the horse stops on you!' He laughs: 'I had one or two loads run back, too, with one particular horse, so one day I said "Well, boss, I'm going to try a bit of holly under his tail, and when he's holding his tail out I'll just give him a little bit of a cut and if he draws his tail down, he won't stop. By God, he was at the top of the bank before you could say "Look out!" though 'twas 'armless, cos I did take it out then. But the next time on the hill he hadn't forgot what I'd done, and although I didn't put any holly under his tail I only had to pull the rein like that, and he thought he was going to get stuck into, and he didn't jib, no, he never jibbed again!'

Farm horses gradually became redundant after World War II when tractors became increasingly popular. Jack recalls sadly: 'I remember we heaped a lot of farm waggons in a pile in an old badger pit and buried them. I reckon they are still there, and not rotten. They were Michael Cox waggons with oak beds.'

I ask Jack if, looking back, he has any particular happy memory of his time with horses. He replies, 'I once trained a racehorse, called "Happy"! He belonged to Mr Lane, and when the army came to take horses for World War II they took Mr Lane's other horse, Lucky Star, but we hid Happy – we took him down with the old carthorses in their barn. Happy won in three classes, the $1\frac{1}{4}$, the $1\frac{3}{4}$, and the $2\frac{3}{4}$ mile races, with a half-hour respite between. I met some farmers before the races, and they'd put £300 apiece on the 10 to 1 favourite Irish Congress. Happy won at 33 to 1 and the farmers never came near me – but the auctioneer, Pearce Pope, had put money on Happy. After 14 June we stopped flapping to go point-to-pointing.'

From his wallet, Jack takes out a photograph of Happy racing to the winning post. Flossie mildly remonstrates with him that the photo will break up through being kept in the wallet. However, it hasn't to date, and it has had such treatment for the past fifty years.

Finally I ask Jack if he has any regrets, and he confides: 'The only thing I wish I'd done was to have got onto a big farm where it was all horse work.' Lastly he remarks: 'I've never cared about money as long as I've a few things out there [gestures to the outside] to see to.'

It seems that to keep working is a trait of old farm horsemen. Jack's friend, 76-year-old Harry Peters, is still working on the farm where he has worked for the past fifty-five years!

A WELSH PONY BREEDER

The Countess of Dysart, Grosmont, Gwent

The approach road to the Countess of Dysart's farm balances on a narrow strip of rock. As it ascends, the ground on either side sweeps down and away into the irregular fields and hedges of the Welsh countryside. It is undeniably border country, because a few miles eastwards, picturesque by the River Monnow, there is a castle built by the Normans as a defence against marauding Welsh.

The spine of road eventually flattens and drops to the lower slopes of Graig Hill and Lady Dysart's farmyard, and in the high fields surrounding the house are her Welsh ponies. Their coats – some glossy chestnut, some grey, others strawberry roan – show up clearly against the green hills. The ponies and their 'families', the dynasties which Lady Dysart has bred, have long been her work and love. She is in fact an Honorary Life Vice-President of the Welsh Pony and Cob Society which has almost 9,000 members. Lady Dysart also keeps attractive Welsh Black cattle, and four-legged creatures have always been a part of her life:

'I've had animal friends around me from birth. One of the first I remember was a sandy, smooth-coated greyhound-type lurcher; he was called Bruton, because my father came across him near Bruton Street. My mother and father had come to London from the country because at that time I was imminently expected. I was in fact born in February 1914, not long after Bruton's arrival!

'In those days there were still horsedrawn cabs in London. The doormen at Hotels would give one whistle on their fingers for a hansom, and two for a "growler", a four-wheeled vehicle. It was a piercing whistle like a shepherd's, and it's a skill I've never mastered, how to whistle on my fingers, although my father did try to show me!

'My father's impulse buy of Bruton was typical of him – he loved animals. He'd been in the Household Cavalry, but at that time had been out of the army for a few years. However, when

I was six months old and war was declared, he had to go to France because he was on the reserve. He took his groom, Jimmy Weston, and his charger which was called "Quenby" after my father's home Quenby Hall in Leicestershire. Quenby was killed, however, so two more horses went out as replacements. Battle Axe and the Little Brown Horse.

'My own interest in purchasing and breeding ponies began when I was staying on the Lovat estate which belongs to friends and is in Inverness-shire. I started by buying any attractive pony, but favoured Shetlands and Welsh. It was during those days that my stud prefix "Polaris" came into being. Polaris is Latin for the "pole star" and I thought it should be the ponies' lucky star!

'In addition to building up my stock of ponies I was helping Glenda Spooner. She was a wonderful woman, and did an enormous amount for horses which without her help could have been in a very sorry state. She founded the Ponies of Britain Society and had considerable influence with the government, and because of this a great many rules and regulations came into being regarding the welfare of ponies.

'Trekking centres had sprung up like mushrooms after World War II, and Glenda Spooner was afraid – and she was right – that people who didn't know how to treat horses would start them for tourists. She had a group of people to inspect trekking and riding centres and asked me if I'd work in the Highland area. I didn't drive a car, but nevertheless I said "Yes" – one should always do that sort of thing in life! I asked the local taxi man to drive me, and he was marvellous! We used to go off sometimes over two or three days. You really couldn't do more than two centres in a day, although they might not be far apart as the crow flies, you often had a sea loch between them and a long drive round it by road.

'I never told a trekking centre that I was coming; usually I'd arrive as they were about to begin their morning ride with their guests. I'd apologise for holding them up, then I'd have the saddles taken off and look at each animal carefully, and have it run out to see if it was sound. Sometimes it wasn't, and then I'd have to say, 'I'm sorry, but this one can't go out today.' The centres soon caught on, and after a while I only had one place that was really difficult, and in the end it gave up. Most were well run and received high marks in my reports.'

Breaking off her narrative, Lady Dysart gathers up a rope halter and we set off to see one of her stallions, Polaris Fagus. The long winter had left a legacy of tractor ruts in the entrance to the field, but beyond the uneven ground the slopes were lush and grassy, and he was grazing here surrounded by mares and foals. He soon saw Lady Dysart approaching and trotted to meet her, the morning sun highlighting the gloss on his dark bay coat and the natural sheen on his long black mane and tail.

Fagus is a Welsh riding pony, known as Section B in the Welsh Pony Club and Cob Stud Book. The Section B ponies were the result of crossing the small native Welsh Mountain pony, known as Section A, with a larger type of quality animal with a more 'riding horse' action, to produce an ideal pony for older children or lightweight adults; its height limit in the show ring is 13.2hh. Section B is now a fixed category and uses its own stallions. Lady Dysart breeds Section A and B ponies, but although she knows the historical background to both breeds, she always refers those interested enough to pursue the subject to the definitive book Welsh Ponies and Cobs, by breeder and judge Wynne Davies.

The arch of Polaris Fagus' neck as he explored Lady Dysart's pocket for pony nuts suggested a touch of Eastern blood in his own ancestry. I ask Lady Dysart if she remembers her first-ever foal. She replies, laughing:

'No! That's lost in the mists of time; but I do remember sitting up every night for a week with a foal born prematurely to a very nice Arab mare I had. It was her first foal, and she was twenty years old! Hers was an interesting story. I'd bought her when she was a three-year-old, and kept her riding and driving until she was nineteen years old, and then I went to a horse sale in a suburb of Aberdeen called Kitty Brewster. There was a railway siding at the market there; if you slept at the nearby inn, you heard the trains shunting with boxes of herrings all night long. We were mostly Scots buyers and sellers at Kitty Brewster, and in the evening before the sale we'd get up a little concert with a squeeze-box and people singing!

'On this particular sale day I saw a lady with an Arab stallion for sale. The horse was rearing and shrieking, which no doubt put off a lot of people, but not me! I could see he was a quality animal, and later, when his papers arrived, I found out he was a son of Indian Magic, an Arabian horse which had done everything he possibly could in this country, and which had then gone to Australia.

'I was lucky, I bought that stallion – his name was Indian Sun – for very little money; if he'd been for sale in the South of England he would have been snapped up. My nineteen-year-old mare was healthy, and after checking with the vet I let him cover her. When her time came she unfortunately foaled too early and hadn't any milk, so I had to feed the new arrival, a colt, every two hours throughout the twenty-four, for a week. Then, mercifully, a very good friend took over night duty for me! We called the foal Rising Sun, but he was always known as "Sunny" because he was born in the early morning; he became a very dear friend for at least twenty-eight years.

Wynne Davies showing Dinarth What Ho! in 1952

Fondling Fagus' muzzle, Lady Dysart explains how she began to concentrate on breeding Welsh ponies:

'In the beginning I thought "Well, I've got these lovely little mares, I might as well have a good stallion for them!" So I went to see a lady in Aberdeenshire and bought a stallion called Fayre Playmate from her. I was also fortunate because I knew Miss Brodrick, who owned the world-famous Coed Coch stud – every stud that's worth anything today has Coed Coch blood somewhere in it.

'Miss Brodrick had exceptionally good grooms, almost all of whom came from a wonderful family who had served her own family for many years. The one known as "Old John" Jones advised her when she began the stud in 1924. He was known as "Old John" to distinguish him from another groom named John Jones, but no relation. That John Jones, "Old John" and Old John's son, named Shem, made a wonderful team. Today, John Jones, Shem and Shem's son Wynne, breed Welsh ponies and judge. They are experts in the field, and I'm still learning from them!

'When Miss Brodrick died a number of her horses were sold and eventually there was a disposal sale of all the horses at Coed Coch stud. I went to the sales, and saw her stallion Coed

Welsh Mountain Pony stallion Coed Coch Madog

Coch Bari sold for 21,000 guineas; the auctioneer at the time said it was the highest price ever paid for a horse other than a Thoroughbred. It went to Australia, as did many Coed Coch horses. Old John was convinced he'd never see them again, but some years later he and Shem were invited to judge in Australia; they went to one particular show, and to their surprise and delight, all the ponies of the Coed Coch line born and bred out there had come from their different studs to this show, and were paraded past!

'I bought a mare at Miss Brodrick's sale: she was called Coed Coch Tarian, and was very famous. I still have her offspring.'

By this time circumstances had changed for Lady Dysart, too: she had moved from Scotland to Exmoor, where in addition to having almost a hundred ponies, she kept a registered flock of Devon Closewools and seventy-nine Welsh Black cattle. Then from Exmoor she moved to her present farm on the Welsh border. Back inside the light-filled kitchen with its high ceiling and the window which looks out onto a field of yearlings, I asked her which of her many ponies she recalled with most affection. Lady Dysart replied with no hesitation:

'I think little Sonnet. She was sweet, and she bred very well. Her mother Greddingdon Rhuddos had belonged to Lord Kenyon, who had owned Rhuddos' sire Coed Coch Planed, too. And I remember the occasion when Planed, who incidentally had been bred by Miss Brodrick, was at the same show as *his* sire, the world-famous Madog; they were in the same class, and it was quite a betting issue as to which of them was going to get the prize! They were both marvellous movers. Lord Kenyon's groom was also connected to the Jones's at the Coed Coch stud, and it was thrilling to see each groom running with his pony; the men were young enough to run just as fast as the ponies, and they really moved! You see at shows, the groom's stride must synchronise exactly with the pony's; he is *not* running just any old how. At its best, a Welsh Mountain pony's action is quite electrifying in competition; they seem to leave the ground and float, and have terrific extension from the shoulder with their hocks well up under them.'

On the kitchen dresser there is a letter from a little girl enclosing a photograph of one of Lady Dysart's ponies which the youngster's parents had bought a few years previously. It's a happy grateful note, keeping Lady Dysart up to date with the pony's successful progress.

'I was touched to receive it,' Lady Dysart admits. I've never met the little girl and, well, it's the sort of thing that makes you feel that despite all the ups and downs, all the icy troughs and cold hands you've had, it's worth it, if you can make a child so happy.'

ARMY HORSEMEN

A mounted British army horseman today is likely to be either on guard or on ceremonial duties, and to be from the Household Cavalry or the King's Troop, the last remaining mounted units in the army. Both liaise with the Army Veterinary Corps at Melton Mowbray, which acts as a receiving station for new horses for them and also runs equitation courses.

That the horse is still represented in the British army is quite right and proper, because horses were once its mainstay. In World War I, millions were employed in battle, those on the sands of Palestine acquitting themselves with more success than their fellow creatures in the mud of Flanders. In the early and mid-1930s the cavalry horse was still very much a part of the British army, and new recruits to cavalry regiments learned how to ride and groom a horse, and how to fight with sword, lance and rifle. Service included long periods of duty in India. However, the thirties were in fact the twilight years for the cavalry horse, because the onset of World War II in 1939, with its tanks and aircraft, spelled the end of mounted warfare.

The following is a collection of extracts from army archives and the personal reminiscences of some of the last cavalrymen.

LIEUTENANT J.H. BLAKSLEY
of the Queen's Own Dorset Yeomanry

An extract from the archives of the Queen's Own Dorset Yeomanry submitted by their archivist Major L.E.N. Neville-Jones. It concerns World War I in the Middle East, when on 28 February 1916, in the Western Desert, the QODY found themselves alone on the battlefield faced by the rearguard of a force of Senussi who had invaded Egypt and were commanded by Turkish officers. This is part of the account by Lieutenant J.H. Blaksley:

'We were ordered to "mount" and "form line". Then, and not till then, we knew what was coming. Imagine a perfectly flat plain of firm sand without a vestige of cover, and in front of us a slight ridge; behind this and facing us were the three machine-guns and at least 500 men with rifles. You might well think it madness to send 180 Yeomen riding at this. The Senussi, too, are full of pluck and handy with their machine-guns and rifles, but they are not what we should call first-class shots, otherwise I do not see how we could have done it. We were spread out in two ranks, eight yards roughly between each man of the front rank and four yards between the second. This was how we galloped for well over half-a-mile straight into their fire. The amazing thing is that when we reached them, not one in ten was down. At first they fired very fast and you saw the bullets knocking up the sand in front of you, as the machine-guns pumped them out, but as we kept getting nearer they began to lose their nerve (I expect) and forgot to lower their sights.

'Anyhow, the bullets began going over us, and we saw them firing wildly and begin to run; but some of them – I expect the Turkish officers – kept the machine-guns playing on us. We were within 30 yards of the line when down came my mare. She was, I think, the nicest I have ever ridden – a well known hunter in the Blackmore Vale – and in spite of want of food and water she was bounding along without the least sign of fear, as though she had left the stable. Down she fell, stone dead, fortunately, as I saw next morning, with a bullet straight through her heart… .

'It would be difficult to describe what was going on in the meantime just behind us – such a scene of terror as it is quite impossible to imagine. The Senussi were running in all directions, shrieking and yelling and throwing away their arms and belongings; the Yeoman after them, sticking through the backs and slashing right and left with their swords. The whole thing was a marvellous instance of the awful terror inspired by galloping horses and steel.'

HARRY BRIGHTWELL
of the Queen's Bay 2nd Dragoon Guards

These are the reminiscences of Harry Brightwell, aged eighty-three of Wool in Dorset. He joined the Queen's Bays 2nd Dragoon Guards in 1931.

'I joined as a recruit. Our daily routine was reveille, followed by a cup of tea. Then we put on a jacket and trousers made of a strong soft canvas to do the mucking out; you put the coat on backwards because you had to carry the wet bedding out to put it under the drying sheds. Then the whole squadron – that is, three troops, one carrying a Vickers water-cooled machine gun – would go out on exercise. This was mostly walking for two hours. When we came back, the horses were fed and watered and we'd have our breakfast.

'Barrack-room cleaning followed, and making your own bed. Each bed was made up with three "biscuits", that is, little coir mattresses like cushions; three made a bed, with a blanket on top. This was in 1931; in later years, men were issued with sheets and pillows. The bed was made from two sections, and if a soldier wouldn't get up in the morning the sergeant could tip the bed up completely and turf him out!

'There was a trumpet call for stables; in fact there was a trumpet call for all sorts, for mail, for water, for feed…. Each troop had roughly twenty-five horses, or slightly more than was needed to make up for the sick, lame and lazy. "Stables" went on from eleven o'clock until about a quarter to one, and sometimes we each had four or five horses to groom because there were the cooks' horses and the officers' horses to do as well.

After lunch, boys who hadn't reached the standard of education required had an hour's instruction, mostly about pride in the regiment. Stable cleaning was from 2pm until 4.15pm. Also in the afternoon we cleaned saddlery and trimmed and clipped horses; I was a horse clipper. We generally used electric clippers, but hand ones for manes and heels.

'Our next task was getting forage. In the summer we took the horses out to graze, but would often be so tired by then that we would fall asleep, one arm up in the air holding the long reins but not noticing that the horse had wandered off!

'On each horse we had a sword-pouch; a horseshoe and four nails; a calico field-bag; a calico water-bottle; a 35in sabre on the left of the saddle; and on the right, a rifle bucket for our Lee Enfield rifle. We wore a carbine for so many bullets, a respirator, a peaked hat (we had a tin helmet which we rarely wore), a jacket with a box collar with a buckrum insert, and breeches with our own cavalry regiment colour on the grips inside the leg. We had putties, which were a nuisance, and normal army boots.

'When it rained we wore an old groundsheet of canvas, but it wasn't really waterproof, and when you galloped it flew up with the breeze. We slept on this behind the horses at night. When fully mounted we carried an overcoat, either on the back arch of the saddle or on the front.

'At 4.15pm at evening stables, one fellow on a bale of hay would feed some out to another who would twist it and break it off and plait it into a wad. Everyone had one of these, and we'd use it to massage the horse, thump in time with the corporal. In winter we rugged the horses up when we'd finished grooming them; then it was bed down, water and feed and putting hay into nets.

'In the stables the horses were separated by a long rail of steel or iron; each horse had a section, and it kept them from biting one another. The end of the rail had a quick-release loop, and if a horse got over, a vertical sheet bar could be activated by lifting off a little loop, and the rail would then drop to the floor so that you could lift the horse's leg back over.

'As a troop corporal I was with twenty-five men, and each night put up a list telling each man which horse he was going to ride. Horses used to be numbered with indelible ink on the gum; in my time, however, they had QB (standing for Queen's Bays) on the flank and their number, and they also had a number on their leg.

'The cavalry consisted of blue-blooded officers who rode, played polo and hunted, and did nothing else. It was a good life for an officer. We did the work, had their horses ready – they were the kings.

'You couldn't get married until you were twenty-six, and then you had to apply to the squadron leader; moreover your fiancée had to sign a certificate affirming that she was of good moral character and not a prostitute.

'I was due to be made a full corporal, but unfortunately the custom was that an officer took precedence, and a fellow who had been an officer in the infantry but had relinquished his commission through financial difficulties, took the job which would have been mine. It broke me.'

CYRIL EDGHILL
of the 16th/5th Queen's Royal Lancers

Here are some reminiscences of Cyril Edghill, aged eighty-two, of Heworth, York. In 1931, when he was sixteen, Cyril joined the Cavalry of the Line as a band boy. He then became a trooper, a regimental scout and latterly a SQMS [Squadron Quarter Master Sergeant] in the 16th/5th Queen's Royal Lancers.

'My father had been a regimental equitation officer, that is, a rough-riding sergeant-major. He wore a spur on his arm and was responsible for new horses to the regiment. He was killed in World War I. I told my mother that I wanted to join the army, and after much weeping and wailing she wrote to the colonel of my Dad's regiment – and I was in.

'After a medical I was later issued with a railway warrant and some ration money, and told to report to Beaumont Barracks in Colchester. I arrived there at about 7pm on a Friday night, and asked the porter at the station the way to the barracks. He said "Son, next door to this station is a loony bin; either go there, or go home whilst you've got a chance . . ." He also told me that I would cry many an hour for my Mum – and believe me, I did!

'Our food was dreadful: stews mostly, and they were all fat. As a boy I was always hungry. We used to go to the cookhouse after meals and offer to do the washing-up in return for some stodgy pudding such as "spotted dick". I was earning 7s a week, but 2s 6d of that had to pay for cleaning equipment, and the rest was put to credits for paying for equipment lost or needed. As soon as we were paid we'd rush to the corner shop and buy a small loaf and a quarter of margarine!

'On the other hand the horses were always looked after. I remember a scheme we'd been on, when the RSM had to report to the colonel at the end of grooming, and the colonel said, "Are the horses and men fed, sergeant-major?" And the RSM replied, "The horses are fed, but the men's food is not quite ready." The colonel replied, "Feed it to the buggers raw!" You've no doubt heard of the phrase "swear like a trooper"; well, troopers did know a choice word or two, but officers were worse.

'People may be astonished to know that before a recruit goes anywhere near to riding a real horse he starts on a life-size rocking horse. It had all the accoutrements of a proper nag, but it also had an extra one, a large pad attached by strong elastic at each side of its chest; if you relaxed your knee-grip on the pad, it would be pulled forward by the elastic.

'Rocking horses were one thing, but we even sat on non-existent horses! Recruits like us weren't given a lethal sabre and expected to get on real horses and do arms drill. We squatted as though – pardon the expression – we were having a crap, with sword belts and sword ready for drill, on the regimental square. Talk about feeling like clowns, the civvies loved it! When you were told to stand at ease, your knees felt as though they were locked. And when the colonel passed you out as good enough, you had to learn it all again on a real horse.

'There was even a command given and taught "To make much of your horse": pat the animal on the neck by numbers... one – one, two...

'The trumpeter (me) sounded the trumpet for different times of the day and the different tasks associated with each particular time. The "call for stables" was very long, in fact the same length of time that it took to chant the following doggerel which was handed down over the years:

> *Come to your stables boys*
> *Come if you're able*
> *And give your poor horses some water and corn.*
> *If you don't your CO will say*
> *"Down to the guardroom tonight you must stay."*
> *Come to your stables boys*
> *Come if you're able, and*
> *Give your poor horses some water and corn.*

'My trumpet horse was called Charity, but he was always known as Chocolate and he was a real old darling. He knew more about soldiering than most of us. We boys used to get a mug of soup for supper, and I use that word advisedly, because one often found a black pea in it to prove its contents. Chocolate loved it, he'd drink it straight from my mug as long as I held it properly for him. Also, the sergeant-major was a good old stick and he used to buy extra fodder for his mount; I knew what time he used to give it to him, and after he had, I used to sneak in and pinch the extras for Chocolate. The sergeant-major suspected this, and one evening came back and caught me red-handed. He said, 'Trumpeter, I don't mind in the least someone doing that occasionally, *if* he has a thin horse, but for that great lump of yours – no!' I didn't do it again.

'Nobody could ride Chocolate without my say-so; all I had to do was to say "Wheee", and old Chocowocks would buck them off. I loved that horse, and I'm sure he loved me – and then

the time came when he was too old for service and was to be taken away and shot. I was heart-broken, and asked my squadron leader if I could buy him. He asked me if I had the money to buy him, and where I'd keep him, and could I pay for vets' bills and winter fodder? Of course, I couldn't. I cried many a night over old Chocolate. I still have a relic of me and him together – it's the only photo I have of my cavalry days.

If there aren't any horses and dogs in heaven, well, I don't want to go. I don't expect I'll get there, anyway.'

Cyril is currently writing his autobiography and in it, vividly describes his army days.

NORMAN BARNES
of the 16th/5th Queen's Royal Lancers

The following reminiscences are from Norman Barnes, aged seventy-nine, of Ely, Cambridgeshire. Norman joined the 16th/5th Queen's Royal Lancers at York in 1936.

'I was in the signal troop, each squadron had one. We used a heliograph, a mirror-type instrument which is used by manipulating the sun's reflection on its glass. A little arm which has squares on, comes out from it, and there is a tiny spot on there about as big as the top of a little finger; the position of the spot told us if we were hitting the other station. We also used flags, and what we called "pot and pan", a plastic thing with flaps which opened, with a message written inside which aircraft could read. In fact it wasn't used much, we mainly used the heliograph and lamp.'

Norman supplied the following extract from the 1937 edition of the regiment's journal *Scarlet and Green*; it concerns George VI's coronation.

THE CORONATION

Everyone will realise what an immense amount of work was caused by the Coronation. To the average spectator the Cavalry regiments were very inadequately represented by one officer and seven men in the procession, and the mounted bands of the Royal Scots Greys and ourselves. In addition, the regiments from Aldershot and Tidworth and ourselves found small street-lining parties of about 40 men.... The weather was so bad in the camp at Kensington Gardens that a party of 40 men, under Capt. R.M. Fanshawe, were sent up the day before the Coronation to help turn out the men and horses of the mounted detachment... .

The weather two days before the Coronation was wet and cold, and the camp and horse lines became a quagmire. Coronation day itself was fine but dull. Reveille was at 4am and the mounted detachment had to be on parade at 6.50am and be in position by 7am... .

Norman adds his own memories of this occasion:

'The drummer in the mounted band was actually a civilian; he had been Corporal Priddy, and had left the regiment some months previous. However, because there was too short a time in which to train another drummer, he returned to the regiment for a few weeks to take part in rehearsals of the parade.

'On the morning of the coronation the rain had stopped; however, the horse lines in the park were muddy so our task, being part of the reserve street lining party, was to saddle the horses, get them onto the hard ground and assist the mounted party to mount. The horses were not very helpful, as when we saddled and tightened the girth they wanted to roll; however, they were all prepared without mishap and the riders carried and lifted onto the horses, then the final brush-down of hooves and so on before they moved off to the marshalling area.

'After this we were able to change into our uniforms and get to our allotted station in a side street.

'It was our task to help control the crowd after the parade had passed. The rain actually poured down after the parade had ended and the Scots Greys horses became streaky grey; I believe it was some sort of powder which they used to enhance their colour, and naturally that started to run.

JIM SEYMOUR
of the Royal Hussars

Jim Seymour, aged eighty-two of Winchester, Hampshire was a trooper in the Royal Hussars. He writes:

'I was born in London, and the only horses I'd seen before joining the army were ones pulling milk floats or carts. I enlisted on 11 January 1933 at Brighton in Sussex, where I had a medical and an education test and was given the grand sum of one shilling [5p]. I was sent to the 3rd Hussars (recently returned from India), in York. It was an old cavalry barracks, and we slept above the horses; you could hear them kicking, stamping and sneezing in the night and the night guard telling them to be quiet.

Jim in his dress uniform in 1936

'I had three months basic training – "square bashing" – marching, rifle drill, sword drill and on the rifle range learning how to shoot. All the drill was done in a tight-fitting, high-necked tunic with a leather ammunition bandolier across the shoulder and chest.

'There were thirty of us in the new intake and that was when we learned about "mucking in" together; we were all in the same boat and we helped each other. We were told by the sergeants and corporals in charge of us that they had been ordered to treat us with kid gloves, and to use "sympathetic" training. All I can say is that sympathy was not in their dictionary. We really went through the mill – the slightest mistake and we were jumped on. It was no good complaining or writing to your MP because you had been sworn at and called a rude name; there was one stock answer to any moaning: "It's your own fault, you shouldn't have joined." I forgot to mention that we also had to do one hour a day physical training. Your body might be soft when you started, but they soon toughened you up in the "muscle factory"; you could do a five-mile cross-country run without raising a sweat.

'When we had finished and passed out of our basic training, we then went to riding school for eight weeks' training in horsemanship. We always said that the sergeant-major riding instructor had two horns under his hat and a long pointed tail in his breeches; but to give the devil his due, he could ride any horse going.

'He always said that you are there to make the horse do as you want, not vice versa. 'They are all fully trained cavalry horses and can do everything expected of them, not like any of you lot, if they can dodge out of anything they will.' We had a perfect example shortly afterwards of how well they'd been trained. We were being taught how to jump, and had to take a row of obstacles 2–3 ft high, follow-the-leader style. The first couple or so, very nice, and then one chap riding all slappy, his horse hit the fence and the rider came off and in doing so, KO'd himself right in front of the jump. Naturally, we all stopped. The sergeant-major came storming up: "Who the blankety-blank told you to stop?" So we pointed at this chap lying on the ground. He said "The horses have got more sense than you, they won't stand on him, so follow me!" Which we did: about eight of us jumped over him without touching him.

'We did a lot of drill in the indoor riding school. The horses knew every word of command, and the troop sergeant would say "Let the horse have his head – he knows what to do, even intricate moves!" We had to learn sword, lance and revolver training, and to my mind it was a waste of time, only good for competitions.

'Once our training was over, most of the time we spent exercising and cleaning saddlery and grooming. We used to go to camp once a year for about three weeks on Catterick Moors in Yorkshire. I really enjoyed that, riding most of the day.

'Once a year we used to take part in a military tattoo, dressed up in period costumes.

'In November 1934 I went to Lucknow in India, to the 10th Hussars, known as the "Shiny 10th" or "Shiners" owing to the amount of "bulling-up" they did. After a month of settling-in training we were considered good enough to be the 10th Hussars.

'Life in India was one long skive. Whereas in England we had to keep all our equipment clean, not so in India: we had a bearer who did it all. When we got back from exercise at about 7.30am all beds were made up, mosquito nets rolled, clean clothes laid out. If you were on guard that night he would give you your equipment which he'd cleaned. We would have about six chaps to look after us, and we'd each pay one rupee to each, that's about 12p a week. We had a syce, or groom, who used to clean our saddlery for a rupee a week. We didn't have the normal chores to do as in England, nothing to relieve the boredom.

Jim with his mount at Lucknow in 1935

'Make no mistake, however, I enjoyed my time as a cavalry man. Undoubtedly there is no more awe-inspiring spectacle than a squadron of cavalry, everything highly polished and shining – but that was really all that the cavalry was good for, because after the Napoleonic wars of the nineteenth century they were a spent force; they were only kept on for show.

'It was a very good life for the officers, who were all wealthy; they had to be, to afford to be in a cavalry regiment. The 10th Hussars returned to York in November 1936 to be mechanised, as were all cavalry regiments. They all became tank regiments, and all gave a very good account of themselves in the last war.'

Lt Col SIR DELAVAL COTTER Bt DSO
of the 13th/18th Royal Hussars

The following recollections are from Lt Colonel Sir Delaval Cotter Bt DSO Blandford Forum, Dorset.

'In 1931 when I was twenty I left Sandhurst and went to the north-west frontier of India as a subaltern in the 13th/18th Royal Hussars. They were already out there, and had been for a month or two, having come from Egypt to quell some sort of disturbance in Kashmir. I was assigned to a troop in a squadron: a troop is approximately twenty-eight men and twenty-eight horses. I had a very good sergeant who'd been there for years, and he taught me everything.

'I didn't ride the same horse all the time; as troop leader I had twenty-eight to choose from – although I certainly wouldn't have taken the sergeant's!

'The men – that is, the soldiers – looked after the horses, although there were a few Indian syces who helped to clean the stables and do the watering; they were excellent, and particularly good with horses that were difficult. The horses were a mixture of Indian-bred ones and Australian horses. In India it was always one man to one horse; over here, one man had two or three horses to look after. I had a groom back at my bungalow; I also owned some polo ponies.

'At first during the summer we had a 5.15am start for exercise because that was when it was

The horse lines

coolest; later the temperature could climb from 90° to 110°F. However, we found that that was a great mistake, because it was between 5am and 6am that the horses got the most rest. After the first year we went out at 6.30am, and found that both horses and men did better.

'Troopers carried a sword and rifle, officers a sword and pistol. A trooper would ride towards the enemy, dismount and fire. The horses were used to people firing rifles.

'When on manoeuvres, a horse carried two feeds strung on the back of the saddle, barley rather than oats as it was customary to feed barley in India. There were two blankets underneath the saddle, one for the horse and one for the rider; so in all, the horse had quite a weight to carry.

'At night a long line was put down, well staked, and the horses tethered to it, one troop on one side, one troop on the other, so fifty horses altogether. A sentry watched over them.

'When we went to Risalpur near the frontier we had a pack of hounds which had been run by the regiment we'd relieved. The hounds were English foxhounds, though over the years a lot had been bred in India. We hunted jackals. It was a marvellous time for a young person.

'We left India in 1938 to come back to England and small tanks; I believe that the Indian army took over the horses. There were still some horsed regiments in World War II. Some went to Palestine at the beginning, but it didn't last.'

184

WILLIAM BROOKS
of the 16th/5th Queen's Lancers

William Brooks comes from Jacksdale, Nottingham; he was a farrier in the 16th/5th Queen's Lancers. I met William at his home, and learned that he had a working knowledge of horses even before joining the army. He was raised in the West Sussex countryside and his stepfather was a blacksmith. He is now eighty-two.

When he left school, William worked with his stepfather in the blacksmith's shop. He worked every day but Sunday, and received 2s 6d [12½p] a week plus his keep. He could see no prospect of progress, and so decided to join the cavalry as a farrier:

'I was always pleased I did it. I joined the Lancers in July 1934 and went to Brighton where I stayed the night. I was sent to Tidworth the next day just in time to see the tattoo with the musical ride. Before the winter we were posted to York. During my stay there we had two weeks' rest camp by the river at Ripon. We farriers took portable fires and anvils and there was a bucket of water to slap your shoe out when it was hot.

'We then went on to Catterick for manoeuvres. Before going out on manoeuvres, or before any moving of horses, as a farrier I put a front shoe and a hind shoe for each particular horse in a leather wallet strapped to its saddle.

'On night manoeuvres you divided the road, and so many horses would go down one side and so many on the other; and very often a horse would go by with its rider fast asleep. The farrier always rode at the back, and whereas the other men carried a rifle in their holsters, the farrier carried a humane killer in his.

'While we were at Catterick we had a forage barn fire. The late Duke of Gloucester was our squadron leader, and he came out of his tent in his pyjamas and fell into a little brook – it was extremely funny! With Catterick being such a large garrison – you can imagine, there were dozens of regiments from throughout the country there – the bugler had to play the alarm "Here's a fire, here's a fire"; and when one regiment heard it they played it, and so did the next, and so all the lot had to stand by.'

After two years in York the regiment moved to Hounslow for one year's rest station and preparation for going to India. During this time William was one of the soldiers who went to the coronation of George VI. At the camp in Kensington Park he prepared his horse for a Commonwealth soldier, a New Zealander, to ride. Mention of Hounslow brought back other memories for William:

'One day I was in charge of about twenty or thirty horses going to the big horse-sales rooms at the Elephant and Castle. You'd ride one and lead one. The horses were unfit for service, and horses in that condition had to have a hole about ¼in in diameter punched in their ear to stop them being sold back to the army. The strange thing was, these horses hadn't had their ears punched. When we got to the Elephant and Castle I pointed this out to the officer who met me there, and he said "Could you do it Brooks?" I said, "I could if I had the right sort of tool!" – and then I suddenly thought of a saddler's star-wheel which has spikes on it from ⅛in to ¼in. So he went off and came back with one. All the horses were tied up at a manger; I stood actually in the manger itself, and using the biggest spike, punched their ears towards the top. I went to give the officer the star-wheel back, and he said "I don't want it!"; so when I got back, I sold it to a saddler for half a crown!

'I went to India three weeks before the rest of the regiment because I was in charge of twenty polo ponies aboard a cargo boat from Tilbury docks. The ponies went up the ramp and into the side of the ship, below deck; inside each pony was divided from the next by four boards.

'On the top deck there were boxes bolted down, and they contained British bloodstock racehorses: they were going first class, you could say, to India and Australia. A little man who'd spent a lifetime with the horses was in charge of these Thoroughbreds.

'Well, we hadn't been going very long, we were only in the English Channel, when one of the ponies developed a temperature of 106° [normally it would have been 101°). So I told the little bloodstock man, also that I'd no medicines, only a hundredweight of Epsom salts. He said, "I'll tell you what we'll do. I'll come down and we'll mix a bucket of mustard and give him a mustard bath." And we plastered him all over his body with this mustard, and do you know, that pony got better.

'But when we got to the Red Sea it was very, very hot. We had like little scoops out through the portholes to try and get some fresh air. All the ponies were sweating, and you couldn't groom them; then the sweat dried up on their ribs and they looked like zebras. An hour from Bombay a pony died. They lowered a derrick and rope down through the square hatchway where all the manure and other rubbish went out, and pulled it through. Then they cut a slit in his stomach so that he'd sink, and dropped him overboard.

'When we got to Bombay there was one Indian to meet each pony. They groomed with just their hands and a damp cloth, no brush. And do you know, when the officers came to see them, those ponies looked marvellous, and I thought to myself "You ought to have seen them at sea!"

William went from Bombay to Secunderabad. He explains: 'Whenever a regiment first went abroad they put them down south because the climate was more or less the same all the year round. There was always plenty of shoeing in Secunderabad because they were polo mad, and all the polo ponies had to be shod.'

After some time at Secunderabad, the regiment moved to Risalpur on the north-west frontier. Amongst his memorabilia of those days William has a photograph taken at Risalpur of the forge staff; on it are two Nepalese, one named Kalou and the other Titch. William recalls the day he witnessed an odd incident which concerned Titch:

'It was a Thursday, and because the Indian mutiny started on a Thursday and ended on a Thursday, they were always a holiday. It was the day you had to debug your bed with a blow-lamp and goodness knows what. Well, on this particular Thursday I was on duty looking after sick horses, and to get to them I had to pass the blacksmith's shop. I saw Titch in there and he'd got a goat. I said, "Are you going to shoe him then, Titch?" and he said, "No, ke-eel him." He'd got some powders, pink and green and yellow and made a design where we shod the horses. He stood the goat in there and it never moved, and he got this curry knife with a big wide blade and made one slash, and the goat's head fell off just like a football. He'd got a saucepan, and he tipped the goat up over it and filled it with blood. Then he threw the blood all over the anvils and the bench and tools. He was blessing all the things he worked with. I suppose it must have been Ramsam, which was a festival of theirs.

'While we were on the north-west frontier I saw my first stampede. We were on parade with the horses when a violent sandstorm blew up; the sand and the cloud went sky high, and many of the horses went spare. Fortunately there were no men riding them, because they ran blind into buildings and pylons. After, we gathered them up. Some had killed themselves and some had to be put down.

'The other stampede was in 1940 when we were back in England. It was in Derby – everyone had turned their horses out to a long water trough, and the forage orderly was carrying tins of food from one stable to another: each tin held 7lb [3kg] of corn and chop, and he was holding about eight or nine tins. He tripped up, and the falling tins made such a noise that the horses jumped over the gate down to the town amongst the traffic. One bus driver could see what was happening but couldn't stop, and a great many horses were killed.'

Turning his thoughts back to India, William recounts the events which saw the end of the regiment's days there. The 16th/5th were in fact the last-ever cavalry regiment to serve in India; with war looming, all the others had returned to England to become mechanised.

The forge staff of William's regiment in Risalpur, 1939

'Before we left, the horses had to be disposed of. Some went to the Indian cavalry, but those too old to be transferred had to be put down. There was a hundred or so of these and we used to take it in turns to do it, knocking so many down every day. You'd walk out to a *mierdam*, which was an open space, say, a dried-up river bed and the vultures would be flying overhead; once a horse had been put down the vultures soon picked its bones clean.

'When they'd been knocked down we used to cut their legs off and boil the hooves so you could scoop out the flesh and bones. You'd get a certain amount of contraction in the hoof which couldn't be helped. Then some of the chaps would fill them with plaster of paris which they'd mixed up in the sick bay. They were for keeping as mementos.'

William stoops down to his hearth and picks up a horse's hoof. 'I did this one before I came away. I made the shoe and nailed it on and made the label.' He turns the hoof to the window. The late September afternoon sun settles on the words engraved on the silver escutcheon:

The Last of
British Cavalry
India, 1939

BIBLIOGRAPHY

Beaufort, Duke of *Driving* (The Badminton Library, 1890)

Christy, Theodore *Random Recollections of an Essex Sportsman* (Benham & Co, c1940)

'Devonian' *Turf Topics* (Postal Libraries Ltd, c1944)

Fairfax, J. *The Complete Horseman or Country Gentleman's Recreation* (1795)

Fisher, Arthur T. *Through the Stable and Saddle-Room* (MacMillan & Co, 1906 ed)

Fitzwygram, Lieut-General Sir F., Bart *Horses and Stables* (Longman's Green & Co, 1911)

Hayes, Alice M. *The Horsewoman – A Practical Guide to Side-Saddle Riding* (Hurst and Blackett Ltd, 1903)

Keen, Richard *Coalface* (Welsh Industrial & Maritime Museum, 1991)

Manners and Tone of Good Society by a Member of the Aristocracy (Frederick Warne & Co, c1880)

Sidney, Samuel *Book of the Horse* (Cassell, Petter & Co, c1880)

Smith, Lady Eleanor *British Circus Life* (Geo G. Harrap & Co, 1948)

The Horse and How to Manage Him (Ward Lock & Co, c1894)

Wynne Davies, Dr E. *Welsh Ponies and Cobs* (J.A. Allen, 1980)

JOURNALS, MAGAZINES, NEWSPAPERS AND PAMPHLETS

Heavy Horse magazine (various editions)

Pit Ponies pub Yorkshire Mining Museum

Journal of the Royal Agricultural Society of England, various editions between 1845 and 1846

Scarlet & Green, the journal of 16th/5th Queen's Royal Lancers, 1937 edition

INDEX

Page numbers in *italics* refer to illustrations